Cast in a Racial Mould
Labour Process and Trade Unionism in the Foundries

To my father and mother
and Luli, Kimon and Alexia

Cast in a Racial Mould
*Labour Process and Trade Unionism
in the Foundries*

Eddie Webster

Ravan Press   Johannesburg

Published by Ravan Press (Pty) Ltd
P O Box 31134, Braamfontein,
Johannesburg, 2017
South Africa

First published 1985

ISBN 0 86975 285 5

Cover photograph: Lesley Lawson
Typeset by: Opus 61

Printed by Interpak (Pty) Ltd., Pietermaritzburg

Contents

Acknowledgements

This study is the outcome of over a decade of teaching and research on race and labour in South Africa. During this period I have accumulated numerous intellectual debts. The following persons require specific mention:

Dr. J. Cock, Dr. B. Bozzoli, and Professor M. Savage for reading and commenting on the original Ph.D manuscript; Dr. A. Sitas, Rob La Grange, Aninka Claasens and Mary-Ann Cullinan for sharing some of their interview material with me; Paul Stewart and Brenda Goldblatt for much of the information on the working lives of Sipho and Josias; the late Judson Kuzwayo, Tina Sideris and Sipho Mhlongo for administering the questionnaires; Les Lawson for taking the photographs; and Leslie Kahn for completing the index.

This study would not have been possible without the readiness of both employers and employees in the foundry industry to cooperate in giving access and time to such an unfamiliar figure as an industrial sociologist. In particular, I must thank the officials and members of the IMS and MAWU for their time and far-sighted decisions to house their records in the University of the Witwatersrand library.

I would also like to thank Bobbie Butterworth for typing the bulk of the original manuscript, and Wendy Cullinan and Arlene Guslandie for the second draft.

Eddie.Webster
September 1985

List of Abbreviations

A. South Africa

Trade Unions

Amalgamated Engineering Union of South Africa	AEU
Amalgamated Society of Woodworkers	ASW
Black Allied Workers Union	BAWU
Electrical and Allied Trade Union of South Africa	EATUSA
Electrical and Allied Workers Union	EAWU
Engineering Industrial Workers Union	EIWU
Engineering and Allied Workers Union	E&AWU
General and Allied Workers Union	GAWU
General Workers Union	GWU
Iron Moulders Society of South Africa	IMS
Metal and Allied Workers Union	MAWU
Motor Assembly Components Workers Union of South Africa	MACWUSA
Motor Industry Combined Workers Union	MICWU
National Automobile and Allied Workers Union	NAAWU
National Union of Engineering, Industrial and Allied Workers Union	NUEIAW
National Union of Motor Assembly and Rubber Workers of South Africa	NUMARWOSA
Radio, Television, Electronic and Allied Workers Union	RTEAWU
South African Allied Workers Union	SAAWU
South African Boilermakers, Iron and Steelworkers, Shipbuilders and Welders Society	SABS
South African Electrical Workers Association	SAEWA
South African Engine Drivers and Firemen and Operators Association	S.A. Engine Drivers
South African Non-European Confederation of Iron, Steel and Metal Workers Union	SANECISMWU

South African Yster, Staal en Verwante Nywerhede-Unie	Y & S
South African Technical Officials Association	SATOA
South African Tin Workers Union	SATWU
Steel, Engineering and Allied Workers Union	SEAWU
Transvaal Radio, Television, Electronic and Allied Workers Union	TRTEAWU
United Automobile, Rubber and Allied Workers Union of South Africa	UAW
Western Province Motor Assemblies Workers Union	WPMAWU

Federations

Council of Non European Trade Unions	CNETU
Council of Unions of South Africa	CUSA
Federation of South African Trade Unions	FOSATU
South African Congress of Trade Unions	SACTU
South African Confederation of Labour	SACL
Trades and Labour Council	TLC
Trade Union Council of South Africa	TUCSA
South African Federation of Trade Unions	SAFTU
Mechanics Unions Joint Executive	MUJE
Confederation of Metal and Building Unions	CMBU

Employers

South African Federation of Engineering and Metallurgical Associations,	SAFEMA
later Steel and Engineering Industries Federation of South Africa	SEIFSA

B. Britain

Trade Unions

Friendly Iron Moulders Society	FIMS
National Union of Foundry Workers	NUFW
Amalgamated Engineering Union	AEU
Transport and General Workers Union	TGWU

Federations

British Trade Union Congress	TUC

C. United States of America

Trade Unions
National Union of Iron Moulders   NUIM
International Moulders and Allied Workers Union   IMAWU
United Automobile Workers   UAW
United Steel Workers of America   USWA

Federations
American Federation of Labour   AFL
Committee for Industrial Organization   CIO

Government Agencies
National Labour Relations Board   NLRB

International

International Metal Workers Federation   IMF

Preface

In the early 1970s an intense debate took place in South Africa on economic growth and its relationship to social and political change. The debate polarized into two opposing views. One view suggested that economic growth would break down apartheid. Industrialization would lead to liberalization. This, the 'conventional' view as expounded most consistently by O'Dowd, was challenged by the 'revisionist' thesis advanced by Johnstone and others which suggested that capitalist development was reinforcing 'white supremacy'. Although these two views reached opposite conclusions, they started from the same basic premise: an exclusive focus on the dominant institutions and groups in South Africa. Whereas in the first view these groups were seen as more or less inevitable agents of change, the 'revisionist' case was that they were more or less irremovable obstacles to change. Neither view recognized sufficiently the possibility of organizations emerging, notably from the black working class, that could take advantage of the contradictions generated by capitalist development to influence the pace and direction of change.[1]

In the post-Wiehahn period the centre of the industrial relations stage shifted unequivocally towards these emerging unions. Drawing largely on unskilled and semi-skilled black, predominantly African workers, these unions have expanded rapidly since 1979. While recruitment has been rapid the total membership is still small at approximately 400 000. Their significance, however, lies in the fact that, for the first time in South Africa, they have laid the foundations of national, mass-based unionism within the core of the manufacturing industry — the metal, motor, textile, food, paper, and chemical sectors — as well as in the retail, mining and transport industries. If we include the 800 000 workers who are members of the established unions, nearly 1200 000 workers (12,2% of the economically active population) now belong to trade unions in South

Africa.[2]

An important feature of the emerging unions is their concentration on building shop steward structures in selected workplaces. They now have an organized presence in over 750 workplaces, while in 420 of these formal agreements have been signed between management and the unions representing workers in that plant. Shop stewards, now numbering over 6000, and their committees have become the pivot of the organizational structures of these unions.

These organizational achievements have increased the bargaining power of labour and opened up, on an unprecedented scale, the opportunity for black people to participate democratically in organizations that have significant potential for change. The growing numerical strength of their organizers, their daily access to rank and file members, and their location in strategic sectors of the economy: these advantages allow them to mobilize more effectively at present than any other organization within the black population. In essence these organizations are independent schools of democracy where substantial worker leadership has developed, with the potential to play a central role in change in South Africa.

A number of journals, in particular the *South African Labour Bulletin* (*SALB*), have attempted to record the struggles of these unions over the last decade. However, with the exception of Lewis, no one has attempted to locate the different forms of workplace organization in the context of the transformation of work, i.e. the labour process.[3]

The aim of this study is to undertake such an analysis through an examination of a particular production process. Foundries were selected as a case study for two reasons. Firstly, foundries form part of the largest industrial council in the country and provide an important, if not the most important, arena for contesting the changing pattern of industrial relations in South Africa. The second reason is more practical and relates to access. The Transvaal is the centre of the engineering industry, and foundries in particular. The Metal and Allied Workers Union (MAWU) established a branch in the Transvaal in 1975 and soon began to recruit among the contract workers on the East Rand, many of whom work in foundries. This study was conceived when I realized that the history of the changing labour process in the foundry lay in the records of the foundry craft union, the Iron Moulders Society (IMS), housed in the University of the Witwatersrand library. The direct access I have had to the records, leadership, and membership of these two unions provided the foundation upon which this study was built.

What began as an exploration of the effect of the labour process on workplace organization was to lead (in Parts II and III of this study) beyond the immediate terrain to take into account three additional determinants.

Firstly, the form workplace organization takes is crucially shaped by divisions within the working class and the relationship of each of these class segments to the state. To account adequately for internal class cleavages it is necessary to link changes in the labour process to segmentation of the labour market.

Secondly, an analysis of the labour process needs to be located within the political economy. The emergence of economic crisis profoundly shapes the response of worker organization. This is of particular importance in South Africa where the effects of recession are magnified by the existence of a large 'reserve army' of unemployed not cushioned by an adequate system of social security.

Thirdly, conjunctural struggles that go beyond the labour process as such — the 1976 Soweto uprising, for instance — may be crucial in shaping the pace and form of workplace organization. The capital-labour relation in production cannot be generated and sustained wholly within the workplace; it is reproduced within the social formation as a whole through a variety of state apparatuses.[4] Although this study has been widened to take into account these three determinants, my central concern has been to fill a gap in our understanding of work and worker organization in South Africa.

The book is divided into three parts. It begins by suggesting, in the introduction, that most studies of the labour process have neglected worker resistance. In particular they have neglected to focus on resistance to deskilling and the bargaining leverage conferred on semi-skilled workers in the wake of the mechanization of the labour process. Part I traces the changing forms of job protection among iron moulders in the face of machine technology between 1896 and 1968. Ultimately the IMS resorts to *de facto* job reservation to defend its members against deskilling.

The persistence of 'racial despotism' under conditions of monopoly capitalism creates a crisis of control in work relations. The 'challenge from below' equivocally supported by the 'international factor', and the need to restructure the racial division of labour, is discussed in Part II. In the face of strong managerial resistance black semi-skilled workers proceed to organize themselves independently, taking advantage of the bargaining leverage created by machine-based production.

The deep nature of the crisis facing South Africa leads to the appointment of two Commissions of Inquiry (Wiehahn and Riekert) to search for a new form of control in the workplace. The solution they eventually propose, discussed in Part III, is designed to incorporate some and exclude other black workers in a strategy of 'reform from above'. The contradictions generated by the limited nature of deracialization and the 'challenge from below' accompanying the rise of the shop stewards' movement leads to demands for a more fundamental restructuring of the industrial relations system. The complex nature of the interaction between division within the working class, the labour process, and workplace organization are illustrated in the final chapter through the work and home lives of five foundry workers.[5]

The use of biography is not, of course, novel in sociology; what is perhaps distinctive in this study is the way in which these working lives are used in the conclusion to illustrate the structures of work and worker organization delineated elsewhere in the study through documentary and survey questionnaire techniques.[6] Because they defined the problem in historical terms, existing documentary sources became central to this study. To gather contemporary data, four semi-structured surveys were administered. However, in the course of cross-checking documentary sources, and confronted by the inability of survey questionnaire techniques to come to grips with real life experiences in the foundry, I turned to biography. This technique aimed at eliciting first-hand experience collected in unstructured in-depth interviews and illustrated through photographs. The technique proved useful not only in illustrating the experience of foundry workers but also in exemplifying the consciousness of ordinary workers — and thus illuminating the mould in which their consciousness has been cast. These three techniques are used in this study as distinct but complementary methods.

Notes

1   For a summary of this debate see L. Schlemmer and E. Webster, editors, *Change, Reform and Economic Growth in South Africa* (Ravan Press, Johannesburg, 1978).

2   For further details of the trends, activities and potential role of these unions see E. Webster, 'New Force on the Shop Floor' in *South*

African Review 2 (Ravan Press, Johannesburg, 1984).

3   J. Lewis, *Industrialization and Trade Union Organization in South Africa 1924 – 1955* (Cambridge University Press, Cambridge, 1984).

4   Brighton Labour Process Group, 'The capitalist labour process', *Capital and Class* 1 (1977), p.24.

5   The idea of focussing on the five biographies was derived from Richard Edwards, *Contested Terrain. The Transformation of the Workplace in the Twentieth Century* (Basic Books, New York, 1979).

6   For a description and discussion of my method see Appendices A – E of my Ph.D thesis, 'The labour process and forms of workplace organization in South African foundries', University of the Witwatersrand, 1983.

CHAPTER 1

Introduction:
Class Struggle in the Foundry

The foundations for an analysis of the transformation of the labour process were laid over a century ago by Marx in Volume I of *Capital*. It is thus appropriate to begin with an exposition of that forbidding, unavoidable book. This chapter is not, however, an exercise in social theory so much as an attempt to provide the non-specialist reader with an understanding of the concepts which constitute the theoretical ground of this study.

Capitalism exists when the process of production is organized in terms of a market on which commodities, including labour itself, are bought and sold according to standards of monetary exchange.[1] Such a process emerges when a class of men and women who do not own the means of production are forced to sell their labour power. In terms of the normal contract of employment the worker does not agree to do an exact amount of work; he surrenders his capacity to work and it is the task of management, through its hierarchy of control, to transform his capacity into actual productive activity. It is this process of transforming labour power into productive activity that is central to capitalism, and yet it is at the same time *hidden*. Let us therefore 'leave this noisy sphere of the market' and examine 'the hidden abode of production'.[2]

Let us begin 'by stating the first premise of all human existence, and therefore of all history; the premise, namely, that men must be in a position to live in order to be able to make history. But life involves before anything else, eating and drinking, a habitation, clothing and many other things. The first historical act is thus the production of the means to satisfy these needs, the production of material life itself.'[3] The process of producing the material means to satisfy these needs — 'purposeful activity aimed at the production of use values' — Marx calls 'the labour process'.[4] The labour process is a universal condition of human existence and is not in itself peculiar to capitalism.

Capitalist production however has a twofold objective — to produce a use value that has exchange value (i.e., can be sold as a commodity); and to produce a commodity greater in value than the sum of commodities used to produce it.[5] This latter process — the difference between the value of labour power and the value created in the course of the working day — is the source of surplus value. Capital accumulation takes place where a portion of the surplus value is converted to additional capital.[6]

How does the capitalist then increase the rate of surplus value? Marx drew a distinction between what he called *absolute surplus value* and *relative surplus value*. Surplus value, he said, can be increased not only by lengthening the working day — absolute surplus value — but equally with a given length of the working day, by reducing the length of the period of necessary labour time. This increase, which he calls relative surplus value, can be accrued by reducing the value of the labour power (i.e., the amount of labour time required to produce the worker's means of subsistence).[7] This depends on an intensification of the productivity of labour. The core of his argument in Volume I of *Capital* is how the labour process is progressively transformed as capital takes hold of it. It is this progressive transformation that leads to the steady increase in the productivity of labour and so to the production of relative surplus value.

Marx identifies three phases in the transformation of the labour process — cooperation, manufacture, and machinofacture.[8] Each phase is characterized by a series of impediments to accumulation which are overcome by a transformation of the labour process. 'Through a combination of class strategies by the capitalist state, and individual strategies by individual capitalists attempting to maximize their profits, these impediments are overrun and the accumulation process continues in new forms.'[9]

Before the phase of cooperation arrives there are limits to the creation of surplus value as the worker still has control over the pace of work (handicraft or guild production), as well as the precise location of production (the cottage, for example, in the putting-out system). Landes describes the contradictions created by trying to increase output under petty commodity production — 'he [the employer] had no way of compelling his workers to do a given number of hours of labour; the domestic weaver or craftsman was master of his time, starting and stopping when he desired'.[10] The lack of supervision under conditions of 'cottage industry' meant that capital had little control over exactly how much the worker worked per day. It was also exceptionally easy for the worker to embezzle raw materials. As Marglin has argued, the creation of the factory provided the structural solution to the first of these constraints. Workers were brought under one roof and closely supervised in their work. Thus, Marglin concludes, the major impulse for the creation of factories was the desire to undermine workers' control. The factory was the central mechanism in securing control of the labour process and lengthening the working day.[11]

While the rise of the factory — what Marx called 'cooperation' — overcomes some of the impediments to accumulation by bringing workers under capitalist control it also creates the potential for resistance to capital. 'As the number of cooperative workers increases, so too does the resistance to the dominance of capital'.[12] For Marx, cooperation is the logical foundation and historical starting point of capitalist production, which 'only really begins when each individual capitalist simultaneously employs a comparatively large number of workers'.[13] Under cooperation, then, the factory as an institution emerges for the first time as large numbers of workers are brought together at the command of a single capitalist. In its earliest stages the factory labour process 'can hardly be distinguished from the handicraft trades of the guilds, except by the greater number of workers simultaneously employed by the same individual capitalist. It is merely an enlargement of the workshop of the master craftsman of the guilds'.[14] But cooperation, by bringing together large numbers of workers, necessitates supervision. 'The work of directing, superintending, and adjusting becomes one of the functions of capital from the moment that the labour under capitalist control becomes cooperative'.[15] This function of capital is also, however, a necessity because of the inherently antagonistic nature of production under capitalism where the driving motive is maximization of surplus value. 'The control exercised by the capitalist is not only a special function arising from the nature of the social labour process . . . but it is at the same time a function of the exploitation of the social process, and is consequently conditioned by the unavoidable antagonism between the exploiter and the raw material of his exploitation'.[16] It is this twofold nature of capitalist control that gives it a 'purely despotic form'.[17]

At the centre of capitalist production, then, is a contradictory process of cooperation and conflict. Some degree of cooperation is necessary for production to take place; at the same time a basic conflict exists between those who own the means of production and those who do not and have to sell their labour in order to survive. The source of this conflict lies in the fact that what is income for the worker, namely his wage, is a cost for the employer, which the capitalist naturally seeks to minimize. This is what class struggle in production is about — the continuous power struggle over how much work is to be done and for what reward.

In the early period of transition from cooperation — or simple cooperation, as Palloix categorizes it — to manufacture, the craftsman still retains a degree of control over the content and performance of work.[18] With manufacturing, the various work activities centred upon the crafts are broken down into a series of distinct tasks, thus introducing the division of labour and job fragmentation even though the craft remains the foundation of work. 'Handicraft remains the basis, a technically narrow basis which excludes a really scientific division of the production process into its component parts, since every partial process undergone by the product must be capable of being done by hand and of forming a separate handicraft'.[19] Three consequences follow this division of labour: the productivity of labour is increased, the value of labour power is cheapened, and a class of unskilled labourers excluded from handicraft production is introduced. But manufacturing comes up against certain impediments to accumulation that are not only technical but also arise out of prolonged apprenticeship training.[20] The introduction of machinery was to provide the structural solution to the impediment of handicraft production.[21]

In Chapter 15 Marx turns to the most highly developed form of capitalist production based on the machine — machinofacture. With the introduction of machines instead of tools 'the motive mechanism also acquired an independent form entirely emancipated from the restraints of human strength'.[22] The worker becomes a mere appendage of the machine. 'In manufacture the organization of the social labour process is purely subjective; it is a combination of specialized workers. Large scale industry, on the other hand, possesses in the machine system an entirely objective organization of production, which confronts the worker as a pre-existing material condition of production'.[23] Under manufacture, increases in surplus value are restricted to lengthening the working day (absolute surplus value) and piece-work (increasing the intensity of labour). Under machinofacture exploitation is emancipated from 'human subjectivity' allowing for further prolongation of the factory's working day through the shift system and the intensification of the individual worker's labour through the compulsory shortening of the working day arising out of the Factory Act.

Marx then analyzes the development of social relations within the factory: the new form of the division of labour that appears through the employment of women and children, the replacement of craft skill by machines (deskilling), the domination of man by machine, the separation of mental from manual labour, the use of the machine as a weapon in the struggle of capital against labour, and the worker's illusion that it is the machine, rather than capital, that oppresses him.[24]

The discussion of the transformation of the labour process culminates in the distinction between formal and real subsumption [subordination]. By formal subordination Marx meant that control over labour was not firmly in the hands of capital, i.e., capital had not yet seized control of the labour process on the shop floor. 'The production of absolute surplus value turns exclusively on the length of the working day, whereas the production of relative surplus value completely revolutionizes the technical process of labour . . . a mode of production arises . . . on the basis of the formal subsumption of labour under capital. This formal subsumption is then replaced by real subsumption'.[25] While the production of absolute surplus value is characteristic when labour has been formally subsumed, it continues with real subsumption and the production of relative surplus value. In some respects absolute and relative surplus value cannot be distinguished; all surplus value is both absolute and relative. However, the distinction is useful when we consider the need to increase surplus value, and the capitalist's choice between lengthening the working day or intensifying the productivity of labour.

For Marx then, transition from the phase of manufacture to that of modern industry or machinofacture was bound up with the shift in the dominant mode of surplus value. But this connection, Maxine Berg reminds us, should not be understood in simple chronological form, identifying manufacture with the raising of absolute surplus value and modern industry with the raising of relative surplus value.[26] A labour process controlled by machinery could be made more productive by allowing for overtime, although it is the machinery, by transcending human limitation through generating relative surplus value, that allows for limitless surplus creation. 'Marx, in setting out manufacture and modern industry as phases of the capitalist labour process, was using a broad sweep of history to illustrate the immanent tendencies of the capitalist mode of production. The phases delineated by Marx formed a part of his model of capitalist development. The phases of manufacture and modern industry were abstractions and were not, therefore, meant to sum up any particular historical period'.[27]

Braverman and Beyond

So successful was Marx in Volume I of *Capital* in identifying the broad tendency of capitalism to transform the labour process that his work in this sphere remained largely unchallenged and, until the 1970s saw a 'rediscovery' of the labour process, undeveloped. Braverman, whose book *Labour and Monopoly Capital* contributed so much to the renewal of interest in the labour process, makes this point clearly in the introduction to his study: 'so well did he [Marx] understand the tendencies of the capitalist mode of production and so accurately did he generalize from the as yet meagre instances of his own time, that in the decades immediately after he completed his work, Marx's analysis seemed adequate to each special problem of the labour process, and remarkably faithful to the overall movement of production. It may thus have been, in the beginning, the very prophetic strength of Marx's analysis that contributed to the dormancy of the subject amongst Marxists'.[28] Of course a focus on work is hardly new in sociology: the roots of industrial sociology — plant sociology as it was called in the early days — lie precisely in Elton Mayo's attempt to isolate the factory and identify the mechanisms of output restriction at Western Electric nearly sixty years ago.[29] What is distinctive about post-Braverman interest in work is that it takes as its point of departure the link between capitalism and work. Braverman, says Nichols, 'reunited capitalism and work'.[30] He did this by linking the major change within capitalism — the transformation from its competitive to its monopoly phase — to the major change within work — the growth of science in production. 'Scientific management', Braverman says, 'and the whole movement for the organization of production on its modern basis, had their beginnings in the last two decades of the last century. A scientific technical revolution based on the systematic use of science for rapid transformation of labour power into capital, also begins . . . at the same time. Both chronologically and functionally, they are part of the new stage of capitalist development, and they grow out of monopoly capitalism and make it possible'.[31]

Although Braverman has been criticized for not clarifying his understanding of the connection between scientific management and monopoly capitalism, his major contribution to our understanding of the capitalist labour process since Marx is his analysis of the former.[32] It is, he says, an attempt to apply the methods of science to the increasingly complex problems of the control of labour in rapidly growing capitalist enterprises.[33] It lacks the characteristics of a true science because its assumptions reflect nothing more than the outlook of the capitalist with regard to the conditions of production. Taylor, Braverman argues, was to raise the concept of control to an entirely new plane when he asserted as an absolute necessity for adequate management the dictation to the worker of the precise manner in which work was to be performed.[34] A major obstacle to the ability of employers to maximize the labour performed by their workers lay in the difficulty of knowing how long any particular piece of work actually required. The ability of workers to keep this knowledge from their employers formed the heart of the system of worker regulation of output described by Taylor as 'soldiering'. Taylor and his 'efficiency experts' believed that through a careful study of individual jobs and careful selection of incentive or bonus pay, employers could structure the workplace so that 'soldiering' would be eliminated. Management could strengthen its hand in the struggle to speed up production if it followed three principles that underlay scientific management.

The first principle was that 'the managers assume . . . the burden of gathering together all of the traditional knowledge which in the past has been possessed by the workmen and then of classifying, tabulating and reducing this knowledge to rules, laws and formulae'.[35] We may call this principle the dissociation of the labour process from the skills of the workers.

The second principle was that 'all possible brain work should be removed from the shop and centred in the planning or layout department'.[36] This we may call the principle of the separation of conception from execution.

The third principle was that 'the work of every workman is fully planned out by the management at least one day in advance, and each man receives in most cases complete written instructions, describing in detail the task which he is to accomplish, as well as the means to be used in doing the work'.[37] The third principle, then, is the use of this monopoly over knowledge to control each step of the labour process and its mode of execution.

Braverman was to incorporate these arguments into a far-reaching critique of what he called 'the degradation of work in the twentieth century'. Although the thrust of his argument is concerned with the manner in which scientific management and the scientific technical revolution have rendered craft skill superfluous in modern industry, he addresses himself directly to the conventional view that technical change and mechanization increase skill levels ('the upgrading thesis') in his final chapter. His central critique is summed up in the concluding pages:

> The break up of craft skills and reconstruction of production as a collective or social process had destroyed the traditional concept of skill and opened up only one way for mastery over the labour process to develop — in and through scientific, technical and engineering knowledge'.[38]

The upgrading thesis rests on two trends, he suggests: the first is the shift of workers from some major occupational groups into others; the second is the prolongation of the average period of education.[39]

This general tendency of greater control over labour was taken further when Henry Ford inaugurated the first continuous assembly line for the Model T Ford in Detroit in January 1914, four years after Taylor's death. Within three months the assembly time for the Model T had been reduced to one-tenth of the time formerly needed and by 1925 an organization had been created which produced almost as many cars in a single day as it had produced in an entire year. The quickening rate of production in this case, says Braverman, depended not only upon the change in the organization of labour, but on the control which management, at a single stroke, attained over the pace of assembly, so that it could now double and triple the rate at which operations had to be performed and thus subject its workers to an extremely intense form of labour.[40]

Sohn-Rethel's verdict is that 'Fordism', or the flow method, is the mode of production most perfectly adapted to the economy of time in monopoly capitalism.[41] The entirety of a workshop or factory is integrated into one continuous process in the service of the rule of speed. Ford put it simply: 'the ideal is the man must have every second necessary but not a single unnecessary second'.[42] Ford, says Aglietta, deepened and therefore surpassed Taylorism in the labour process by the application of two complementary principles: the integration of different segments of the labour process by a system of conveyors and handling devices, ensuring movement of the materials to be transferred and their arrival at the approximate machine tools; and the fixing of the workers to jobs in positions rigorously determined by the configuration of the machine system. The individual worker thus lost all control over his work rhythm. The continuous linear flow prohibited the formation of buffer stops between jobs and subjected the worker to the collective rhythm of the uniform movement of the system.[43]

The limits imposed by human subjectivity were to lead to what Palloix calls a fourth stage of automated production. This fourth stage, Palloix says, 'aims to eliminate all manual intervention by the worker by means of electronic techniques, so that the worker's intervention is now limited to overall supervision and control'.[44] In the most sophisticated theoretical contribution to this debate the Brighton Labour Process Group challenge the idea of a fourth stage. They argue that 'developments in the labour process such as high speed continuous flow mass production, automation, etc. do not signal the emergence of a "new era" in which the brutalities of machine-based production would be left behind'.[45] They offer an account of the transformation of the labour process which is strongly influenced by Chapter 16 of *Capital*, Volume 1, and which is explicitly organized in terms of the distinction between formal or real subordination. When the labour process is only formally subordinated to capital, they suggest, 'the objective and subjective conditions of labour are such as to provide a material basis for continual resistance to the imposition of valorization . . . real control of production is not yet firmly in the hands of capital. There is still a relationship between labour and the conditions of labour within production which provides labour with a degree of control and hence with a lever with which to enforce its class objectives, which may be objectives of artisan labour — craft prerogatives over recruitment into the trade and over the content and performance of work'.[46] This they contrast with real subordination, which they call 'valorization in command' — where capital has power in the very heart of production itself. This, they argue, is achieved on the basis of a series of linked and mutually interdependent developments: the extraction of relative surplus value; the employment of machinery; the conscious application of science and technology; the mobility and replacement of labour (the formation of the reserve army of labour); and large scale production.

The formation of a reserve army of labour forms a crucial part of

Marx's argument in *Capital*, Volume 1 — functioning, along with deskilling, as a mechanism that disciplines the working class in the phase of real subordination. Marx argued that the industrial reserve army was both a condition and a consequence of capital accumulation, 'but if a surplus population of workers is a necessary product of accumulation or of the development of wealth on a capitalist basis, this surplus population also becomes, conversely, the lever of capitalist accumulation, indeed it becomes a condition for the existence of the capitalist mode of production'.[48] To put it simply, Marx argued that the process of capital accumulation led to machines replacing men and women and thus to unemployment. At the same time, the existence of unemployment was crucial in keeping wages down and disciplining workers.

Worker Resistance

While the arguments so far in this chapter have been concerned to demonstrate how capital has increased its control over the labour process, real subordination is never complete. By calling labour power 'variable capital' Marx made it clear, Nicols suggests, that surplus value was not determined in a mechanical way. The employment relationship is one that gives the employer the right to issue orders while imposing on the workers the duty to obey. 'If powerful enough employers can vary the surplus value created. If they are strong enough workers can vary this too. The term 'variable' draws attention to the fact that the surplus actually created varies according to the relative strengths of the combatants.'[49] In particular Marx believed that the evolution of industrial capitalism provided the pre-conditions for collective organization by throwing workers together in large numbers and creating deprivations which spurred them to combination. However, the limited economic achievements of these trade unions lead workers to adopt more political forms of action and ultimately to challenge directly the whole structure of class domination.[50]

Subsequent experience failed to confirm this 'optimistic' prognostication of the revolutionary potential of trade unions: unions were to become exclusive preserves of the aristocratic minority of privileged craft workers.[51] Marx and Engels never produced a comprehensive revision of their early writings; rather, they tended to treat the development of trade unions in the second half of the nineteenth century as a deviation from the natural course. Since the death of Marx and Engels the development both of trade unions and capitalist society has further undermined the credibility of the simple thesis propounded in their early writings.[52] The most influential accounts of twentieth century socialist theory (Lenin, Michel, Trotsky) and industrial sociology (Wright-Mills, Lester, Flanders, Bell, Coser, Kerr, Dahrendorf, Lipset) have focussed on some aspects of trade unions which appear to inhibit any overt challenge to capitalism. With organization, they suggest, comes oligarchy, a decline in militancy and integration and incorporation of trade unions into capitalist society.[53] Braverman shares this 'pessimistic' interpretation:

> the unionized working class weakened in its original revolutionary impetus by the gains afforded by the rapid increase in productivity, increasingly lost the will and ambition to wrest control of production from capitalist hands and turned ever more to bargaining over labour's share of the product . . . the critique of the mode of production gave way to the critique of capitalism as a mode of distribution. Trade unions were prepared to accept increased control over production in return for better wages. Conceding higher relative wages for a shrinking proportion of workers in order to guarantee uninterrupted production was to become, particularly obvious after the Second World War, a widespread feature of corporate labour policy, especially after it was adopted by union leaderships.[54]

The re-emergence of industrial conflict in advanced capitalist society in the 1960s was to lead to a critical reappraisal of the pessimistic one-sidedness of industrial relations orthodoxy. Foremost amongst these critics of the dominant structural functionalist view was Hyman, who emphasized the ambivalence inherent in the trade union function. Strongly influenced by the militant rank and file challenges to union officials in Britain in the late 1960s and early 70s, he drew attention to the potential of trade unionism. 'Pure and simple trade union activity *does* pose a substantial threat to the stability of the capitalist economy in certain circumstances', he concluded. 'The iron law of oligarchy is subject to important constraints. Attempts to extend the process of incorporation do meet significant obstacles to success. To this extent, the "optimistic" interpretation of trade unionism cannot be rejected outright'.[55] Yet Marx's 'optimism' was not an article of faith; his analysis of the revolutionary role of the working class rested on a materialist account of the contradictory nature of capitalist development. The precise effect of the changing labour process on forms of workplace organization is not explored, though Marx's theory postulates such a link. What is the relationship between the abstract and the concrete, between the labour process and class struggle?

Although class struggle is central to Marx's analysis of the transformation of the labour process, with the exception of Chapter 10 in Volume I it is capital not labour that is the central actor. This has led some commentators to see in *Capital* only abstract laws of motion 'in that it completely ignores the way actual working class power forces and checks capitalist development'.[56] The absence in Braverman's study of an account of the way in which the development of machine-based production has generated important sources of leverage for effective workplace organization is a serious omission.

> The point is not that he fails to focus on worker consciousness — this after all is a self-proclaimed limitation. The weakness of Braverman's account is that the working class struggle is accorded the status of a merely transient or frictional reaction to capital, rather than being located as the articulation of contradictions within the forms of valorization dominating a specific period of capital accumulation. For Braverman it was only the existence of craft skill that presented an obstacle to capitalist development; consequently the transformation of the labour process is conceptualized in terms of a switch from thorough-going craft control to pervasive capitalist direction of the labour process.[57]

Forms of worker competence and initiative lodged within the real subordination of the labour process may constitute significant bases of worker resistance and counter-control — and these, as Elger argues, are ignored in Braverman's account.

A number of post-Braverman studies have attempted to rectify this neglect by focussing on the effects of worker resistance. Penn, for example, indicates a considerable amount of resistance to deskilling.[58] Such resistance, he shows, was quite successful in retaining levels of skill, with the key role being played by the craft union through the mechanism of social exclusion. To understand how this takes place it is necessary to move from the sphere of production to the market — from Marx to Parkin's reformulation of Weber's notion of social closure.[59] By closure Parkin refers to the capabilities of groups to exclude outsiders (exclusion) and to monopolize resources denied to others (usurpation). In capitalist society, according to Parkin, there are two predominant modes of exclusion — control of property and control over professional qualifications and credentials. It is precisely this latter mode of exclusion that Penn and others describe craft workers using to protect themselves against deskilling. In particular, by methods of labour market closure, limiting recruitment to an occupation, and demanding lengthy training, craft workers have been able to protect established interests. The result is the survival of a higher number of 'craft' jobs than the deskilling thesis would appear to indicate.

Labour market theorists have developed as a means of explaining the persistence of differentiation within the working class. There is common ground among these theorists in the assertion that segmentation creates a number of distinct sectors, usually distinguished by some variety of the terms primary and secondary. Edwards suggests a three-fold segmentation — a secondary labour market of unskilled and casual labour, and subordinate and independent primary labour markets of more skilled and stable workers.[60] Importantly, Edwards links the segments of the labour market to the nature of the labour process. 'Labour markets are segmented', he says, 'because they express a historical segmentation of the labour process; especially, a distinct system of control inside the firm underlies each of the three market segments'.[61] Thus, for Edwards, the fundamental basis for division into three segments is to be found in the workplace, not in the labour market.[62]

A second, and more important, aspect of worker resistance neglected by Braverman is the new bargaining power conferred on unskilled and semi-skilled workers when mechanization replaces craft skill. What are often retained, Elger suggests, are specific dexterities which still involve levels of training, if for no other reason than that they are the 'tricks of the trade'. Forms of expertise may be narrower than traditional skills, but they can still 'constitute effective obstacles to capitalist initiative.'[63] This line of argument is developed more fully by Edwards who argues that the growth in size of the firm that accompanies the transition to monopoly capitalism creates a crisis of control.[64] The crisis emerges from the contradiction between the firm's increasing need for control on one hand, and its diminishing ability to maintain control on the other. The practical solution to this crisis, Edwards suggests, lies in making management's power invisible in the structure of work — what he calls technical control.[65] However technical control — where the entire production process of a plant, or large segments of it, are based on a technology that paces and directs the labour process — greatly facilitates a new form of unionism, industrial unionism. 'Technical control linked together the plant's workforce and when the line stopped every worker necessarily joined the strike — technical control thus took relatively homogeneous labour (unskilled and semi-skilled workers) and technologically linked them in production. The combination proved to be exceptionally favourable for building unions'.[66]

These two forms of worker resistance — the resistance of deskilled craft workers and the new forms of workplace organization among semi-skilled and unskilled workers — provide the basis for this study. Through an examination of the relationship between changes in the labour process in South African foundries and in the labour market, the nature of these forms of workplace organization will be explored. To understand changes in the foundry, production must be conceived not only as a material process — involving the instruments of labour — but also as a social process — involving activities whereby people transform both their circumstances and themselves.[67] Thus while change in the social relations within which individuals produce is linked to change and development in the material means of production, the relationship between them is not a mechanical but a dialectical one. This view of the role of technology in capitalist society is more subtle and compelling than the technological determinism of the Webbs.[68] It also allows us to recognize the specificity of each labour process and to avoid the 'juggernaut' view of capital's all-pervasive control presented by Braverman. It suggests instead that the contradictory nature of capitalist development offers new opportunities for workplace organization.

Our hypothesis then is that while machine technology undermines the craft unions' bargaining leverage, leading to real subordination and relative surplus value, it also transforms unskilled labour into semi-skilled labour. By increasing the proportion of workers strategically involved in the mechanized production process it increases the bargaining power of a large section of the workforce. The new semi-skilled workforce now represents a threat to the deskilled workers who either try to recruit them or redraw the boundaries to exclude them. If they choose the latter course, semi-skilled workers will proceed to organize themselves independently. However, the pace and form of this change is uneven and craft competence may well remain embedded within the labour process. With this theoretical framework in mind let us now turn to an examination of the foundry.

Five Faces from a 'Hidden Abode'

Roughly twenty thousand people work in the 142 foundries in South Africa.[69] They cast the metal products of South Africa's industrial economy, which increasingly involves munitions production.[70] Five men who have worked in these foundries and reflect the different working lives of foundry workers are Bob, Len, Morris, Sipho, and Josias.[71] They share a common condition of all workers, past and present: they do not own sufficient means of production to survive and must, therefore, sell their labour power to live. But here the similarity between these men ends. Not only did they all enter the foundry from different starting points and with different levels of education, skill, and political and economic power; but the organization of foundry work has changed, exacerbating and further altering the cleavages between the five, both at work and at home. These differences within the working class express themselves in different forms of workplace organization. These five men's experiences demonstrate in capsule form, not only the history of foundry work in the twentieth century, but also the complex nature of the interaction between division within the working class, the labour process, and workplace organization.

Bob and Len, both white, started their working lives as journeyman moulders — skilled craftsmen. Bob was born in Uitenhage in 1906 and 'served time' as an apprentice for five years between 1922 and 1927 — the heyday of the 'labour aristocrat'. His father had immigrated to South Africa from England at the turn of the century and had eventually settled and raised his family in East London. Bob attended Selborne College until Standard Eight, when he left school to start his apprenticeship at the local foundry. He started at 12s6d per week, reaching 15s in the second year and £1 10s from then until he completed his apprenticeship. Once qualified, and with an earning power of £6 a week, Bob left East London for the Transvaal, the centre of the foundry industry. With his journeyman's ticket, Bob was to enter the Transvaal foundry industry as a 'labour aristocrat'.

Len is a younger man than Bob but is now close to retirement. He was born in Benoni in 1924 of Afrikaans-speaking parents. His father worked on the mines on the East Rand. In 1940 Len followed his brother into the East Rand Proprietary Mine (ERPM) as an apprenticed moulder. He was drawn into the production of strategic materials during the Second World War when a chronic shortage of skilled labour for strategic industries prompted the government to move swiftly to secure 'dilution'. Initially dilution of the moulding trade was secured by employing non-union 'emergency workers' at lower rates. But employers soon took advantage of this breach in union rules to link the employment of 'emergency labour' with mechanization and therefore deskilling. Thus the trade was on the decline when Len entered it, as deskilling kept pace with the more rapid introduction of machine technology. Unlike Bob, who retained a deep pride in his craft skill, Len approached moulding in a more instrumental way. His only interest, he said, was money.

Morris is a coloured man whose experience of race discrimination inside the union and the industry was to embitter him so much that he eventually left the union and the industry. He began his working life as a production moulder in Durban Falkirk (now Defy) in 1946. He wanted to become an appronticed journeyman moulder but was unable to persuade the foundry manager in his home town of Pietermaritzburg to take him on. This angered him as some foundries in Natal did accept coloureds as apprentices. He decided to leave Pietermaritzburg and found employment at Durban Falkirk where he had heard management employed large numbers of coloureds as production moulders. (The establishment of Durban Falkirk in 1936 as South Africa's first large-scale mass production foundry had opened up a demand for a new type of worker, the machine-operating production moulder.)

Sipho and Josias are both Zulu-speaking migrant workers whose families live in KwaZulu. Although they have responded to their situation in different ways, they share the common lot of migrant life: the geographical separation of day-to-day working life from child-rearing.

Sipho first came to Boksburg in 1959 from Mhlabatini where his family had lived for generations. He has worked sufficiently long in Boksburg (15 years) to acquire Section 10/1(b) rights, but he lives in Vosloorus Hostel while his wife is forced to remain on their plot of land in KwaZulu. He works as a 'cast-boy' in Rely Precision.

Josias is the youngest of the faces from the 'hidden abode'. He was born in 1950 on a white farm in Vryheid, Natal, where his father was a tenant labourer. But, he says, 'we were chased from these lands because the government said the land could only be used by big white farmers'. The family was relocated to Nondweni, a resettlement camp in Nqutu, KwaZulu. However, because of the desolate living conditions and the difficulty of making a living there, he went to work in Durban in 1970. It was here that he first came across worker militancy when he participated in the strikes in Durban in 1973. He came to the Reef in 1975 in search of work on the East Rand. As a contract worker he found it easiest to find employment in the foundries. Josias says he has worked at most of the unskilled and semi-skilled jobs in the foundry.

These five faces from 'a hidden abode' illustrate the transformation of the labour process and its effect on workplace organization in South African foundries. Although they are mentioned only occasionally in this study, it is from the testimony of men like Bob, Len and Morris (in Part I) and Sipho and Josias (in Part III) that the process of class struggle in the foundry is understood. Bob and Len illustrate the privileged but at the same time vulnerable nature of the craft moulder in the face of a changing labour process. Morris, Sipho and Josias illustrate a new type of foundry worker whose role within the social relations of production offers new opportunities for workplace organization. The different work and home lives of these five faces illustrate the specific racial nature of the division of labour. These differences are conceptualized in this study in terms of three racially segmented labour markets — the independent primary labour market (Bob and Len), the subordinate primary market (Morris), and the secondary labour market (Sipho and Josias). We will return to these men in the concluding chapter to illustrate the changes that have taken place in the foundry.

To understand why workplace organization has taken a racial form it is necessary to go back to the origins of foundry production in South Africa with the following questions in mind. How did craft moulders in South Africa respond to the process of 'deskilling'? Did craft workers attempt to organize the new class of machine operators that emerged, or did these machine operators organize themselves independently? Above all, does an examination of South African foundries confirm the possibility which Braverman neglected: that machine-based production generates important sources of leverage, thus providing the terrain for the new form of workplace organization?

Notes

1   Karl Marx, *Capital, A Critique of Political Economy*, Vol. 1 (Penguin Books, London, 1976), pp.270-280.

2   Marx's exact words are: 'Let us therefore, in company with the owner of money and the owner of labour power, leave this noisy sphere, where everything takes place on the surface and in full view of everyone, and follow them into the hidden abode of production, on whose threshold there hangs the notice "No admittance except on business"'. Marx, *ibid.*, pp. 279-280.

3   Karl Marx, *The German Ideology*, Part 1, in *The Marx-Engels Reader*, edited by Robert C. Tucker (W.W. Norton & Co., New York, 1972) p.120.

4   Marx, *Capital*, p.290.

5   *Ibid.*, p.293.

6   *Ibid.*, p.302.

7   *Ibid.*, p.432.

8   These three phases are covered in Chapters 13, 14 and 15 of Volume 1 of *Capital*.

9   E.O. Wright, *Class, Crisis and the State* (New Left Books, London, 1978), p.163.

10   D.S. Landes, *The Unbound Prometheus* (Cambridge University Press, Cambridge, 1969), p.58.

11   Stephen A. Marglin, 'What do bosses do? The origins and functions of hierarchy in capitalist production', in Andre Gorz, *The Division of Labour, the Labour Process and Class Struggle in Modern Capitalism* (Harvester Press, Brighton, 1978), p.36.

12   Marx, *Capital*, p.449.

13   *Ibid.*, p.438.

14   *Ibid.*, p.439.

15   *Ibid.*, p.449.

16   *Ibid.*, p.449.

17   Marx's actual words were: 'If capitalist direction is thus twofold in content, owing to the twofold nature of the process of production which has to be directed — on one hand a social labour process for the creation of a product, and on the other hand capital's process of valorization — in form it is purely despotic'. Marx, *ibid.*, p.450.

18   C. Palloix, 'The labour process: from Fordism to neo-Fordism' in *The Labour Process and Class Struggle* (Stage 1, Conference of Socialist Economists pamphlets, London, 1978), p.51.

19   Marx, *Capital* p.458. For a discussion of the consequences of this division of labour see pp.458-470.

20   Palloix, 'The labour process', p.52.

21   Marx, *Capital*, 1976, p.491.

22 *Ibid.*, p.499.
23 *Ibid.*, p.508.
24 See, for a discussion of the shift system, *ibid.*, pp.526-533; for the compulsory shortening of the working day, pp.532-542; for the development of social relations within the factory, pp.547-564.
25 *Ibid.*, p.645.
26 M. Berg, *Technology and Toil in Nineteenth Century Britain* (CSE Books, London, 1979), p.5.
27 *Ibid.*, p.5.
28 H. Braverman, *Labour and Monopoly Capital. The degradation of work in the twentieth century* (Monthly Review Press, New York and London, 1974).
29 For an account of the rise of industrial sociology in the United States, see L. Baritz, *Servants of Power* (Wiley, New York, 1965).
30 Theo Nichols (ed.), *Capital and Labour. A Marxist Primer* (Fontana Paperbacks, Glasgow, 1980), p.273.
31 Braverman, *Labour and Monopoly Capital*, p.252.
32 See T. Elger and B. Schwarz, 'Monopoly capitalism and the impact of Taylorism', in Nichols, *Capital and Labour.*, for a critique of Braverman along these lines.
33 Braverman, *Labour and Monopoly Capital*, p.86.
34 See Frederick W. Taylor, *Scientific Management* (New York and London, 1947) where Taylor discusses his three-year struggle as foreman with the pieceworkers in Midvale Steel Works to overcome soldiering. The conclusions he derived from this experience formed the basis of his life-long propagation of Scientific Management. They are discussed at length in three book-length documents: *Shop Management* (1903); a public document, *Hearings before Special Committee of the House of Representatives to investigate the Taylor and other systems of shop management* (1912); and *Principles of Scientific Management* (1911).
35 Braverman, *Labour and Monopoly Capital*, pp.112-119.
36 *Ibid.*, p.113.
37 *Ibid*, p.118.
38 *Ibid.*, p.443.
39 *Ibid.*, pp.424-449.
40 *Ibid.*, p.148.
41 A. Sohn-Rethel, *Intellectual and Manual Labour, A Critique of Epistemology* (Macmillan, London, 1978), p.161.
42 H. Beynon, *Working for Ford* (Allen Lane, London, 1973), p.19.
43 M. Aglietta, *A Theory of Capitalist Regulation: The US Experience* (New Left Books, London, 1978), p.122.
44 Palloix, 'The labour Process', p.54.
45 Brighton Labour Process Group, 'The Capitalist Labour Process', *Capital*

and Class, Vol. 1, 1977, p.20.

46 *Ibid.*, pp.6-7.

47 *Ibid.*, p.9.

48 Marx, *Capital*, 1976, p.784.

49 Nichols, *Capital and Labour*, p.35.

50 These sentences are a summary of Marx and Engels, 'Manifesto of the Communist Party', in *The Marx-Engels Reader*, pp.342-343.

51 Tony Lane, *The Union Makes Us Strong* (Arrow Books, London, 1974), pp.63-90.

52 For a distinction between what the author calls the 'optimistic tradition' and the 'pessimistic interpretation' in Marx and Engels, see Richard Hyman, *Marxism and the Sociology of Trade Unionism* (Pluto Press, London, 1971).

53 *Ibid.*, pp.25-37.

54 Braverman, *Labour and Monopoly Capital*, p.150.

55 Hyman, *Marxism*, p.37. Writing a decade later Hyman was to qualify what he sees as a romanticized and idealized conception of shop floor organization and action. In particular he emphasizes the bureaucratization of the rank and file in the wake of the Donovan Commission's attempt to incorporate shop stewards. Hyman, 'The politics of workplace trade unionism', *Capital and Class*, Vol.8, Summer 1979.

56 Harry Cleaver, *Reading Capital Politically* (University of Texas Press, Houston, 1979), p.28, sums up this approach as the 'political economy' approach to *Capital*.

57 Tony Elger, 'Valorization and "deskilling": a critique of Braverman', *Capital and Class*, Spring 1979, p.84.

58 P. Penn, 'Skilled manual workers in the labour process, 1856-1864', in Stephen Wood (ed.), *The Degradation of Work. Skill, deskilling and the labour process* (Hutchinson, London, 1982).

59 F. Parkin, *Marxism and Class Theory — a bourgeois critique* (Columbia University Press, 1979), pp.44-73.

60 Richard Edwards, *Contested Terrain: the transformation of the workplace in the twentieth century* (Basic Books, New York, 1979), p.166.

61 *Ibid.*, p.178.

62 *Ibid.*, p.178.

63 Elger, 'Valorization', p.76.

64 Edwards, *Contested Terrain*, p.51.

65 *Ibid.*, p.110.

66 *Ibid.*, p.128.

67 Marx is emphatic that production is a social, as well as a material process: 'In production men not only act on nature but also on one another. They produce only by cooperating in a certain way and mutually exchanging their activities. In order to produce, they enter into definite connections

and relations with one another and only within these social connections and relations does their action on nature, does production, take place'. *The Marx-Engels Reader*, p.177.

68   The Webbs believed that the perpetual revolution of technology was creating conditions in which the boundaries between jobs were always shifting and the 'skill' gap between journeymen and labourers was progressively narrowing, thereby undermining claims to property rights in the job. The victory of the imperatives of technological change would eliminate antiquated skill and restrictive craft unions. This summary is drawn from Chapter 1 ('The Webbs') in Alan Alridge, *Power, Authority and Restrictive Practices. A sociological essay on industrial relations* (Blackwell, Oxford and London, 1976).

69   There are no official figures available as the statistics give figures from basic metals as a whole. This estimate is based on figures derived from the Steel Engineering Industries Federation of South Africa (SEIFSA) and the Foundry Welding and Production Journal (FWP).

70   In 1982 castings were distributed as follows: Defence 37%, Mining 25%, Motor 15%, South African Transport Services 6%, Forestry 4%. (Source: *Die Beeld*, 1.9.1982.)

71   In the course of cross-checking documentary sources, and conscious of the inability of survey questionnaire techniques to come to grips with real-life experiences in the foundry, I began collecting biographies of some of the workers I met between 1980 and 1983. The five biographies emerged from the unstructured interviews with men identified in the union records (Bob, Len and Morris), or at union meetings (Sipho and Josias). Bob, Len and Morris were visited at their homes in Van der Bijl Park, Boksburg and Durban respectively. Sipho I met during the strike at Rely and Josias at a Shop Stewards' meeting. Numerous biographies were collected in the course of the unstructured interviews but only five were chosen as they contain in capsule form the main themes of the study I was pursuing at the time. For a general overview of the study the reader should refer to my Ph.D, thesis: Webster, 'The labour process and forms of workplace organization in South African foundries', University of the Witwatersrand, 1983. The account of Sipho is drawn largely from P. Stewart, 'A Worker Has a Human Face', Honours dissertation, University of the Witwatersrand, 1981. The account of Josias is drawn in part from an interview by B. Goldblatt, Industrial Sociology Project, University of the Witwatersrand, 1981.

PART I

The Colour of Craft

Early craft production in the foundry was monopolized by European immigrants who had learnt the technique of union protection in the period of intense struggle against deskilling in their home countries.[1] These craft moulders were to become a privileged stratum of the foundry labour force — a labour aristocracy. Blacks, on the other hand, had been subordinated in the late nineteenth century through colonial conquest and were now entering wage labour on a weak and unorganized basis. They were to enter the foundry as unskilled migrant labourers whose prolonged absence from their rural homes was to lead to the progressive deterioration of the productive capacity of these areas, creating a growing reserve army of labour dependent on wage labour. The division of labour that was to emerge in the early foundries was thus shaped by the differential proletarianization of black and white workers rooted in the colonial origins of South African society. The colour of craft was white and those who performed the subordinate labouring jobs were black. However, the beginnings of mass production were to transform the labour process, breach craft control, and open up job opportunities for 'coloured' machine operators. The central focus of Part I is on the response of the labour aristocracy of the foundry to these changes; in Parts II and III attention shifts to black workers increasingly at the centre of a transformed labour process.

Notes

1   For a detailed description of these responses see Chapter 1 of E. Webster, 'The Labour Process and Forms of Workplace Organization in South African Foundries', Ph.D thesis (University of the Witwatersrand, 1983).

CHAPTER 2

The Heyday of the Labour Aristocrat: The Stage of Manufacture 1896 — 1930

Up to the outbreak of the Second World War, the engineering industry in South Africa was essentially a jobbing and repair industry and did not, with the exception of a few establishments, engage in the manufacture of engineering supplies.[1] In the early years, before South Africa's base mineral wealth was known, it was dependent on the importation of its requirements and was confined largely to the coastal areas.[2] The earliest recorded foundry, Cape Foundry, was advertising its products, such as church bells, as early as 1831. Foundries also existed in Port Elizabeth, Grahamstown, Durban and Pietermaritzburg.[3] The discovery of diamonds in Kimberley and gold on the Witwatersrand led to the spread of the engineering industry inland. However, prior to 1900 the 189 establishments that existed were either repair shops or blacksmith shops.[4]

It was in the context of this simple division of labour between artisans and unskilled workers that the Iron Moulders Society of South Africa was established on 25 September 1896 as a craft union 'for the protection of the trade of iron, brass and steel moulders in the case of oppression and accident'.[5] At this stage of formal subordination 'real control of production is not yet firmly in the hands of capital. It is still a relationship between labour and the conditions of labour which provides labour with a degree of control and hence a lever with which to enforce its class objectives — [which may be] craft prerogatives over recruitment into the trades and over the content and performance of work'.[6] A craftsman exercises control over production through his possession of the instruments of production, that is, the tools of the trade, which are an extension of his hands and over which he attempts to maintain exclusive control. Three tools are central to the moulder's trade — the trowel and the heart-and-squeeze, used for sleeking, and the cleaner, used for blacking into the mould.[7]

The IMS was involved in a constant struggle to maintain this monopoly of control and attempted to draw lines of demarcation between the craftsman and his labourer. In 1918 the Executive Committee (Exco) summoned Smith, an IMS member, to account for his alleged breach of this line of demarcation by carrying castings. 'Smith explained that he had not personally carried castings from Knox to Bonds but had merely directed a native to the latter shop. This explanation was considered satisfactory by the meeting.' Similarly we find Jock Naysmith writing to the shop steward at East Rand Proprietary Mines (ERPM) warning him of the importance of maintaining this demarcation. 'It has been brought to the knowledge of our society that in the making of white metal bearings . . . the usual moulder's tools are used — by a plumber — we do not know how this has been initiated and allowed to continue by our moulders in the ERPM as my society has always considered anything of this nature as an infringement of our trade.'[8] With the introduction of moulding machines during the First World War the society tried to draw the line of demarcation so as to include these machines, demanding exclusive jurisdiction over them. In 1918 a resolution was passed that 'our members should work machines and that we should take care that we do not lose the machines'.[9]

The mechanism for establishing control over the job is twofold: the closed shop and the apprenticeship system. From its inception the IMS was concerned to establish a closed shop among moulders by ensuring that all moulders in the Transvaal belonged to the society. At the second recorded meeting of the IMS Exco a dispute was recorded at a shop where a moulder refused to join the union.[10] A meeting was held two days later when the men in the shop went out on strike and were supported by the embryonic IMS. The Exco wrote to the shop informing them that one of the employees had scabbed.[11] Similarly the shop stewards from Parry and Co. raised the case at the Exco meeting of a man who had been taken on as a labourer but spent most of his time at moulding.[12]

Part of the closed shop strategy involved establishing a recognized rate of pay. In March 1899 Exco decided to invite several moulders on the Rand to their next meeting because they were working for less than the recognized rate of pay. Similarly in April 1905 a member was called to appear before the Exco and questioned in regard to his working on the Sunday without receiving double pay. He said he was in ignorance of the society rules but would take care not to transgress them in future.[13] By May 1913 the chairman was able to claim that

100 percent of the moulders in the Transvaal belonged to the society and that no member of this trade was allowed to work under the standard rate of pay of £1 per day, whereas in other trades they worked for £4 per week.[14]

Initially the IMS responded to the challenge of coloured moulders joining the union by defining the closed shop in racial terms. In 1906 a resolution was passed declaring that if a coloured person started in the shop, the foreman should be told that it was 'against the principles of the society' and if the coloured was not removed that the shop had 'the full sanction of Exco to cease work'.[15] However, the increase in the number of coloured moulders from 1910 divided the membership between those who saw the issue in traditional unionist terms and those who believed that protection must take a racial form. On 18 April 1913 a Special General Meeting was called to discuss the transfer of a coloured man from Salt River in the Cape to the Pretoria Railway Foundry. Smart, putting the 'separatist' case, stated that he considered the government had introduced the thin end of the wedge by bringing coloured moulders from the Cape to the Transvaal. 'We will be forced out of our jobs by these men.'[16] Pomfert, putting the non-racial case, said 'he was prepared to work with any man provided he got the standard wages and lived under similar conditions as himself'. Besides, he said, 'the man was recognized to be a white man and had the same privileges as he himself, he was a registered voter in the Transvaal and was served openly in any public bar. In fact, he had partaken in a European hotel, Pretoria, liquid refreshment with him'. Smart replied that 'it doesn't matter whether he was three generations removed or not, we should keep the society white as these men were eventually going to do us out of our jobs and it should be put a stop to'. Pomfert, arguing that he could not stop the coloured man's advance, proposed the motion that if a coloured earned the same wages, he be accepted in the union. This motion was eventually withdrawn and the proposal accepted that if *this man* applied for membership he would be accepted.

The 1906 resolution seems to have been retained as the society's position throughout the First World War. In 1919 the secretary found it necessary to write to an employer reprimanding him for employing a coloured man as a moulder. 'If white men are going to employ coloured men in preference to white men as skilled mechanics, the white standard is soon going to disappear in South Africa and future generations of whites are going to be left a legacy of a coloured standard of life'.[17]

No debate took place on Africans joining the society during this period but sharp responses were made when the lines of demarcation were breached by Africans. The shop steward of Rand Foundry reported in May 1909 that 'a native had been set to make cores in the Rand Foundry and that he [the shop steward] had had an interview with the manager. The boy was stopped that afternoon'.[18] The practice of employing an African 'helper' was an established custom in the moulding trade. 'It has been customary now for a number of years for each moulder on bonus work to have a labourer . . . . He has to keep the moulder supplied with sand, clay, work moulding boxes, help to lift boxes over the patterns, shovel sand into the boxes, help lift on and off boxes, both by hand and with the crane, make beds for green sand and dry sand boxes, clean and oil patterns, assist to load and unload completed moulds . . . . He has also to clear up the superflous sand around each box, assist in carrying hand shanks and see that the shop is clean.'[19]

The racial forms of union protection which emerged during this period were neither irrational nor permanent — they represented the contradictory nature of the white workers' location in the labour process and society at large. On one hand they are an index of their privileged position in the racially discriminatory hierarchy in the division of labour and within a racially segregated society. On the other hand, they are also an index of their vulnerability — the different patterns of proletarianization between black and white, the rigid controls over black workers which created the basis for a cheap and unorganized black labour force, ever ready to undercut the 'privileged white worker'. It is also important to understand that the racial basis of union protection was not permanent — in fact, the union responded to the forces of change, first by opening its doors to coloureds in the 1930s, and then, in 1979, with the amendment to the Industrial Conciliation Act, to Africans.

The second aspect of craft control over the job, the apprenticeship system, was established from the inception of the union. Until 1922, when the Apprenticeship Act was passed providing for the control of apprenticeship by joint management-union committees, the reproduction of skilled moulders was entirely in the hands of the IMS. Rule Sixteen laid down the length of apprenticeship (six years), the ratio of apprentices to journeymen (one to three), their entrance fees and subscriptions, and the rule that they could not leave an employer without his consent. These rules were drawn largely from the rules and customs of the FIMS of the U.K. Their enforcement depended on custom and the society's capacity to enforce these rules. It is clear from the society's minutes that they struggled to achieve this and in most cases the society was forced to rely on employer goodwill.

In 1909 it was reported that Wright Boag and Company were employing one too many apprentices. The IMS decided that the present apprentice be allowed to continue and that the 'shop steward ask the foreman as a favour to adhere to the rules as far as possible as the number of apprentices employed were altogether out of proportion to the requirements of the trade'.[20] Their only sanction was to threaten withdrawal of their labour if the apprentice was not removed,[21] and thus where the foundry was well organized the society could enforce the ratio system.[22] But their dependence on employer cooperation is clear from attempts to enforce other apprentice rules. In November 1910 it was reported that an apprentice had left Metropolitan Foundry for another employer, thus breaking society rules. This foundry appealed to Exco 'to take steps to have him returned to complete his term of apprentice'. The society agreed to write to the shop steward and the new employer to allow the apprentice to return to Metropolitan Foundry.[23] Similarly the society struggled to enforce the six year apprenticeship rule. In 1914 the society was forced to write to Wright Boag that they had heard that their apprentices were only doing five years. The creation of a skilled moulder, the secretary wrote, 'is a step in a direction that must appeal to employers equally as much as to us as a body'.[24]

The power of the craft union depends on its success in establishing direct control over the supply of labour. In 1904 the society found it necessary to write to the Rand Foundry protesting against their method of advertising through an employment agency, stating that the society 'would be pleased to supply their needs if they were notified of their requirements'.[25] The fear of undercutting was particularly strong in periods of recession such as 1912. Proposing an Idle Benefit Fund one member said: 'There were large numbers of men out of work and unless something was done to relieve these men they might prove a menace to our trade, for there was no greater factor than hunger that drove men to work for less wages.' The motion was carried.[26] In June 1912 the Idle Benefit Fund was established.[27] However, the society drew the line at paying the passage of unemployed moulders to Australia, in spite of a plea by one Exco member to 'remove a danger of lowering the standard rate of pay in our union'.[28]

The passing of the Apprenticeship Act in 1922 was to end the period of union autonomy over recruitment and training of apprentices and usher in a period of joint union-management regulation. While the union had lost exclusive control over the intake of apprentices, it had gained better enforcement of the rules. In the days of union autonomy, employers were to argue later, 'there was a tendency in some trade unions to limit the authorization of apprentices to the number that they believed the industries were capable of absorbing, thus protecting the economic situation of the artisan, rather than to the number an establishment was technically capable of training. This tendency was concerned with maintaining full artisan employment'.[29] The intention in passing the Act was to curb this autonomy, as the Department of Labour noted: 'The Act has also exercised a moderating influence on the trade union practice previously in operation, of stipulating for a ratio of minors to journeymen who might be employed in certain skilled trades. The Act deprived the unions of this assumed right and gave them in exchange the statutory right to control through the Apprenticeship Committee system under which the registration of a contract is dependent on the ability of the employer to provide adequate training over an extended period.'[30]

In the early period of manufacture, the craftsman still retained a degree of control over the content and performance of work. Expansion of absolute surplus value — increases in surplus value resulting from the extension of the working day and the intensification of work — constituted the most obvious and effective way to increase the rate of exploitation.[31] However, the limits of this expansion were set by the strength of shop floor organization which determined the extent to which unions could achieve their objective of a 'fair day's work for a fair day's pay'. The concept of a 'fair day's work' was determined, says Hobsbawm, by custom rather than the market.[32] A moral code defined the moulder's notion of economic justice and this was protected by the autonomy of the craftsmen. When faced by output restriction some years later, the chairman reminded Exco that: 'The men should determine what is too much, or what is too little, or what is a fair day's output.'[33] Moulders who, like Bob, went beyond this moral code were faced with abusive epithets such as 'tear arse'. Associated with the moulder's autonomy was his pride in his job and his insistence on being left alone to complete a job free from interference by the foreman.[34] Moulders who worked extra time without pay were believed to have breached this moral code.[35]

Consequently during this period major struggles took place over the length of the working day, eventually culminating in a thirteen and a half week strike in 1918 over a demand of two weeks' paid holiday. The other area of struggle over the intensity of work was the piece work system, a forerunner of Taylorism and scientific management. The IMS maintained a constant opposition to the piece work system on the grounds that it ultimately forced moulders to work more for less money. In 1902 a dispute took place over the piece work system when moulders refused to accept it at Crown Mines.[36] In 1909 the Railways, including the moulders, went on strike over piece work, arguing that their wages were being reduced and the working day lengthened by the system.[37] The IMS gave support to the strike and maintained its opposition to the piece work system even after the men returned to work on the basis of certain guarantees.[38] They argued that any acceptance of piece work was the thin end of the wedge. The increased wages that accompany the extra expenditure of effort, they believed, delivered the worker into the hands of the employer, who now increased the rate of surplus value through cutting piece work rates.[39] This is what Burawoy calls the piecework trap.[40] In order to earn a subsistence wage workers must strain their labour power, which then provides the employer with a justification for cutting prices. Surviving today means working harder tomorrow for the same wage. The only way to avoid the piecework trap is for workers to combine and collectively reject it. This remained the policy of the IMS until piece work was forced upon them during the Second World War.

The struggle over the length of the working day led in 1908 to the establishment of a select committee of the Transvaal Legislative Assembly which rejected the demand of an eight hour day.[41] In February 1910 the IMS called a general meeting in which a motion for a 48-hour week was proposed but defeated in favour of a demand for a 50 hour week.[42] In May 1916 the IMS collaborated with the Amalgamated Society of Engineers (ASE) and SABS in making a joint demand for a 48-hour week. In December 1917 the IMS put forward five demands to the newly formed Engineering Foundry Association that were to lead to a major confrontation. They demanded a minimum wage of £7 10s per week, a war bonus of ten shillings, a ban on all overtime, two weeks holiday on full pay, and no victimization of the society's members. The demands were put to the ballot and unanimously approved in January

1918. In February the employers conceded all these demands except the holiday pay, which was then conceded on arbitration by the chief magistrate, McFee. Though he had found in favour of the IMS, the employers hesitated. The IMS believed that this was a breach of faith and consequently went on strike in September, eventually winning their demands in November 1918.[43] The First Factory Act had been passed earlier that year, granting less favourable holiday pay conditions than those won by the IMS.

This thirteen and a half week strike was to be the high point of militancy in the union's history. During the First World War a shop steward movement had developed in the engineering industry and by 1918 shop stewards were operating in most engineering establishments. W.H. Andrews, a leading trade union militant, had returned to South Africa from Britain where after discussions with, amongst others, the Clyde Workers' Committee he had become an enthusiastic advocate of the shop stewards' movement as it existed in Britain.[44] But the more significant outcome of the 1918 strike for the future of industrial relations was the recommendation to form Joint Boards which would draw up and police industry-wide agreements.[45] These joint employer-employee bodies were to be the forerunners of the Industrial Councils in the engineering industry a decade later.

The First World War created a basis for expansion in the engineering industry in the next decade with the establishment of 132 new foundry and blacksmith shops. Capital investment in machinery almost doubled during the war years.[46] Optimism after the war was running at an all-time high as regards the engineering industry. Many products never previously made in South Africa were being produced and by the end of the war solder and white metal were being produced on the Rand.

Yet engineering was to remain, in the 1920s, a labour-intensive industry. In 1920, in basic metals, the value of machinery was 2,5 times smaller than the value of wages.[47] The size of these establishments remained small with only eleven per cent having more than fifty moulders. (See Table 1 below).

Furthermore, production remained organized on jobbing lines. Bosman, writing in 1929, despairingly concludes that 'the conditions under which the engineering industry is working enable it to develop along lines of the general jobbing shop, while the other lines which might become more lucrative and lead to developments of real national importance are entirely eliminated from its programme'.[48] Jobbing implies that concerns do not 'produce any one product, but

Table 1. *Classification of engineering factories according to the number of workers employed*

Number of Workers	0-4	4	5-10	11-20	21-50	51-100	101-200	201-300	300+
Number of establishments	135	107	289	147	123	42	22	10	26

(Source: Board of Trade and Industries Report No.94 of 1924.)

involve themselves in the production of various products, usually markedly different. Production is only done to order, that is, very little stock of any one product is held. The products produced may necessitate different processes of production, depending upon the specific product involved. It is the non-specialization on the part of engineering concerns that encourages the continuation of jobbing'. For instance, Bosman says, 'one plant may carry as many as 25 000 different patterns'. Manufacture was based 'on contract' — the result of a 'sell and make' policy. Most of the orders were special in character, given according to particular specifications. No stocks of finished products were carried, and a steady production was not maintained. Thus the industry suffered 'ups and downs and the idle machine factor becomes a great waste'.[49] But with the increasing introduction of moulding machines, the juxtaposition of two forms of production emerged — one continuing to be based on craft work and located in jobbing; the other involving the replacement of the craft moulder by the machine.[50]

It was during this period — when labour was not yet subordinated to capital and had a degree of leverage to enforce its class objectives — that the decomposition of craft work began. By 1916 nearly half (12 589 of a total of 26 343) of those employed in engineering establishments were already working in establishments employing more than 100, with a mean size of 270 workers.[51] The lack of opportunity for apprentice training had become a problem in some of these establishments, such as the African Iron and Steel Rod Company. 'The opportunity of giving apprentice moulders an all round training to become an efficient moulder was totally impossible. The shop was run on repetition lines.'[52] Similarly Exco received a letter from an apprentice in East Rand Engineering complaining of the type of work they were getting which gave them no opportunity of being journeymen,[53] and a complaint from an apprentice in 1932 that he and his fellow apprentices 'were not given a good class of work, being confined to the use of machinery'.[54]

During the phase of manufacture, Palloix writes, employers come up against 'the contradictory process of reproduction of labour power, which remains organized around the crafts, so that it is still necessary for there to be a broad stratum of skilled workers, prolonged training and autonomy of this stratum of artisans — all this at a time when it is simultaneously necessary to devalue this labour power now that the process of fragmentation and dequalification is under way'.[55] The Apprenticeship Act was an attempt to facilitate this control by limiting the autonomy of the craft union. Capital's objectives, however, were ultimately to be achieved by the introduction of machinery.

This process of 'deskilling' emerged during the First World War and became an issue within the union in the 1920s. Reminiscing forty years later, a moulder described the introduction of moulding machines during the First World War in these terms: 'Men were required to clock in and out and machine moulding had arrived. I must confess that these innovations depressed the old-timers in the trade. Many of them found it beyond their capacity to adjust themselves to these conditions. The introduction of operatives and machinery was more than they could cope with and many of them retired or were pensioned off.'[56] In May 1921 Exco recommended to the general meeting that all machine moulders be approached in regard to membership of the society. 'We feel', they said, 'that it is time we had some control over the machines.'[57] The following week Exco instructed the secretary to write to the members of the South African Railways foundry in Pretoria to get their opinion on the admittance of machine moulders into the society.[58] In 1925 the shop steward in Vereeniging reported that a moulder had started working on a machine and that he had informed members of the shop that he had no intention of applying for membership of the society. The shop steward also stated that two handymen were starting that Monday to work the other machine.[59] Exco decided to write to the manager of the works, asking him if he would meet a deputation from the society to discuss the rate of pay for moulders working the machines. It was recorded in the minutes soon after this incident that the secretary had written a letter to the NUFW of Great Britain to obtain information on pay and conditions of machine moulders.[60]

At the next Quarterly General Meeting the secretary tabled the reply from the NUFW of Great Britain informing the moulders of their lost opportunity in not tackling the machine moulding issue in its infancy. He trusted that the moulders of South Africa would not make the same mistake as they had. This was followed by a letter from the Engineering and Foundry Association requesting permission to change the ratio of apprentices 'on account of the development of the industry'. Naysmith then appealed to members to consider seriously what the employers were doing and take note of the warning that had come from the British union. He said 'our aim should be to grapple with the questions before us and not to think we are all powerful. We had the signs of the times around us in the aluminium works. African Steel Products, Denver, Dunswart, and Wright Boag were all introducing machines for moulding'. He appealed to members not to rest in the position of false security, 'but to face the question before it is thrust upon us unconditionally'. Discussion seems to have ended when the secretary reported that 'on account of the iron fields opening up the number of journeymen today compared with the situation two years ago showed a good deal of increase. The sign of the times was that the moulding trade was developing'.[61]

No further discussion took place on the question until six years later when the minutes of the Exco meeting recorded a decision on the possibility of changing the union to a foundry workers' union. The minutes recorded the following:

> The Exco decided to draw up the following scheme to place before the next Quarterly General meeting.
>
> 1. The organization of all workers connected with foundries.
> 2. The name of the union be changed to the Foundry Workers Union of S.A.
> 3. The reason for this was that in the near future the Pretoria Steel Works would be opening and the result of this would be the creation of a large army of unskilled workers who would eventually encroach on the various skilled occupations. The introduction of modern machinery would also tend to require semi-skilled supervision in the place of skilled mechanics.[62]

There is no further record in the union minutes of the outcome of this discussion, but the adoption by the Pact government of the 'civilized labour policy' diluted the moulder's trade and was, as we shall see in Chapter 3, a major threat to skilled moulders.

In 1926 the society visited Dunswart to discuss with the foreman a dispute over who was to work a new moulding machine and at what rate. The foreman informed the secretary that it was his intention to keep a moulder working the machine at the standard rate of pay. The secretary replied that the society intended keeping control of these machines and any member who was asked to work them must do so.[63] A month later Exco received an application from a machine moulder at Dunswart for membership. He stated that he had commenced work on the moulding machine in 1915 in South African Railway Foundry in Pretoria and worked the machine until 1922. He had been placed on the present moulding machine eighteen months before and had been constantly on it while there was work for the machine. He was receiving 17*s* 6*d* a shift and his overtime rates were one and a quarter. He said he was anxious to be made a member of the society and claimed the same rate of pay.[64]

However, by the end of the decade, the pressure on the part of both capital and the state for transition to mass production was building up. Capital's strategy was to breach craft control by defining machine moulding and core making in the 1928 Transvaal agreement as operative work at a rate of 2*s* 1*d* an hour, while artisans received 2*s* 9*d* an hour. In 1928 the secretary reported an invitation from the manager of East Rand Engineering Works to visit the shop to discuss a complaint from a moulder who was not satisfied with working the small squeezing machine. Management considered that any moulder who had served an apprenticeship was too ambitious to be content with machine moulding. They suggested that output would be increased if the handyman was employed because he would be a satisfied man. The secretary stated that it was an instruction from the society to their members to work these machines and that moulders could give the best results from these machines provided conditions were equal.[65]

A union meeting was held three weeks later with the men and the foreman from the shop present. The foreman told them that he did not feel that he was getting his fair return from a day's work from the men on the moulding machine. He was prepared to cooperate with the union by employing moulders if they would assist him by increasing output. The shop was being reorganized on a production basis and all the machines would be put in one place in the shop and some men would then be required to work permanently on the machine. Some of the men working on the machines confirmed their dissatisfaction, others were not dissatisfied. The secretary argued that these machines were on the increase and that they should devise a strategy that allowed them to control the machines by giving as little as possible of the unskilled and semi-skilled aspects of the job to operators. A form of job fragmentation was then accepted by members.[66]

The intervention of the union in this shop seems to have strengthened shop floor resistance to management's strategy of employing non-moulders on the moulding machines. A year later the secretary reported that men in the East Rand Engineering Works were not prepared to accept management's attempt to employ a non-moulder on a machine. He said 'the grievance of the members was that Barlow [the new man] was an interloper, not having served an apprenticeship and so was not eligible for membership'. The meeting proposed that Barlow should not be allowed to continue working there. This was accepted.[67]

By the end of the decade, the society's fears that it would lose control of the machines were increasing. In September 1930 a delegation visited the SAR Foundry in Pretoria, reporting back to Johannesburg on machine moulding. One alarmed member stated that the days of 'white slavery' were not finished and that the men completed a day's work with their hands covered in blisters. Furthermore, management was putting obstacles in the way of moulders working these machines, while the unskilled labourers were getting every assistance.[68] In October the minutes recorded the society's successful designation of moulding to include core making and machine moulding in the Industrial Council Agreement. However, this was only after a considerable battle within the Industrial Council established two years earlier. Discussing the proposed 1929 agreement the IMS delegates (the Industrial Council consists of joint employer and employee delegates) reported that the employers were pressing for core making and machine moulding to be classified as operative work.

Similarly a complaint was presented at the meeting that a core maker employed at the Salt River workshop of the SAR, although a fully qualified moulder, was receiving less than the artisan's rate of pay because a lower schedule had been introduced. This schedule rate, the report said, allowed the man to work as a core maker at lower rates than had been in existence for some years. 'There was always a danger so long as it existed it would be a way of employers overcoming the requirements for core making without the recognized period of apprenticeship. Every effort should be made to remove core making from Schedule B to Schedule A.'[69]

The state's strategy towards scientific management first emerged in the Department of Labour's journal, *The Social and Industrial Review*, in the mid 1920s. The Department of Labour, set up after the

Pact government's victory in 1924, and following on the defeat of white labour in the 1922 strike, rapidly became a highly articulate propagandist for scientific management. In January 1926 the journal commissioned an article titled 'Are Skilled Trades Dying Out or Growing?' After discussing the disappearance of some skills and the creation of new skills, the author concludes 'that the belief that labour is being degraded by machinery is nothing but a myth. The field of skilled labour is now vastly greater than it ever was'.[70] In December the *Review* reported on a time and motion study in the Sweet and Confectionery industry suggesting ways of reducing the number of movements involved in making chocolate.[71] By 1927 scientific management was the major topic in the journal. In the May edition the new Institute of the Scientific Organization of Industry, in Geneva, was mentioned.[72] In July a mechanical engineer from Johannesburg, S. Couzens, described the development and methods of scientific management in an article entitled 'High Wages and Low Costs'.[73] He concluded by quoting Lenin's support for Taylor and felt that labour's attitude had now become sympathetic towards scientific management. In a later article, the author considered the application of scientific management in South Africa. He gave examples of 'soldiering' by artisans in South Africa and then proceeded to advocate removing the tools from the care of the artisan and storing them in the tool room.[74] In 1928 the Department of Labour held a conference on mass production. In 1929 an article on mass production from an overseas journal was summarized, the author concluding that 'the proportion of skill is not in fact being very seriously upset. I believe that as fast as the one type of skill is eliminated other types of skills are called into being'.[75] In June the chairman of the Wage Board, Hotz, wrote an article calling for the establishment of an organization to promote the rationalization movement in South Africa since 'the discussion which has been carried on in the engineering industry in connection with the question of work, specialization and mass production are evidence of the fact that South African industry has not been altogether oblivious of scientific management'.[76] One of the striking features of the debate as conducted through this journal was its derivative dependence on developments elsewhere in the world. In August an article was reproduced which summarized the rationalization movement as it had manifested itself in the USA, Germany, France, Great Britain, Spain, Italy, Australia and Japan.[77]

While it was clearly concerned to present capital's perspective on scientific management, the Department of Labour's commitment to implement the Pact government's 'civilized labour' policies led it into the contradictory role of continually having to reassure its political bosses that (white) skilled labour would not be displaced by this restructuring of the labour process.[78] The clearest statement in favour of scientific management was made in 1929 when Bosman, a Pretoria engineer, presented the Board of Trade and Industries report on the engineering industry. Bosman argued that the engineering industry of that time was designed for jobbing and that if South Africa was to become less dependent on imports, then a transition to mass production was required. 'A local industry, which has reached a high point of development along the lines of general engineering, is at present seeking wider markets and new fields of manufacture. It is quite capable of entering such fields if the conditions are made favourable . . . several plants in fact are in a partial transition stage towards this type of work. Such firms find conditions extremely severe and find it difficult to compete with foreign competition'.[79] Bosman identified three obstacles to mass production. Firstly, *lack of standardization*. 'In industry high labour costs are to a very large extent due to lack of standardization. Each particular job has its own value, some more lucrative than others.'[80] Secondly, *no scientific management existed*. 'The system is dangerous and depends to a large extent for its success on the human element. In large scale organization a system of this nature becomes impossible. A proper costing system, time sheets, accurate statistics are required.[81] Foundry practice, except in one case, is carried on along 'rule of thumb' lines. No scientific control is in evidence.'[82] Above all, to prevent restriction of output a scientific study of timing based on each operation must be done. Thirdly, *the power of the artisan was inhibiting the use of semi-skilled operators*. Bosman then isolated five examples of restrictions imposed on the use of operative labour by the craft unions. The locus of power was, according to him, the Apprenticeship Committee which was set up in terms of the Apprenticeship Act of 1922 and which controlled entry into the trade. This contributed to the massive disparity between the wage levels of skilled workers and labourers in South African industry.

His solution to these obstacles was a transition to mass production. 'The basic function of mass production methods is the saving of time. All forms of management centre around this factor. A saving of time in any direction and under any conditions involves an increased turn-

Table 2. *Average Weekly Wage in Engineering Industry (1925 - 1926)*

	U.S.A.		S.A.		U.K.		Amsterdam		Paris	
	s	d	s	d	s	d	s	d	s	d
Skilled	155	0	144	2	64	0	53	6	38	1
Labourers	69	3	21	3	43	8	42	9	24	1
Percent	45%		15%		70%		80%		70%	

Source: Board of Trade and Industries Report No.92 of 1929.

over per workman for any particular period and accordingly reduced costs.'[83]

The impediments to capital accumulation and the strategies devised by the state and capital to overcome these impediments in the 1920s have been identified in this chapter. The progressive introduction of machines into the production process identified the transition from manufacture to what Marx called machinofacture. Following Marx, this is defined as a transition from formal to real subordination of labour to capital. Moulding was no longer the exclusive task of the craftsmen. Moulding machines were beginning to displace the privileged position of the aristocrat of the foundry. Although machine-based production was not yet dominant, the heyday of the labour aristocrat was about to pass.

Notes

1   Board of Trade and Industries Report (BTI), No.286 (Pretoria Government Printer, 1946), pp.175, 206.
2   *Ibid.*, p.1.
3   H.J. van Eck, 'The Foundry Industry in South Africa', supplement to the *Engineer and Foundryman*, February 1958, p.76. According to the *Eastern Province Year Book* of 1883 three foundries existed in Grahamstown: Albany Iron and Brass Foundry; Andrew Elliot (brass founder, machinist and gunsmith); J. Jolly (engineer, iron and brass founder).
4   Industrial Census, U. 917/1910. Two exceptions that were to survive to the present day were the East Rand Foundry (later Rowe, Jewell and Co. Ltd.) founded in 1893, and Phoenix Foundry, established in 1895.
5   Rules of the Iron Moulders Society of South Africa. A number of craft

unions were established in the 1890s — Witwatersrand Mining Employees and Mechanics Union (1892); South African Engine Drivers Association (1894); Witwatersrand Tailors Association (1896); Amalgamated Engineering Union (1896); South African Typographical Union (1898).

6   Brighton Labour Process Group, 'The Capitalist Labour Process', in *Capital and Class*, Vol.1 (1977), p.7.

7   Interview, 7 March 1980, with Bob Thorpe. Other tools used by the moulder are the square corner, round corner, fillet tools, top edge and boss tool.

8   The Iron Moulders Society of South Africa (IMS). Housed in the Historical and Literary Papers, University of the Witwatersrand Library, Accession No. A1008/e, Letterbooks, 18.10.1918 and C 7, 8.10.1918.

9   A 1008, C 8, 12.12.1918.

10   C 1, 29.1.1898.

11   C 1, 31.1.1898.

12   C 1, 7.4.1898.

13   C 2, 28.4.1905.

14   C 3, 23.5.1913.

15   C 2, 19.1.1906.

16   C 4, Special General Meeting, 10.4.1913. Smart's anxieties about coloured artisans were based on the fact that coloureds had dominated skilled occupations in the Western Cape with the abolition of slavery in the early nineteenth century, and he feared a similar pattern developing in the Transvaal.

17   E 1, 11.9.1919.

18   C 3, 5.5.1909. There was a similar case at the Eagle Brass Foundry on 27.8.1909 and again at the Rand Foundry on 29.6.1911.

19   B, Rule 13, IMS 1949 Biennial Conference Minutes.

20   C 3, 11.2.1909. Similar situations are recorded in the Executive Committee Minutes on 11.5.1919, 15.5.1919, and 25.8.1919.

21   C 3, 21.7.1914.

22   C 3, 5.12.1910, Globe Foundries.

23   C 3, 31.10.1910. Two weeks later it was recorded that this apprentice had not returned to his former employers. The society was clearly angry that his new employer had not forced the apprentice to return, particularly as the employers were ex-members of the society. 15.11.1910.

24   A,1008/F, Correspondence, 17.11.1914.

25   C 2, 2.2.1904.

26   C 4, 15.5.1912.

27   C 4, 6.6.1912.

28   C 4, 22.8.1912.

29   *Engineer and Foundryman*, Vol.1, No.9, pp.63-64.

30   Department of Labour, Annual Report No.43, December 1933 (Pretoria, Government Printer), p.33.
31   See Chapter One for a discussion of the distinction between absolute and surplus value.
32   E. Hobsbawm, 'The labour aristocracy in nineteenth century Britain' in *Labouring Men* (London, 1964), p.348.
33   Exco Minutes, 17.7.1947.
34   Exco Minutes, 30.7.1909. On 22.9.1908 it is recorded that a moulder was fined by the society for bad work.
35   In 1911 a dispute was declared when a moulder breached society rules by working incentive without any extra pay. 11.11.1911.
36   C 2, 11.10.1902.
37   C 3, 7.5.1909.
38   C 3, 21.5.1909.
39   See Karl Marx, *Capital*, Vol.1, p.1072 for an expansion of this argument.
40   M. Burawoy, 'The Politics of Production and the Production of Politics: a comparative analysis of piecework machine shops in the U.S. and Hungary', in *Political Power and Social Theory*, Vol.1 (1980), p.266.
41   E. Katz, *A Trade Union Aristocracy*, African Studies Institute, University of the Witwatersrand (Johannesburg, 1976), p.332.
42   C 3, 16.2.1910.
43   C 5, 27.5.1919.
44   R.K. Cope, *Comrade Bill — The Life of W.H. Andrews*, Workers' Reader, pp.188-199.
45   A. O'Quigley, 'Engineering on the Rand 1914 - 1924', 1978, mimeo.
46   SEIFSA, *The Origins and Structure of the Metal and Engineering Industry in South Africa* (1968), p.10.
47   Figures derived from *Union Statistics for Fifty Years: 1910 - 1960*.
48   BTI Report No.94 (1929), p.74.
49   *Ibid.*, p.26.
50   Mechanization of moulding was introduced because it lowered the cost of production by reducing the time involved in the casting of a mould and improved the quality of the mould.

   A moulding machine properly installed offers the following advantages compared with ordinary hand ramming from a loose pattern:
   (a) Output is increased considerably though using the same manpower.
   (b) Castings are much more accurate and are regular in weight.
   (c) Finish is much improved.   *Engineer and Foundryman* (Nov. 1930).

   It will be obvious how each of these three advantages contributed to the general reduction in cost. Of course mechanization has the added advantage of undercutting the craftsman, although not always successfully in South Africa, as this foundry employer wrote in 1940:

> At the outset I may state that the foundry trade is one of the few trades of a real craftsman nature, with the exception of machine moulding which, although today operated by skilled tradesmen, is a semi-skilled job in any other part of the world outside South Africa.
>
> *Engineer and Foundryman* (February, 1940).

51 South African Statistics of Production: Statistics of Factories and Productive Industries in the Union for the year 1915 - 1916. First Industrial Census.

52 C 10, 30.4.1926.

53 C 10, 11.2.1926.

54 C 10, 13.5.1932.

55 C. Palloix, 'The labour process: from Fordism to neo-Fordism' in *The Labour Process and Class Struggle* (Stage 1, Conference of Socialist Economists Pamphlets, London, 1978), p.52.

56 'Fifty Years in the Foundry Trade', *Engineer and Foundryman*, July 1958.

57 C 8, 11.5.1921.

58 C 8, 20.5.1921.

59 C 9, 11.12.1925.

60 C 10, 8.1.1926.

61 C 9, 26.3.1926.

62 'We believe', C.S. Richards writes,

> 'that this policy [of giving preference to white labour] would yield better results in a modern highly mechanized works such as are being built at Pretoria and our estimates of production costs are based on white labour entirely....
>
> Furthermore ISCOR being established in the Depression 1929 - 1932, when serious unemployment existed, recruitment of local men took place under difficult circumstances. The management engaged European labour [many taken over from the contractors constructing the works] to a much larger extent than it would have done under normal economic conditions... on operations generally performed by non-Europeans... on humanitarian and not economic grounds... and at wages much higher than are usually paid to non-Europeans for the same class of work.... [After the dispute in 1936] the arbitrators characterized the excessive wages paid for unskilled work as "unjustified on economic grounds" and argued that "general labourers (natives) should be employed on unskilled work and most of the semi-skilled work where the degree of skill is low", and condemned any attempt to introduce a purely white labour policy and the attitude of the men that each was entitled to continuity

of employment irrespective of the work available.... ISCOR should therefore not be conceived as a training machine or a means of sub- sidizing European labour.'
C.S. Richards, *The Iron and Steel Industry in South Africa* (Johannes- burg, 1948), p.293. Reference in minutes from Exco, 13.9.1931.

63   C 10, 1.10.1926.
64   C 10, 29.10.1926.
65   C 11, 28.9.1928.
66   C 11, 20.10.1928.
67   C 11, 1.6.1929.
68   C 11, 12.9.1930.
69   C 12, 13.9.1931.
70   *Social and Industrial Review* (SAIR), Vol.2, 1 (1926).
71   *Ibid.*, Vol.2, 2 (1926). Davies writes that by 1933 the Wage Board was able to record that the sweet making industry was 'considerably more mechanized'. He attributes this in part to the fact that the Wage Board was raising wage levels, ignoring the propaganda role of the Department of Labour in encouraging scientific management. R. Davies, *Capital, State and White Labour in South Africa, 1900-1960* (Brighton, 1979), p.222.
72   SAIR, Vol.3, 17 (1927).
73   SAIR, Vol.4, 19 (1927).
74   SAIR, Vol.4, 20 (1927).
75   SAIR, Vol.3, 14 (1927).
76   SAIR, Vol.7, 42 (1929).
77   SAIR, Vol.7, 44 (1929).
78   The contradictory nature of the Pact Government's encouragement of mechanization and its support for the 'civilized labour policy' is discussed at greater length by Davies, *Capital, State and White Labour*, pp.119-232.
79   BTI Report, No.94 (1929).
80   *Ibid.*, No.14.
81   *Ibid.*, No.17.
82   *Ibid.*, No.32.
83   *Ibid.*, No.28.

CHAPTER 3

Contesting Skill — Deskilling and the Transition to Machinofacture

Between 1932 and 1950 South African manufacturers invested heavily in machinery, which rose in value by over 1 500 percent. Employment increased at only half this rate (700 percent) in the same period.

Table 3. Basic Metal Industries (1933-1950)

Year	Establish- ments	Mach- inery	Employment		Salaries		Net Output
			Total	Whites	Total	Whites	
1932/33	322	1 465	11 900	5 153	1 620	1 305	2 737
1933/34	359	3 162	15 886	6 865	2 346	1 906	3 797
1934/35	373	3 825	20 086	8 644	3 100	2 514	5 490
1935/36	410	4 087	24 925	10 151	3 807	3 047	7 112
1936/37	433	4 360	27 895	11 435	4 245	3 367	8 222
1937/38	445	4 306	29 958	12 088	4 690	3 672	9 748
1938/39	448	4 692	29 340	11 744	4 621	3 604	9 285
1939/40	453	5 418	33 878	13 185	5 471	4 251	11 313
1940/41	484	6 078	41 068	15 687	7 111	5 386	15 091
1941/42	514	7 711	46 898	17 930	9 197	6 905	17 441
1942/43	515	9 182	52 158	19 662	11 150	8 156	19 873
1943/44	567	12 443	55 744	20 824	12 308	8 775	21 689
1944/45	579	13 552	59 075	21 767	14 286	9 856	25 557
1945/46	623	14 756	61 835	22 642	14 904	10 272	26 308
1946/47	667	15 858	63 884	23 841	16 153	11 319	29 406
1947/48	812	17 386	70 861	26 231	19 344	13 782	35 030
1948/49	926	20 703	77 200	28 641	22 360	16 207	40 130
1949/50	990	22 611	83 603	30 846	24 714	18 054	45 162
		(£000)			(£000)		(£000)

Source: Union Statistics for 50 Years: 1910 – 1960.

Technological innovation in the European and American foundry industries in the 1920s laid the basis for this South African drive to mechanization a decade later. The experience of Union Steel illustrates this process of change. In January 1932 an IMS member reported to Exco that a new operation, 'hollow drill steel', had been introduced in the Union Steel Company foundry in Vereeniging.[1] Another member reassured the meeting that the cores for this job were made and handled by moulders. Exco's anxieties remained — delegates expressed the opinion that Union Steel was employing Africans in these various operations, and the secretary was instructed to place on the agenda for the next quarterly meeting a resolution urging the government to impose a tariff on all machinery imported into the country. Nine months later these fears were confirmed when the secretary reported that the Industrial Council representative for Union Steel had stated that 'unskilled youths' were employed in this operation which was not considered to be core making. The society delegates had challenged the employers' representatives at the Industrial Council meeting: in their view the work was skilled, and could only be performed by moulders and apprentices.[2]

The issue was raised again in December, when Exco discussed Union Steel's statement that the making of numerous runner cores and the assembling of the permanent moulds was outside the province of the moulding trade. The meeting decided to adhere to its previous decision that the making of runner cores for hollow drill steel was part of the moulding trade.[3] A year later the secretary reported that the matter had been discussed again at the Industrial Council. Faced by delegates who had been instructed by Exco that under no circumstances were they to agree to this operation being classed as semi-skilled, the council had not been able to agree on the question. A sub-committee appointed to reach a decision had then recommended that the hollow drill steel operation be removed from the foundry into the steel manufacturing section. Various members expressed the opinion that United Steel was using this operation as the thin end of the wedge for the dilution of the moulders' trade. Naysmith, the president of IMS, stated that he believed that the company would be prepared to spend a large amount of money to force that point.[4]

Contesting Skill in the Pretoria Railway Foundries

The main contest over skill was to be fought out in the Pretoria Railway Foundries. An analysis of the debate over machine moulders and core makers in these foundries illustrates the nature of this contest.

The background to dilution on the railways was the Pact Government's 'civilized labour' policy. Under a directive issued on 31 October 1924, government departments were instructed to seek ways of replacing African employees by whites, partly within their own budgets and partly with the aid of subsidies made available through the Department of Labour. Between 1924 and 1932 the number of unskilled white labourers increased from 6 363 to 12 042, while the number of Africans employed fell from 35 532 to 17 467.[5] Dilution of the moulding trade formed part of this strategy. During the period 1928 – 1934 the railway administration introduced a new moulding machine in the foundries, with the result that considerably more work was given to machine moulders.[6] In 1928 the IMS formed a branch in Pretoria, submitting a memo shortly afterwards which sought to obtain a guarantee from the administration that in future moulding machines would be worked by moulders.[7] A meeting was then held between the chief mechanical engineer and delegates from the Pretoria branch, at which the society received a guarantee that the latest Peacock machine would be operated only by moulders. It was also agreed that a conference be held between the officials of the administration and one representative from each of the foundries in Pretoria.[8]

The following year a meeting was held to discuss encroachment in the railway foundries. The minutes read as follows:

> The men had decided that things had gone much too far and the time had arrived for them to stop any further action on the part of the railway administration to introduce unskilled labour into the moulding trade. Mention was also made of core makers and machine moulders in the railway services and it was thought that the time had come when the society should seriously consider accepting machine moulders and core makers into the society. Brother Sutton spoke on the question and said that the railway administration had for some time been putting forward their 'poor white' policy and introducing the men to the different trades. At a conference some two years ago, the Minister of Railways had told delegates that the artisans were highly paid and would have to allow some of the poor white element to come into their trade to increase the output and that comparisons between their wages were so great that the artisan would have to accept a reduction to allow the unskilled man to be raised to a higher standard. He hoped that the members of our

society working on the railways would stick together and show a united spirit in any negotiations which might arise. Many members spoke and all seemed in agreement that the time was ripe to accept machine moulders and core makers in the society so that we could control them.[9]

Meetings with the administration, however, seemed to be having very little effect. At the quarterly general meeting in December 1930, Pretoria officials complained that the SAR was inclined to ignore the trade union. In fact, they reported that at their last meeting with the chief mechanical engineer he had left the meeting and the discussions had taken place with the piece work engineer. A number of meetings had been held since then and it had now been decided to approach the Minister of Railways to appoint a conciliation board to go into railway moulders' grievances.[10] In June 1931 the report of the meeting with the Minister of Railways was tabled at the quarterly general meeting. The Pretoria delegates informed the meeting that in their opinion the minister was attempting to bring about a further reduction of pay and also to shorten the hours.[11]

An intensification of work had begun with the introduction of the itemized bonus system in 1929:

Immediately the itemized system of bonus working was put into operation, rationalization became the order of the day. Patterns were simplified and improved, moulding boxes were made to suit most patterns, gang core boxes were introduced, hooks, nails, clamps and tackle in general were made and supplied to the moulders in abundance. All this resulted in a 'speed-up' and a reduction in moulding time.[12]

During the depression (1929-1932) the moulders' bargaining position weakened and the society was forced to accept a reduction in the number of labourers attached to a moulder. Instead of each moulder having an assistant, two moulders were forced to share one assistant. As the society noted:

The depression had improved production methods more than any efficiency engineer would have done. But with the return of prosperity and plenty of work . . . disputes between the supervisors and the union took place.[13]

Reflecting on the effect of this, two decades later, a delegate at the Biennial Conference concluded that:

Invariably a settlement was arrived at by giving the moulder extra assistance in the form of a labourer to himself. This practice was gradually carried on until it became the practice and custom for each moulder to have a labourer.[14]

In 1932 the Pretoria branch reported that new machines were being introduced which were so simple that practically anybody could work them.[15] The question of the degree of skill involved in these new operations had been raised on a previous occasion when a discussion had taken place over whether 'chilled moulds' could be defined as moulders' work.[16] The Industrial Council inspector, however, declared that chilled moulding required no skill and was very strenuous work.[17] With regard to the new machines in the Pretoria foundry, members seemed to see the degree of organization as crucial.

> Various members were of the opinion that the railway men were not as well organized as they should be and that the administration were taking advantage of this. It was also pointed out that the moulders in SAR had refused to work the machines when they were introduced in 1914.[18]

The theme of organization was taken up again at a joint meeting between Pretoria and Johannesburg in 1933 to discuss encroachments on the trade in the Pretoria foundries. The discussion is worth recording:

> Brother Wallace stated that if the Pretoria men had been fully organized at this time, they would have been able to withstand any encroachment of unskilled labour, but, unfortunately for themselves, not being organized the full weight of any protest could not be brought to bear on the administration. 'You must know and have seen employers from the Rand visiting railway shops, and noting conditions of labour as they existed in the railways. They used this as an argument on the Rand in an endeavour to introduce similar methods there, and thereby break the strength of the society. We have fought for the railway men tooth and nail, and have spent far more money fighting for the railway men than ever we have received from them.' Plunkett said 'employers visit Great Britain and see the change in the foundries there owing to the introduction of unskilled labour into the trade, and if it were not that the moulders on the Rand were strongly organized, they would not hesitate to introduce similar methods here'. In the railway shops in Pretoria some of the moulders were members, and were contributing to the society,

but owing to the state that existed they were unable to withstand the attacks that were being made. The worst features were that the men were cutting away the feet from one another, one man tried to earn a larger bonus than his fellow shop mate, thus destroying the brotherhood that should exist with moulders. Brother Boyder referred to the inauguration of the Pretoria branch in 1928, when the moulders were enthusiastic to organize and withstand the encroachment, and now another meeting was being held for a similar purpose. He viewed with alarm the future in industry because of the changed conditions that existed world-wide. Opinions expressed by several prominent people in South Africa is that there is too large a difference between the wages of the skilled and unskilled workers. Because of the expression of opinions such as these, and the decision of the Minister of Labour that the Wage Board should hold an enquiry into the wages and conditions existing in the engineering industry in South Africa, there was a definite need for the workers to organize. The working conditions of the moulders in the railways were being attacked and as long as a difference between the workers continued, the administration would be successful in having their own way. Wiltshire stated that organization was a wonderful thing. Every institution has its own rules, and the constitution of the society should be altered to enable the railway members to join at a cheaper rate of contributions. He was speaking for the men who were not able to express views on this matter as he considered that organization of the railways was necessary.[19]

In September 1933 Plunkett reported that the SAR was intensifying its policy of encroaching on skilled work and that the moulders were not receiving any support from the other craft unions (the AEU, for example). In order to stop the rot a meeting of all railway artisans had been arranged.[20] In September a second-class core maker was employed in the brass foundry to make cores on the machine.[21] This occasioned a one-day strike of all the Pretoria moulders as a protest against the employment of a labourer on core making. The union advised a return to work.[22]

On 15 January 1934, the secretary reported to Exco that further encroachment had taken place in the steel foundry and the men were determined to resist it. The men from Pretoria at the meeting reported further that unskilled labour was being introduced and that they anticipated more, particularly men from the Special Service Battalion who would be placed as core makers and machine moulders.[23] At a special executive meeting called on 18 February, the men decided to go on strike.[24] On 22 February, it was reported by Exco that all members in the railway shop were out on strike.[25] The following demands were submitted to the Department of Labour: the abolition of encroachment; reinstatement of the apprenticeship system; that machine moulders and core makers be paid the artisan rate of pay; that all previous agreements be cancelled.

The dilemma facing the union, of resisting encroachment when the task had been deskilled, re-emerged in the joint discussions between the Johannesburg and Pretoria executives on 28 February 1934.[26] Again the logic of the situation led them to argue for opening the union's rules to allow these new workers in as members. Core makers and machine moulders were working in the trade and were serving an indentured apprenticeship. It was suggested at the meeting that they should be organized in order to be controlled, otherwise the administration would swamp the trade with underpaid men. This was the only way to stop unskilled men from working under the standard rate. Eventually the meeting endorsed a proposal first made by Exco in 1921: 'that the policy laid down some years ago whereby machine moulders and core makers could join our society, be put into operation and that we strongly oppose any further encroachments'.[27]

On 2 March the Department of Labour official attended the meeting with an offer from the general manager of the Railways to meet the IMS and open negotiations for a settlement. However, on 5 March the Pretoria branch decided that there would be no return to work until negotiations had been completed. On 15 March the terms of settlement were submitted to the Pretoria strikers. A commission of inquiry was set up and the moulders returned to work.

In trying to draw a line between skilled and semi-skilled work, the commission of inquiry was faced by the complex question of trying to establish objective measurements of skill.[28] From the evidence of foremen and works managers, and the arguments of the commissioners themselves, three elements that characterize skill were identified: that it was based on knowledge that required some period of training; that the worker was able to conceive of the job as a whole and make a decision on what had to be done; that the worker exercised some degree of independent control over the work process. But ultimately the commission conceded the difficulty of trying to identify in isolation from the concrete labour process how skill is to be defined. They realized that formal definitions were less important than the strength of the respective parties in a specific historical context.

After noting the extent to which jobs in Pretoria were defined as artisan, whereas elsewhere they were semi-skilled, Skillocorn said 'this impressed him as an extraordinary state of affairs, and enquired what was the reason for Pretoria's practice in this respect differing so much from other centres'. Plunkett said that this was due to the men at Pretoria being organized. There was always strong protest when any encroachment took place. The importance of organization was confirmed by the foundry manager of Pretoria who said that at foundries overseas, where there were strong societies, cores were made by moulders; where there was no union, women made the cores.[29] It is of interest that the strike began in the steel foundry, where more jobbing was done than in any other foundry in South Africa. It would therefore have the largest concentration of craft moulders in the country, including those who had not yet been deskilled, who were both more threatened by encroachment and more able to resist it.[30]

The outcome of the 1934 strike was inconclusive — the South African Railways had not been able to establish that the artisan moulder had become a semi-skilled moulder because of the introduction of modern moulding machines, nor had the IMS been able to prevent a large number of jobs from being retained by machine moulders. In November 1937 the IMS proposed to the SAR Conciliation Board that, should the board be unable to agree to raise the pay of machine moulders and core makers to that of artisan moulders, the board consider raising the pay of machine moulders by 20 percent and that of core makers by 7 percent, thereby raising them to the level of the semi-skilled employees in the machinist trades.[31] While it had become obvious to all that the labour process was being transformed, what the 1934 strike established was that the transformation would not take place entirely at management's pace. During the commission of inquiry, the IMS delegates agreed to accept the proposal that changes in the status of the artisan would be brought in gradually.

> It was thereupon agreed that as there are a number of instances where work, now designated by this committee as semi-skilled, being done by artisans, and it is undesirable that any sudden change in past practice should be made, the committee's findings are subject to the administration agreeing not to displace artisans by semi-skilled men until such time as the artisans can be suitably provided for as a result of increased work or wastage in their ranks due to retirement in age limits, or ill health, resignations, death or transfer.[32]

While it is clear from this commission's deliberations that a certain notion of specialized competence was retained, the evidence suggests that the concept of skill was *contested* by management and labour. This supports the view that the concept is socially constructed: thus different interpretations can be advanced by the differing contestants. This is implied in Marx's caution concerning the ideological and organizational features of skill when he wrote that:

> the distinction between higher and simple labour, skilled labour and unskilled labour rests in part upon pure illusion, or, to say the least, on distinctions that have long since ceased to be real, and that survive only by virtue of a traditional convention; in part on the helpless conditions of some sections of the working class, a condition that prevents them from exacting equally with the rest the value of their labour power.[33]

The Rise of Mass Production at Durban Falkirk

In 1936 the establishment of Durban Falkirk as South Africa's first large-scale mass production foundry began a new phase in the transformation of the labour process. 'The period between 1933 and the Second World War', SEIFSA records, 'can truly be said to have witnessed the vital development of the metal industries. It was the period wherein the main activity of engineering jobbing commenced its transition to mass production, mostly through the establishment of a few substantial plants, the operation of which more or less coincided with the commencement of production in the first ISCOR plant located in Pretoria'.[34] Falkirk was to make more pressing the crisis in the society: was it to breach craft control and open to non-journeyman moulders? Plunkett, a veteran member, 'considered it inadvisable to organize the Falkirk moulders under the present circumstances as it would not be beneficial to the society, and he could not see how it could be done without radical changes to the constitution'. He was followed by another veteran, Jock Naysmith, who said 'that up to the present we had not given away any of our craft and in spite of the difficult aspect of the industrial movement today . . . we should still retain the craft union aspect'.[35] It was then decided that the secretary should visit Falkirk. On his return the debate continued. The chairman noted that similar firms existed on the Reef (notably City Engineering Works and Eclipse Tube Mill Lines), which were 'purely repetitive shops and if the position was accepted at Falkirk it would mean a certain weakening of the society'. The secretary then proposed a separate branch for machine moulders.[36]

The debate was eventually settled by the pragmatic arguments of the Pretoria branch. Although the Falkirk moulders, they said, were a 'motley crew', 'as a matter of self preservation it was necessary for the society to organize them . . . . If we left the men unorganized they might prove a menace'. The same danger, on a smaller scale, they said, existed on the Reef. At the Exchange Engineering Works there were a number of men employed as moulders who had not served their apprenticeship.[37] It was decided to establish a separate Light Metal Section along the lines of the NUIM in the United States. They insisted that lower contributions and entrance fees be paid and that no transfer from General to Light be possible.

In support of this diluting of the craft nature of the union, members cited the SAR case. 'When the society decided to organize core makers and machine moulders in SAR, there had been a lot of opposition but it had turned out to be in the interests of the society.'[38] The society, however, was not prepared to accept labourers from Falkirk as members.[39]

The emergence of an industrial union for coloured and Indian metal workers in the wake of the 1937 Falkirk strike was an important factor in persuading the IMS to open its membership to coloured production moulders. In 1937 the South African Tin Workers' Union (SATWU) and the Iron and Steel Workers' Union (ISWU) were formed.[40] In 1941 ISWU merged with the AEU to form the No.5 branch of the AEU.[41] In 1957 when the coloured members were removed from the AEU they all joined this No.5 branch and in 1961 the first coloured parallel union in the engineering industry, the EIWU (Engineering Industrial Workers' Union) was launched.[42]

The rise of mass production had transformed the labour process, creating a new task in the foundry, that of machine operator or production moulder. These new unions and the IMS's decision to open to non-craft moulders are the landmarks of this change.

It was in this context of dilution that employers were to request a meeting with the society to discuss a 'shortage' of moulders in the industry. The society agreed to meet the employers but were unanimous that what employers desired was dilution of the moulding craft. They were also adamant that no shortage existed.[43] The society refused to agree to any further dilution at the meeting but agreed to allow apprentices in their fourth year to be placed on journeyman rates.[44] At a further meeting they agreed that if foundries similar to Falkirk were established, the society would grant them the same facilities.[45]

This was to lead to a prolonged debate among members. Some felt the society had made a mistake 'as the employers' interest is to flood the trade with cheap labour in the foundries and Falkirk was the pretext for this'. Others agreed that employers 'were after cheaper labour' but that they had no choice but to organize production moulders. They cited an example where a foundry was unable to find moulders willing to work on machines and had asked permission to 'start anybody off the streets for the production of kaffir pots'.[46] Although the society was eventually able to fill these vacancies, it had become clear that repetition foundry work was growing and that the craft skill in these foundries had been irreversibly undermined.

The Second World War, Munitions and Mass Production

If by 1939 the impediments to capital accumulation on a mass production basis had been breached, the war provided capital with the opportunity to go on to the offensive.[47] 'The war of 1939', A.G. Thomson writes, 'did not come as a complete surprise. It had advertised its arrival for almost six years and the more frequently recurring crises immediately preceding it gave rise to a strange assignment for a local manufacturer'.[48] He goes on to describe the construction of a mass production foundry in less than six weeks to produce field mortar bombs.

> The specification and reduction of all operations to an absolute minimum was essential, in order to ensure more output with the least room for error. This necessitated considerable planning beforehand in regard to layout, pattern and moulding for design and construction, pouring methods, and fettling arrangements, etc. A proper flow-through had to be secured by the avoidance of any bottleneck in the various stages of manufacture from moulding, drying, closing, pouring, etc., stripping, fettling and annealing.[49]

As South Africa entered the war, the demands for munitions escalated rapidly, most orders being placed by the Director General of War Supplies. The quantities demanded necessitated the introduction of mass production rather than jobbing. Most foundries were converted to manufacturing heavy armaments supplies, materials and shell cases. Between 1938-9 and 1944-5 the net output in basic metals rose from £9 285 000 to £25 557 000. (See Table 3).

The war strengthened the hand of the employers as a chronic shortage of skilled labour for strategic industries prompted the government to move swiftly to secure dilution. 'In an emergency', ran an editorial in the August 1940 issue of *Engineer and Foundryman*, 'people can be taught to carry out a limited number of skilled operations . . . . it speaks volumes for the patriotism and realism of trade unions that they should be willing to accept the principle of dilution during such emergency periods as this'. Employer enthusiasm for this mechanism for overcoming labour shortage was thinly disguised. 'It would be calamitous', the editorial continues, 'for the unions if a shortage of labour were allowed to hamper a period of internal industrial development likely to result in permanent expansion with the creation of more jobs for the rising generation and a consequent increase in the prosperity of the country.'[50] Thomson sums up the change:

> Before the war the majority of South African foundries were engaged mainly in jobbing work and it was the general practice for moulding to be carried out by hand. The repetition work involved in the execution of large orders for the Director General of War Supplies has stimulated the use of foundry machinery. Since the war a considerable number of moulding and core-blowing machines of various types have been imported. Some types of machines for foundry work are also being manufactured locally, among them core sand mixers and jolt stripping machines of which several are already in operation.[51]

Employer appeals to worker patriotism announced, in reality, a serious setback for the organized working class. The Emergency agreement of 1939 was passed because the unions realized that the alternative to a voluntary agreement was state regulation.[52] At a special general meeting a delegate expressed the magnitude of the defeat which the society had suffered. 'The society was faced with the biggest crisis in its history. The employers had always desired dilution and at this stage if backed by the Director General of War Supplies the society must be broken up.'[53] This was certainly the feeling of a delegate to the annual conference in 1941, when he said:

> . . . the IMS had made great sacrifices in sacrificing the principles of the craft to open the trade to others to assist in the war effort. This had been

done in good faith, but they would have to fight hard to keep what they had got. Conditions had been forced upon the workers, meaning the end of individual liberty, and when objecting, were told they were not helping the war effort, wages were frozen at the lowest level instead of the highest level when commodities were frozen at the highest price. If the workers' wages were limited, profits too must be limited, or 100 percent of profits taken in tax by the state. The war demanded sacrifice by the employers as well as employees. The time had arrived for unions to take part in political action.[54]

Profits in the base metal industries increased by 400.4 percent between 1939 and 1943.[55]

The society did not break up — it chose strategically to accept mechanization and an increasing dilution on condition that craft privileges were retained. Thus one emphasis at the special general meeting of the society in 1939 was on the need to ensure 'absolute control' over the introduction of emergency labour.[56] The means to maintain control were threefold. Firstly, the unions would retain some say in the allocation of emergency workers through their membership of the Industrial Council.[57] Secondly, the unions sought to ensure that emergency labour would not become a cheap labour device, by demanding that these workers should receive journeyman wages.[58] Finally, the executive of the IMS attempted to obtain a strict definition of the scope of emergency labour.[59]

Employer strategy was to conceal a more radical restructuring of the labour process.[60] Initially emergency workers had been employed because of the shortage of skilled labour. However, employers soon took advantage of this breach to link the employment of emergency labour with mechanization and more fundamental processes of deskilling. Often women were used as the pretext for mechanization. One employer observed that 'there appears to be no reason why the manager of a modern foundry should not be able to augment his labour force by women', and went on to argue that the core-making section of modern foundries 'has been mechanized so that work is more suited for the utilization of female labour'.[61] Again an employer observed that in a munitions factory '80 percent of the machinery is already being run by women'.[62] Noting the high percentage of female labour employed in a shell foundry, Thomson remarked that it had 'been facilitated by the use of jigs and by the provision of stops on the machines, the possibility of error being reduced by these means to a minimum'.[63]

This error was, as Lewis argues, to lead to a challenge by the rank and file to IMS leadership on the grounds that the officials had lost touch with the membership on the question of emergency labour. By December 1940 the members had deposed the executive of the society, and voted to repudiate the emergency agreement on the grounds that Clause 2 was being abandoned by employers. However, the moulders' stand was not successful and failed to gain the support of other engineering unions. Although relations between the IMS militants and the leadership stabilized after this, the moulders typified a tradition of rank and file activism which at times transcended the limits of the particular trade union and survived throughout the war years. In 1942 a 'war workers' committee of action' went on strike in the course of a short-lived conflict with the executives of the engineering unions. In 1944 the rank and file movement ran its own newspaper, *The Engineering Worker*, and was blamed for holding up implementation of the piece work provisions of the new national Industrial Council agreement.[64]

By 1940 the capital-labour ratio stood at par, the value of machinery being £5 418 000 and the value of wages £5 471 000. (See Table 3.) In 1943 expenditure on capital surpassed labour for the first time, although the ratio was to decline for the rest of the war. During the war the major area of growth was in black employment and new machinery. Machinery rose by 150 percent (substantially faster than any other industry during the war); overall employment by 74 percent (whites by 65 percent); wages by 161 percent overall (whites by 134 percent); and output by a high 100 percent. The value of machinery in 1950 was only 1.1 times smaller than the value of wages, indicating that the major thrust of expansion since 1920 had been capital-intensive in character. By 1970 the capital labour ratio was 2.7. Basic metals had become the most capital-intensive sector in manufacturing.[65]

The demand for increased mechanization during the Second World War and the difficulties in importing machinery under war conditions led to the manufacture in South Africa of machine tools.[66] Simultaneously pressure built up among employers to make full use of these machines. An editorial in the employers' journal, titled 'The Scandal of the Idle Machines', deplored the 'high percentage of our machine tools [which] are standing idle during hours when they should be working at full speed to cope with the huge requirements of munition production'.[67] It also asked 'whether the way should be open for an extension of the shift system (for example, two daily shifts of eight hours each — say 6 a.m. to 2 p.m. and 2 p.m. to 10 p.m.). Two shifts halve the capital charges upon industrial plant and lessen many other overheads as well. The ability to adapt a two-shift system often makes it worth while to install the best and most costly plant where it would be economically impossible to do so with one shift'.[68] Two further implications follow from growing mechanization — an increase in the number of mergers to provide the capital for expansion,[69] and a steady climb in the toll of industrial accidents — culminating in the inauguration, in December 1951, of the National Occupational Safety Association (NOSA).[70] Budlender argues that '...accidents increased fairly steadily from 1924 to 1945, 256 and 2 796 respectively, while deaths increased from 24 to 84 in the same period'.[71]

The Transition to Machinofacture

In 1944 the IMS finally opened its doors to all production moulders. In doing so the society was simply coming to terms with the development of the non-craft aspect of moulding. The semi-skilled nature of production moulding was by then widely accepted in foundry practice.[72] In amending the constitution, the chairman suggested 'that the time will arrive when the production moulder would most likely outnumber us general members and unless we work with them and together, they would break away and form their own union and perhaps due to numerical strength would have more to say in the framing of a policy with regard to moulding than the general moulder would have'.[73]

By 1949 25 percent of the members were production moulders; by 1971 the proportion had nearly doubled. The strategy of the union was to admit operators only when absolutely necessary in order to protect the skilled members. This had shaped the union's attitude to coloureds in the 1920s, the contest over skill in the Pretoria railway foundries, and the rise of mass production at Durban Falkirk.

What of African workers? Before the war an African Iron and Steel Workers' Union existed 'to bring all workers engaged in the iron and steel trade in the continent of Africa into one union. Special attention to be paid to all the big concerns, that is Pretoria Steel Works [ISCOR], Dunswart and Vereeniging'.[74] In September 1940 this union

Table 4. IMS Membership 1949-1971

Year	Moulders	Appren-tices	production Moulders	Others	Total
1949	1 405	205	526	87	2 223
1955	1 530	148	934 + 7	135	2 754
1957	1 461	118	912 + 5	158	2 649
1959	1 303	134	575	191	2 203
1962	1 198	78	572	214	2 062
1964	1 329	62	858	222	2 471
1966	1 380	92	1 322	243	3 037
1968	1 241	49	979	262	2 538
1971	1 116	0	1 377	333	2 836

Source: IMS Biennial Conference Minutes.

submitted a well motivated memo to the Industrial Council for an increase in Grade 7 operators' wages from sixpence per hour to ninepence per hour (where board and lodging was provided from fivepence to sixpence per hour); and an increase from fivepence to eightpence per hour for labourers.[75] By 1942 at least two black metal unions existed and in April they merged into the South African Non-European Confederation of Iron, Steel and Metal Workers Union (SANECISMWU) and affiliated to the Council of Non-European Trade Unions (CNETU).[76] In 1943 Grade D operatives' positions were opened to Africans under the Industrial Council agreement. By 1946, 3 643 out of 63 545 Africans employed in the engineering industry held operative jobs.[77]

Union growth kept pace with this rapid advancement of black workers during the Second World War. At its height SANECISMWU claimed 35 000 members. The Mechanics Union Joint Executive (MU-JE) began to fear undercutting and in 1943 agreed to support the black unions' demands though in their negotiations these demands 'would not constitute a breaking point'.[78] In the event, the wages given fell far short of black worker demands and a number of strikes broke out in 1946. The longest of these, at USCO foundry in June 1946, in-volved 1 400 members of the union. The attempt by MUJE to intervene on behalf of the strikers failed when employers found themselves 'unable to discuss with MUJE the conditions which should apply to persons who are not workers in terms of the Act, since in its opinion the trade unions do not represent such persons'.[79] Protected by the closed shop and prevented from incorporating them into the Industrial Council by the racially exclusive Act, MUJE's equivocal support was to turn to antagonism when white worker attitudes hardened in the face of technological change under the umbrella of the post-1948 apartheid state. By 1950 the black metal unions' membership had declined to 96.[80]

Faced by the organized challenge of black labour in the 1940s, the United Party government responded cautiously by proposing the 1947 Industrial (Natives) Bill which, if enacted, would have accorded some formal recognition to African unions but excluded them from the Industrial Council system. Although Africans had moved into semi-skilled jobs, they were largely unskilled labourers, easily replaceable in the strikes that were to take place in the immediate post-war period. The 1948 Nationalist government scrapped this bill and appointed the Botha Commission to examine African trade unions. The commission proposed, when its recommendations were eventually made in 1951, that African trade unions should be recognized under stringent conditions. The proposal aroused considerable government hostility and was turned down. By the time parliament was debating the recommendations of the commission in 1952 and 1953, conditions had changed — most of the (CNETU) unions had declined and the state was now on the offensive. This was reflected in the nature of the government's alternative to trade unions — the works committee system — introduced in 1953 in the Native (Settlement of Disputes) Act. In introducing the bill in parliament in 1953 the Minister of Labour, Ben Schoeman, stated the government's position:

> My proposals are the following: first of all we do not prohibit Native trade unions. Consequently the question of freedom of association does not arise . . . what we do in this bill is to create machinery which will ensure justice to native workers, to enable them to channel their grievances and bring them to the attention of the authorities — or some alternative machinery. If that machinery is effective and successful the natives will have no interest in trade unions and trade unions will probably die a natural death.[81]

By the end of the war the production foundry had been well established: a spate of trade and industry commissions reported during this period advocating more scientific methods of production. Report 282, an investigation into manufacturing, recommended standardization, industrial research, and better utilization of labour.[82] This was followed a year later by an investigation into the iron and steel engineering industry which recommended the rationalization of industry through standardization, research, patents and specialization.[83] Then, in 1948, the De Villiers Commission recommended restructuring the apprenticeship system in the light of the rapid technological developments in the industry. The previous method of apprenticeship, in which the apprentice performed all the tasks under the close supervision of an individual artisan and under less pressure to work intensively due to the jobbing character of the work, was no longer possible under the new conditions in the foundry. These new conditions, under which neither employer nor foreman showed any interest in the apprentices, emerge clearly in the following comments from the commission:

> The opinion that the primary consideration should be the interests of the apprentices was general. This would certainly be the ideal, but it hardly seems practicable in these days of keen competition. As one informant put it, the primary idea of a foreman in any factory is to look to his production, and teaching in consequence is neglected. The same can no doubt be said of many journeymen, as a minimum output is usually required of them: individual cases, which do not appear to be unique, were cited where neither the employer nor his foreman showed any interest in an apprentice throughout a period of five years and where an apprentice was kept on a simple operation for more than half his apprenticeship.[84]

A major concern of the commission was to reduce the period of training:

> [There] was practical unanimity that the period of apprenticeship bore no relationship to the amount of skill and knowledge that had to be acquired, and was in general much too long . . . . With the development of technology, the number of positions in the semi-skilled occupations may be expected to increase, but at the same time there will probably be a proportionate decrease in the number of both highly skilled positions and the entirely unskilled jobs, which will more and more be taken by workers of the machine tender type, who are skilled at repetitive processes dealing with only a small fragment of the entire productive enterprise. A large number of semi-skilled workers require training of only a few weeks or months on the job to obtain the necessary manipulative ability. [Para.1015][85]

The commission believed that the Central Organization of Technical Training (COTT), set up during the war, provided a model for technical training. The nature of this training is of some interest:

> The various operations involved in a given exercise or job were fully detailed in instruction sheets and drawings. There was a master operation sheet for each job, together with a shop instruction sheet, each of which gave detailed instructions as to the procedure to be followed and the tools required, and the various operations constituting the complete job were given on the master operation sheet together with the standard time allocated for each item, for which dimensioned drawings were also supplied. On completion of the item this was stamped and returned to the store for future inspection and assessment of marks, and further re-issue to another trainee if further work was required to be done upon it. In the inspection department, marks were assigned according to the accuracy, finish and ratio of actual time taken to the standard time laid down. Weekly time and record sheets were prepared in the case of each trainee, these being signed by the Officer in Charge and filed for future reference. The system of training was based on mass production methods, and while it provided experience in various workshop operations — backswing, chipping, filing, scraping and machine drilling — when the complete job was assembled no trainee could point out that it had been made entirely by himself, although he had made similar constituent parts. In this respect the method differed from that in operation in the trades schools of the technical colleges, where the individual pupils make each part of the assembled job and naturally take a greater interest in an article entirely created by themselves. [Para.1081]

The main proposal to emerge from the commission, which was incorporated into the amended 1951 Apprenticeship Act, was the opportunity afforded to above-average apprentices to curtail their period of training by writing a trade test. The secretary of the society, Crompton, who sat on this commission, opposed its recommendation as he saw it as the end of apprenticeship: 'the thin end of the wedge'.[86] Similarly, the society, along with the other engineering unions, opposed the proposal by the National Apprentice Board to make the test compulsory. The members feared that unsuccessful candidates would become second rate artisans who would undercut their positions. The introduction of the journeyman recognition scheme in 1965, which allowed a trainee to by-pass apprenticeship and become an artisan by the efflux of time, confirmed these fears.[87]

While the De Villiers Report was concerned to stress the 'dequalification' of the craft skill, it also focussed on the contradictory effect of the new technology in creating a demand for a small number of 'hyperqualified' technicians and engineers. De Villiers indentifies this stratum as follows:

> In the case of manufacturing industries, though much of the work can be done by operatives, the organization of production is possible only if there is also available a supply of very highly skilled workers, competent to undertake the difficult and delicate work of making and setting machine tools and installing and adjusting automatic machinery. For these workers, prolonged and thorough training is indispensable. In fact, the growing demand by industry for the semi-professional or technician grade is one of the significant trends in industrialized countries . . . . [Paras. 1018-1020].

These new skills were obtained, not through apprenticeship, but in the technical colleges and the universities.[88] Relying on their professional qualifications, this new stratum of professionals in the foundry did not require the support of a trade union.

One report dealing specifically with the foundry industry regretted the fact that 'work standards established by time and motion studies had barely commenced in the union. So long as the management are able to obtain a sufficiently high price for their products to enable them to show a good profit; so long as the seller's market conditions continue, there is but little incentive to go to the trouble of setting up work standards'.[89] This latter report is central to the changes taking place in production at this time. Referring to the new mass production foundries the authors wrote:

> . . . these production concerns have also taken advantage of the various mechanical means designed to reduce labour costs, so that cores and moulds are prepared by mechanical means under certain specified conditions, and the employment of skilled labour for these tasks is unnecessary. Again, the inter-operational transfer of materials, moulds, and finished products is effected by suitable machinery, so that it is possible to adhere to rigid time schedules with a minimum of labour. Furthermore, the fettling of the finished castings is concentrated in a separate section of the plant and the labour force required for this work is considerably reduced by the use of modern fettling equipment.[90]

The report goes on to regret the fact that

. . . pay work or the flat hourly rate and an absence of work standards mean that the management is operating without effective control. In other words our managers are unable to compare the actual performance of the plant, even though it may be on restricted output, with the standard or target performances for that output.[91]

The argument is clear. The primary source of energy is increasingly mechanical. As part of the deskilling process, skills are now incorporated into and under the control of the machine. The skill of the individual worker is being broken down and incorporated in a machine-dominated process which places the emphasis on collective work. In other words the stage of the 'real subordination' of the worker is reached and labour power is devalued with increasing productivity. The dominant form of surplus extraction is now relative surplus value, hence the gradual appearance of cost accounting, attention to plant lay-out and a system of 'payment by results', ratified in the so-called Premium Bonus System in the 1944 agreement.

This attempt to increase surplus value extraction was to come up against resistance from the iron moulders. In particular the attempt at a more systematic bonus system at Van der Bijl Engineering Corporation (VECOR), which is dealt with in Chapter 4, is an example of this resistance. The post-war period continued the process, with further major changes in foundry technology.

Table 5. Installation Dates for New Foundry Technology

1949	First automatic frequency induction moulding unit.
1954	First automatic shell moulding machine.
1955	First core shooter.
1957	First mass frequency induction furnace.
1960	First hot blast cupola.
1963	First hot box core shooter.
1965	First continuous mixer.
1970	First fully automatic flashless moulding machines.

Source: John Steele, 'The Foundry Industry in South Africa', *Foundry, Welding and Production Journal*, February, 1979, p.67.

By the mid-1950s it appeared as if base metals were about to enter a massive expansion into automatic production.[92] W.F. Boustred, president of SEIFSA, warned that the size of the internal market restricted this transition to automatic production:

> The economic questions relating to automation, including the high costs of the necessary plant, its specialized nature in relation to the end product and its consequent inflexibility are not likely to be overlooked. It is for these reasons that I believe in a country such as ours where only relatively short runs can be undertaken, which call for a good deal of versatility in the moulding, we must emphasize that this is not an immediate problem we have to face.[93]

The juxtaposition of jobbing and mass production defines this phase — the phase of machinofacture — as a phase of combined as well as uneven development. The effect these uneven forms of production, and in particular new technology, had on work place organization in the 1950s and the 1960s will be dealt with in Chapter 5. What is clear is that the transformation of the capitalist labour process is uneven and cannot be understood in simple chronological form. Mechanization had not created a single homogeneous mass of deskilled workers. Where workplace organization existed moulders were able to exclude non-members from handling the new machines. In other cases they were able to contest the definition of skill as in the Pretoria railway foundries, and resist deskilling. While deskilling remained the major tendency during this period, what emerges from this chapter is that this transformation would not take place at a pace set exclusively by management.

Notes

1   C 10, 8.1.1932.
2   C 10, 3.9.1932.
3   C 10, 14.11.1932.
4   C 10, 23.3.1933.
5   Davies, *op.cit.*, p.225.
6   F, 'Proceedings of the Annual Conference of the IMS 1941'.
7   Quarterly General Meeting, C 10, 18.10.1929.
8   C 10, 20.12.1929.
9   C 10, 19.9.1930.
10 C 10, 19.12.1931.
11 C 10, 19.6.1931.
12 Biennial Conference Minutes, 1949.
13 *Ibid.*
14 *Ibid.*

15 C 10, 19.3.1932.
16 C 10, 19.12.1930.
17 C 10, 3.7.1931.
18 C 10, 19.3.1932.
19 C 10, 4.8.1933.
20 C 10, 29.9.1933.
21 C 10, 9.10.1933.
22 C 10, 25.11.1933.
23 C 10, 18.2.1934.
24 C 10, 22.2.1934.
25 Special General Meeting, C 10, 23.2.1934.
26 C 10, 28.2.1934.
27 C 10, 2.3.1934.
28 General Report of the evidence to the commission of inquiry into the moulding trade.
29 *Ibid.*
30 See J. Hinton, *The First Shop Stewards' Movement* (George Allen & Unwin, 1973), for a discussion of the tradition of craft control among engineers in England during the First World War. Hinton argues that a condition for the emergence of a successful local Workers' Committee during the First World War was that the status and privileges of the craftsmen in the area concerned should be intact when the war broke out. The advanced technology of the Midlands motor car industry, for example, had substantially undermined the craft status before 1914, and workers' committees were not successful in the Midlands.
31 F, Annual Conference Minutes, 1937.
32 General Report of the evidence of the commission of inquiry into the moulding trade.
33 Quoted in footnote 12, J. Elger, 'Valorization and "deskilling": a critique of Braverman', *Capital and Class*, Spring 1979.
34 SEIFSA, *op.cit.*, p.13.
35 C 10, 8.9.1935.
36 C 14, 5.3.1937.
37 C 14, 11.6.1937.
38 C 14, 1.7.1937. The Durban branch, of which Falkirk was a member, had made union history 16 years earlier when it was the first to open its membership to coloureds.
39 C 14, 7.12.1937.
40 Interview with R.D. Naidoo and R. Kirsten, both active officials in the AEU, No.5 Branch, and later in the EIWU. Interview, August, 1981.
41 South African Tin Workers' Union (SATWU), Silver Jubilee souvenir brochure, *A Brief History*, 1963.
42 Kirsten was to be its first secretary from 1961-1970. He presented it as a

parallel union of MUJE, although it received finance from the Amalgamated Engineering Union.

43 C 14, 2.12.1937.
44 C 14, 9.12.1937.
45 C 14, 17.2.1938.
46 C 15, 28.7.1939.
47 Not entirely! The existence of cheap African labour remained an inhibiting factor in mechanization. This is stated bluntly in an address to the Institute of British Foundrymen (S.A. branch) in 1941:

> A boy is made to transport castings by hand or barrow, is made to prepare the ground for the hand-moulder, is made to fettle by hammer and chisel, etc. In transportation a lift of some 80 lbs, would, overseas, be considered a reasonable amount for ordinary and more or less continuous handling, but the boy must have an aid and the rhythm of the work is as always the speed of the slower. This is an aside, but the point should be brought out that having this native labour at one's disposal, and the fact that it is always available is, in my opinion, one reason why foundry development in the mechanized sense is, generally speaking, somewhat behind the times in this country.

J. McLane Renwick, 'Foundry mechanization and equipment', *Engineer and Foundryman*, April 1941.
48 A.G. Thomson, *The Years of Crisis* (Johannesburg, 1946), p.207.
49 *Ibid.*, p.31.
50 *Engineer and Foundryman*, August 1940, p.75.
51 Thomson, *The Years of Crisis*, p.114.
52 C 15, 29.12.1939.
53 C 15, 6.12.1939.
54 F, Annual Conference Minutes, 1941.
55 BTI Report, No.286 (1946), p.12.
56 C 15, 6.12.1939.
57 C 15, 6.12.1939.
58 C 15, 5.12.1939.
59 C 15, 27.12.1939.
60 Lewis, 'The new unionism' in (ed.), E. Webster, *Essays in Southern African Labour History* (Ravan Press, Johannesburg, 1978).
61 'Women in South African Engineering', *Engineer and Foundryman*, March 1942, p.579.
62 'Women operators make good', *ibid.*, October 1942, p.459.
63 Thomson, *The Years of Crisis*, p.44.
64 J. Lewis, 'The new unionism'.
65 D. Innes, 'The state, post-war manufacturing and class struggle', mimeo (1978).

66 C 18, 20.4.1944. The *Engineer and Foundryman* reported, in January 1943, that National Engineering (Pty) Ltd. were producing general purpose machine tools at the same prices as imported machines. In June 1944, the *Engineer and Foundryman* reported that East Rand Engineering Company was manufacturing moulding machines. In both cases the machines were being used effectively in production.

67 *Engineer and Foundryman*, December 1940.

68 *Ibid.*, February 1943.

69 *Ibid.*, March 1946.

70 *Ibid.*, January 1941. It is interesting to note that the Factory Act was amended to introduce a chapter entitled 'Machinery and Accidents' for the first time in 1941.

71 D. Budlender, 'Labour Legislation in South Africa, 1924-1945', M.A.Thesis, University of Cape Town, 1979.

72 D.M. Davidson, 'Modern Foundry Practice', *Engineer and Foundryman*, Vol.4, No.9, February 1940.

73 C 15, 20.4.1944.

74 South African Trade Union Congress file, AH646, IDA 57.

75 *Ibid.*

76 M. Stein, 'The South African Non-European Iron, Steel and Metal Workers' Union (1942-1950)', mimeo, 1978, p.1; see also *Guardian* 30.4.1942; *Bantu World* 9.5.1942.

77 D. Hemson, 'Capital restructuring and the war economy', mimeo, 1977.

78 AEU Monthly Report, July 1946, p.504, quoted in M.Stein, 'The South African Non-European Iron, Steel and Metal Workers Union'.

79 Presidential address to the SEIFSA A.G.M., 21.1.1947, quoted in M. Stein, *ibid.*

80 M. Stein, *ibid.*

81 This quotation and parts of this paragraph are drawn from my introduction and Part 5, E. Webster, (ed.), *Essays in South African Labour History* (Ravan Press, Johannesburg, 1978), pp.209-215.

82 BTI Report, No.282 (1945).

83 BTI Report, No.286 (1946).

84 Report of the Committee on Technical and Vocational Education, UG 45, 1948 (the De Villiers Report).

85 The fact that mechanization had made prolonged craft training unnecessary was argued by the Department of Labour and employers in the 1930s. See Department of Labour Annual Report, 1932, p.44 and *Engineer and Foundryman*, Vol.1, No.9; Vol.2, No.9. It was developed more systematically as an argument in the 1940s in a series of government reports of which the De Villiers Report was the most comprehensive. See also UG40/1941 para.161 (Van Eck Report) and Report 282, para.417.

86 Interview, Cliff Crompton, May 1980.

87   Exco, 27.11.1959. The period of apprenticeship had been reduced from six to five years in the 1920s.

88   The University of the Witwatersrand increased its engineering enrolment from 149 in 1922 to 1 351 in 1967. Ad Hoc Committee to Advise on Quinquennial Planning, 1968, University Archives.

89   BTI Report, No.311, para.35.

90   *Ibid.*

91   *Ibid.*

92   F, 10th Biennial Conference Minutes of the IMS.

93   SEIFSA Presidential Address, *SEIFSA Monthly Bulletin*, 1956.

CHAPTER 4

The Theory and Practice of Taylorism in the Early Post-War Period

There are two ways of rewarding labour — either by paying for the time spent at work (time wages) or by paying for the amount of work performed (piece-work). Traditionally, as argued in Chapter 2, the work of the moulder was rewarded by time wages, the amount of work to be performed being set by custom. With the exception of South African Railways (where piece-work had been introduced before the First World War) and Durban Falkirk, the IMS had successfully resisted management's attempts to introduce piece-work among moulders.[1] As the chairman stated at the 1947 biennial conference, 'We as a society have always been opposed to piece-work, our contention being "a fair day's work for a fair day's pay" and with the piece-work system this was not a practical issue.'[2]

The way to avoid the piece-work trap discussed in Chapter 2 was simply, the society argued, to avoid piece-work altogether. However, the demand for increased production during the Second World War led the state to intervene directly in production, creating the Controller of Manpower in 1941. In terms of War Measure No.6 of 1941 engineering, because of the crucial importance of munitions production, fell under the Controller of Manpower, who was empowered to determine wages, conditions of work, resignations, dismissals and transfers.[3]

The regional nature of employer organization prevented the employers from developing a national strategy to combat worker unrest in the wake of the Controller of Manpower's attempt to freeze wages, restrict the movement of skilled engineers and extend the working day. At an employers' conference called by the controller in late 1942

discussions on working conditions proved abortive. The employer association representatives had been confronted by the five trade unions then concerned which were able to speak nationally on behalf of the workers. The employers having no national organization were not in a strong position to meet this situation . . . resultant on this situation the employers resolved to form a national employer organization, which was known as the South African Federation of Engineering and Metallurgical Association (SAFEMA).[4]

The formation of SAFEMA can be seen as part of an employer and state strategy to increase national control over the engineering shop floor in the wake of craft worker resistance.

The defensive nature of this attempt to unite employers to confront organized labour emerged more specifically in the case of the formation of the Industrial Employers' Association by the FCI in 1943. According to its official history, the association was formed in response to labour unrest in Durban in 1942 during which

> it was felt that under the prevailing conditions employers were at a grave disadvantage in labour disputes, as each employer acted on his own without the knowledge of what his fellow employers might be doing. Individual employers were negotiating with representatives of well-organized trade unions, affiliated to the united coordinating council, in possession of full information in all trade union matters in other parts of the country. This lack of organization on the part of the employers resulted often in their agreeing to extravagant demands by the trade unions, only to find out later that trade unions were playing off one employer against another by using their bargaining strength against an unprepared opponent.[5]

In that same year (1943) a National Industrial Council for engineering was formed from the different regional councils and in 1944 the first national agreement was negotiated. A number of features were introduced into the final document providing specifically for different conditions in mass production (or 'repetition') foundries as distinct from jobbing foundries. More controversially, and in response to representations from employers, provision was made for wage incentive schemes, 'which hitherto had been resisted'.[6] 'Expert staff', management said, 'would be engaged to determine scientifically and accurately by such means as time and motion studies, the task that can reasonably be expected from efficient workmen during the course of a working day.'[7] The two delegates representing the IMS were the only delegates who were opposed to the employers' recommendation of a bonus work clause in the agreement. Though the Minister of Labour,

W. Madeley (an ex-AEU official) initially questioned the inclusion of wage incentive provisions 'which in his opinion were not in the interest of workers', he finally approved the agreement.[8] Opposition from the IMS continued and, after consultation with the membership and since the agreement was about to expire, it was decided to go to arbitration on this issue.[9]

The society was divided on what approach to adopt in their evidence before the arbitration board. On one hand the traditionalists were in favour of resisting the bonus system completely and insisting on the right of craft workers to set their own pace of work.

> Dowie questioned what man would be able, after the age of thirty, to stand up to the bonus work system that the private engineering employer was trying to introduce. They were now demanding task work, and what is more, they were getting it, and the membership were to blame. They should stand together, and not give the employer the excessive output that he was demanding.[10]

The pragmatists, represented by the secretary, agreed with Dowie but favoured accommodation as 'the dice were too loaded against the society. We should have a second string to our bow'. He pointed out that bonus work had been accepted by other engineering unions and was a standard practice in every industry throughout the world.

> He personally did not see how we, as an organization, could expect an arbitrator to give a finding which was contrary to the attitude taken in countries such as Great Britain, New Zealand, Australia and even the Soviet Union. He felt that we should by all means put up as strong a case as possible for the elimination of piece-work entirely. But we should not lack a mandate and a prepared case for the arbitration proceedings. In the event of the arbitrator indicating that he would introduce bonus work we should ask for greater safeguards. For example, we should ask for a pricing committee consisting of at least three members, not as the present agreement provides, so that the individual employee could agree with his employer on a price. He felt that all the men in the shop were interested in a price set for any job in that particular shop and should play an equal part in setting the price of any job. We had always expressed that three men could get a better deal than one and if the pricing committee had the confidence of the shop, he felt better prices and facilities would result from such an agreement.[11]

After further discussion it was moved and agreed 'that the society endeavour to remove bonus work from the award altogether, and further that if the society officials, when presenting the case, found the issue going against them, then they should compromise and endeavour to tighten the conditions of the bonus claim as contained in the national agreement'.[12]

The arbitration court met and in the award that followed it was decided that there were no legal grounds in terms of the Industrial Conciliation Act for opposing the introduction of bonus work.[13] However, the award did suggest that a price fixing committee be established, including the man on the job, the shop steward and another man from the society elected by the men. A suggestion was then adopted in the Industrial Council[14] in terms of which the arbitration award became a supplementary agreement to the main agreement. It provided for stricter control of bonus work for moulders, and for an increase of $2\frac{1}{2}$ percent on the bonus. In addition members won a $7\frac{1}{2}$ percent annual leave holiday bonus and production core makers were raised by $2d$ and $3\frac{1}{2}d$ an hour to $10d$ and $11\frac{1}{2}d$ an hour. This guarantee was to prove most timely as two months later management from the newly-formed heavy engineering foundry, VECOR, contacted the society with a bonus system proposal. 'An establishment the size of VECOR (nearly 500) had to have', management said, 'some control over the output.'[15] The mechanisms for extending this control, they believed, lay in time and motion study.

The Promise of Taylorism

In order to establish work standards, Taylor and his associates had developed the techniques of time study discussed in Chapter 1. Using stop watches and mathematical formulas they attempted to establish the time required for any job. Time study results were then used as a basis for setting incentive pay rates. Taylor promised to extend management's control over the work place through scientific study.

Engineering management took these bold claims at their face value and with uncritical enthusiasm spread them before expectant South African audiences. In 1939 the ISCOR Efficiency Bureau read a paper to the Institute of British Foundrymen (South African branch) in which it was said that 'the aim of the father of time and motion study (Taylor) was to show up and eradicate this cancer (awkward, inefficient or ill directed movements of men) gnawing at the vitals of our industrial efficiency'.[16] In March 1944 Dr Berliner read a paper to the Institute of Production Engineers in which he spoke of 'the evolution of a nation (South Africa) becoming aware for probably the first time of the need for scientific organization in production'.[17] Two months later a paper was delivered at the same Institute that reproduced in detail Taylor's method:

> Taylor's method of approach to this problem (conflict over the division of the surplus) was to gather all the great mass of traditional knowledge which in the past has been in the hands of workmen, and in the physical skill and knack of workmen, and to reduce it to laws, rules and mathematical formulas. With this weapon he attacked the systematic loafing on the one hand, and rule of thumb management on the other.

The results of Taylor's work, the speaker concluded, led to high wages, low costs and a fair price for the consumer.[18] Similar papers were read throughout the 1940s — possibly the most enthusiastic example was a man by the name of Spiro who, in analyzing in detail the introduction of time and motion study in the Soviet Union, concluded that 'the Russian experiment showed on a very large scale that if industry and the economy of a whole country is efficiently handled, classical income incentives, developed within the last hundred years of industrial development in engineering countries, cannot be discarded'.[19]

The theme of scientific management was to be picked up by the state in a number of commissions. The 1945 Board of Trade and Industry report (282) summarized the general principles in regard to 'scientific utilization of labour' in Taylorian terms as follows:

> The conditions for the optimum performance of each function in the production process are carefully analyzed. The necessary equipment, procedure and product are then standardized. Planning is basically divorced from the function of execution. The workers merely carry out tasks in accordance with detailed specifications.[20]

Foundry production was the subject of a specific investigation in 1948 which reported, in particular, on the need to introduce 'modern methods of controlling labour productivity'.[21] Stressing the importance of work measurement and wage incentives[22] the report mentioned that 'an absence of work standards means that the management is operating without effective control. In other words, management is unable to compare the actual performance of the plant, even though it may be restricting output, with the standard or target performance for that output'.[23]

In Chapters 2 and 3 the way in which the third principle of scientific management — rendering the labour process independent of craft skill — was already far advanced by 1945 was described. Furthermore, scientific management had been first propagated twenty years earlier by the Department of Labour. Why then did the theory find such a ready audience during the Second World War? The growing mechanization of engineering production which accompanied increasing concentration of production increased the indirect or fixed element of the cost, forcing capital to increase the rate of exploitation of labour. The 'economy of time' had now become a necessity to maintain profitability. The more highly the productive capacity of a given plant is utilized, i.e., the more products are turned out in a given time and, as a consequence, the greater the capital that can be turned over, then the lower is the unit cost of the output and the greater the competitiveness of the enterprise. The speed of operators in utilizing the given plant of a firm is the all important factor in a competitive struggle under conditions of machinofacture. Writing on the economy of time and scientific management Sohn-Rethel said:

> The main reasoning involved is one of the economics of overhead cost. Indirect expenses equal or exceed the wages paid directly and remain approximately constant whether the output is great or small. Greater output justifies higher wages, the diminution of indirect portion of the cost per piece being greater than the increase in wages. The operating economic factor is the effect that the volume of output has on the unit cost, or, as Taylor later puts it in his *Principles of Scientific Management* (1911) 'it pays the employer to pay higher wages as long as the high output does not increase overheads'. And there is no doubt that Taylor grasped the implications of the economics of time with greater systematic consistency from the standpoint of monopoly capital than anybody else from among the would be founders of the appropriate sort of management at that time.[24]

Of course management was to turn to a wide range of mechanisms to increase the productivity of labour. In Chapter 3 the introduction of the shift system during the Second World War was discussed. However, Taylor's innovation was to combine piece-work incentives with systematic time study. His promise was to increase the productivity of labour by scientific methods.

Scientific management thus presented an ambitious agenda. It proposed to extend management's control over the work place and eliminate soldiering. More broadly it claimed to remove the conflict in industry between workers and employers, making collective bargaining and trade unions redundant. On one hand, time and motion study made 'bargaining' and 'horse-trading' hardly necessary.[25] On the other hand, it encouraged 'both sides to take their eyes off the division of the surplus as the all important matter and together to turn their attention towards increasing the size of the surplus until the surplus becomes so large that it is unnecessary to quarrel over how it shall be divided'. That clearly was a solution in which all shared in the attempt to transcend immediate differences by mobilizing scientific management in the projection of a utopian future which made trade unions superfluous. As one of the few public critics put it,

> the situation in 1946 is somewhat similar to that in the industrial countries overseas twenty years ago when everybody expected everything from the magic word rationalization, only now in South Africa scientific management is the slogan of the day. The newspapers are full of it, it is the favourite topic of lectures in professional societies and the stock in trade of business consultants, and the government advises us in an avalanche of blue books that scientific management includes all the basic problems of industrial management.[26]

The Battle at Vecor

Yet if we look at Taylorism as a managerial practice, rather than as a managerial theory, the promise was only partially fulfilled.[27] In the first place the system was far too complicated, in view of the commission appointed to examine incentive schemes by the Institute of Production Engineers. Emphasizing the importance of a system that was easy to grasp and 'free from accounting intricacies, they felt that most of the systems that they had examined were too complex for universal application'.[28] Time and motion study was particularly difficult, as we shall see later, to implement in jobbing foundries where production was not standardized.

The main problem faced by Taylorism, however, was that workers attempted to subvert it. The decisive battle in the foundries was fought at Vecor. Arising out of the foundry arbitration award the IMS was able to enter into an agreement with management that, in effect, subverted Taylor's central objective of locating control entirely in management's hands. In December 1947 the organizer put forward, in his annual report, an agreement between the IMS and Vecor that provided for recognition of a shop steward as a representative of the moulders in the foundry. A bonus system was agreed to with times to be set by a price-fixing committee consisting of the shop steward, two shop-floor moulders and an equal number of management representatives. Disputes over the time or price of any job would be resolved on the basis of a time study by a man selected by the price-fixing committee. Furthermore, the shop steward would be allowed a reasonable time per day to attend to matters arising from bonus work.[29]

In making this proposal the organizer made clear his opposition to piece work. 'I, together with other trade unionists, have a very definite abhorrence of the piece work system but we have to take a realistic view of the position . . . we have held out to the last and have only agreed when very definite safeguards have been given to our members.'[30] This, once again, was to lead to a hotly contested debate with traditionalists, led by Jock Naysmith, resisting piece work on principle. Yet, when challenged, he seemed to retreat from opposition to the Vecor agreement. 'I did not express anything in my remarks in regard to a policy. I gave the conference my personal opinion, just the same as many people believe in their own minds that they would not like to go to work but are compelled, due to circumstances, to go to work.' But, replied the organizer, that was precisely the point: 'The time is passing when our society is able to resist bonus work through its skilled craftsman membership. We have 400 people [production moulders] on our society's book as members and they are at the whims of the management. They are exploited to the utmost, virtually slave labour. Similarly, any controlled system of bonus work is better than task work which is going on in the workshops without payment.' Besides, he said, Vecor offered a house, pension and medical facilities, and other moulders were keen to accept employment there. 'The men will work at Vecor — let us face the realities and get the safeguards.'[31] The pragmatists in the society were correct — men did come to Vecor, and at first their agreement did retain considerable shop floor control over production.

But this attempt to retain control on the shop floor was clearly in opposition to management's strategy. This was made clear in an address by the works manager in October 1948 to the Institute of Production Engineers. Spelling out Taylor's second and third principles — the divorce of conception from execution, and monopoly over knowledge to control the pace of work — he said:

> Each shop has its own detailed planning and rate fixing department under the control of the shop superintendent, whose duty it is to break down the component operations and decide the sequence of operations, all the paper and brain work being done before the job reaches the operator. The detail planners decide which type of machine shall perform the operation, and whether jigs and fixtures shall be used, also the type of fixtures . . . .[32]

With these two antagonistic objectives — the craft workers wanted to retain control while management was determined to relocate knowledge in the planning and layout of the department — open conflict was only a matter of time.

The occasion for the first dispute was management's attempt to bypass the society's long-standing rule by appointing a non-moulder as foundry foreman. Through established custom, foremen were required to be members of the society. In 1943, at the biennial conference, their participation in union activities was questioned for the first time.[33] A motion was proposed, but eventually defeated, that 'any member occupying the position of foreman shall not be allowed to attend a general meeting and shall be exempt from any fines for non-attendance, neither shall he hold any official position in the society'. The objection of the proposer and seconder to foremen as members of the society was that foremen were increasingly taking the side of management.[34] Evidence of this growing pressure from management to define more clearly the role of foremen as part of the managerial function can be seen in employer journals at the time.[35] However, when at the 1947 conference the Pretoria branch proposed that foremen be allowed to contract out of the society, the motion was firmly rejected as members feared that the society would lose control over the shop floor. 'Already', the chairman said, 'larger firms were attempting to supersede the old foreman by a manager, usually a pattern maker.' 'This', he said, 'should be resisted by the membership who should insist on taking their orders from the foreman and not the foundry manager.' Defending the traditional role of the foreman, the secretary described him as someone 'who carried the balance of power between the employer and the employee. Thus a really good foreman would be the man who would protect his man, be a good trade unionist, and at the same time see that the firm had a fair deal and the members were dealt with fairly.'[36]

By appointing a non-moulder as foreman, Vecor management was clearly attempting to shift the balance of power firmly to management's side, incorporating the foreman into its attempt to increase control over the shop floor. Bob Thorpe, a skilled moulder and shop steward, perceived it as a breach of union autonomy and refused to take instructions from the foreman. He was dismissed and the society members supported him by refusing to go on shift. The general secretary came down immediately from Johannesburg where management informed him that since there was no stipulation in the agreement that the foreman had to be a moulder they would take the matter to the Industrial Council. The general secretary appealed to tradition and custom saying that his members 'were fully aware of this lack in the agreement but by fifty-year-old tradition the society had always retained the foreman position and any position under the foreman for members of the society. This was the policy of the society and tradition of the membership, and no conciliation board would settle the matter.'[37] After a meeting between the society and the management, a moulder was made foreman and the old foreman was promoted to supervisor.[38]

Two months later the general secretary was forced to visit Vecor again when a dispute arose over the attempt by management to intensify production by introducing a three-shift system in the jobbing foundry.[39] Management said that a three-shift system was required because the foundry was the bottleneck, slowing down the flow of production from the machine shop. Idle machines cost money, management said, and unless they were running twenty-four hours a day the machinery was not a worthwhile investment.[40] The society replied that 'it was impractical to work a jobbing foundry on a three-shift system, for it was necessary in a foundry to clean up, and that at some period in the twenty-four hours there should be a foundry floor free from moulders'. The secretary went on to argue that 'it is impossible to clean up, knock out and remove castings while moulders are busy working and that if Vecor introduced the three-shift system in the foundry it would mean that the cranes would not be available for the turning and lifting of castings of the moulders' work'. As a result of these stoppages, the secretary said, the waiting time booked by the moulder employees would be excessive and the cost of production castings would be greatly increased.[41]

Management was determined to intensify production at Vecor and in August announced a scheme to import German immigrants. The IMS clearly saw this as an attempt to undercut members' resistance to management strategy. Releasing a press statement opposing the scheme they mentioned the opposition to the three-shift system and the excessive overtime.[42] However, a meeting with management was arranged where the society agreed:

a) we would not give the blessing of the society to the importation but as we were unable to supply men we asked for certain guarantees in writing;

b) if the recession was severe the importees would be sent back in order to prevent unemployment on the understanding that certain outstanding importees would not be sent back if the South African moulders did not measure up to the standard;

c) that management would endeavour to change the three-shift system to a two-shift system.[43]

In addition it was accepted that the immigrants would become members of our society and would have the full protection of the society against exploitation by the firm.[44]

The society's fears that the introduction of immigrant labour would be used to divide the membership was confirmed when management announced a bonus system where 'half the shop would receive a personal rate of up to six pence per hour and the other half no personal rate at all, particularly that the personal rate would be payable to the South African moulder whereas no personal rate would be payable to the immigrant moulder'. This, the secretary indignantly noted, 'savoured bias in favour of the South African member'. He suggested an alternative system — the tonnage system, where all the members participated — which 'did not divide the membership in the Vecor foundry'.[45] Because, said the secretary, members had been disciplined and acted as an entire shop and negotiated through their society, the differential bonus scheme was eventually abandoned.[46]

It was argued in Chapter 1 that a major obstacle to the ability of employers to increase production was management's ignorance of exactly how long a particular job took. It was the unplanned and unforeseen tragedy to Bob Thorpe, a key craft worker in the foundry, that was finally to swing the balance of power in favour of Vecor management. Because he earned in excess of the limit stated in the Workmen's Compensation Act (£750) he was not entitled to compensation for the permanent disability he suffered to both his hands after falling into a pool of molten metal.[47] Unable to continue with his craft and unable to claim compensation from the commissioner, Thorpe was in a vulnerable position at Vecor. At the end of 1950 he accepted the position of rate fixer in the foundry. After initial resistance to Thorpe, the superintendent of the foundry assured the author, the moulders were forced to accept his timing of the job.[48] 'He was a top artisan', said the superintendent, 'a very honest chap. He differed with the men on timing of jobs. But he was tough.' Thorpe explained how he did it in a manner reminiscent of Taylor's famous example of Schmidt and the pigiron.

> My job was to estimate how long a job took. You cannot calculate this — you know through experience. When I first took over the job, one of the moulders went to the shop steward and said he can't do the job in the allowed time. The shop steward went to the superintendent saying that one of the workers had challenged the time. He demanded that I demonstrate if it can be done or not. In spite of my disablement [a 42 percent disablement] I said to the superintendent that if I set the time I'll do the job. So I went ahead and did the job. I made a real fool of him. The man got fired. The price-fixing committee was never tried again while I was there. The times went unchallenged.[49]

Although management had overcome a major obstacle to increasing productivity, it had not done so through scientific methods, but through Thorpe's craft knowledge. Vecor had attempted to do this when they employed a time and motion expert from Germany who re-rated the jobs and put them on a graph. But, Thorpe said, the timings were unrealistic and the graphs were abandoned.[50] Similarly when Taylorites moved into Scaw Metals to introduce the bonus pay plan and began stop-watch timing on particular jobs, conflict immediately flared.[51] A few moulders refused to be timed and the manager, Boustred, agreed 'that if that was the feeling of the men he would give instructions immediately that the stop watch be withdrawn'.[52] Moulders learnt to be on the lookout for time-and-motion men in the foundry. When management eventually did achieve a better understanding of the pace of work in Vecor it was on the basis of Thorpe's craft experience, determined by the wholly unscientific concept of competition.

At the 1951 biennial conference the secretary announced that the society now accepted bonus work. At Vecor, management had abandoned the individual bonus in favour of the group tonnage bonus suggested by the society.[53] Earlier in that year the organizer had reported that the members at Vecor were not prepared to give up their time on Sundays to attend meetings.[54] The following year the secretary reported that the shop stewards were no longer able to collect susbscriptions and they were going on to a stop-order system.[55] It seems that once individual bonuses were abandoned timing of jobs ceased to be a major issue — the shop floor agreement fell away and the issue was now handled by the Industrial Council. The foundry management summed up the situation today as follows:

> We do rate fixing still in the planning department. We still set a time on a job but it is not done for individual bonus purposes. We don't have piece-work. Piece-work is only practised when you have sufficient mechanization for the cycle of each worker's job to be similar. We are still a jobbing foundry where every mine wants its own specification. We have to give a time for the job. The weekly return sheet of all jobs completed is handed into the planning department. If the time is over-spent we must have a reason. We let people know that we are worried about time. Times haven't been challenged since the early fifties.[56]

The foundry manager then went on to reveal a more subtle form of intensification of work:

> We now prefer the merit system. This gives recognition to the individual. One man recently resigned — he found that his friend was getting one cent more than him. He packed up his tool box and left. Informally they rank themselves. They tell each other what they are earning. Recognition is the key. A man feels proud if he is the top moulder on the job. There is a high degree of job satisfaction in jobbing work. We use Herzberg's theory of the hierarchy of needs here.[57]

What was to emerge in Vecor in the course of the fifties were two forms of control of foundry production: a jobbing foundry where a bonus system operated with individual motivation of workers through a management controlled merit system; and a mass production foundry where continuous assembly-line production existed and workers were paced by the machine. Piece-work had been resisted and found unworkable in its original form in the jobbing foundry and eventually, as we shall see later, was superseded in the mass production foundry. This juxtaposition of two forms of control over production in the foundry industry was to continue throughout the 1950s. It had become clear to the organizer at the 1947 conference that production moulders would grow more numerous in the mass production foundries as mass production increased. He believed that the pragmatic approach was to encourage artisan moulders to accept production moulders fully into the society:

> At present we are unable to replace 400 production moulders with artisan moulders and if the policy of equal pay for the producers of equal casting could be established, the competition between the two sections would clearly disappear. But the move must come from the artisan moulders as the production moulder is incapable of such activities and outside a very few they do not attend meetings or take part in deliberations and discussions.[58]

But while mechanization was increasing, jobbing still remained the predominant form of production at the end of the decade. In an investigation of wage incentive systems in 1960 the Industrial Tribunal found that 62 percent of engineering firms had no incentive scheme and did not intend introducing one. This was, the report said, largely because

> the majority of the South African undertakings perform jobbing work on individual orders or manufacture small quantities at a time. The general opinion seems to be that wage incentive schemes cannot be practically applied to a production unit where the work is continually changing. It is difficult to determine the standard times, there is a continual readjustment of workers from machines and employers are not continuously kept busy on the same process. Furthermore, the administrative costs of such a system would be disproportionately high because such a large supervisory staff would be necessary to assess the skills required in the different types of work.

The Development of Personnel Management and Technical Control

It has been suggested in this chapter that in South Africa Taylorism presented an ambitious agenda that was only partially successful because of the persistence of jobbing production and the resistance of organized moulders in the foundries. One important element that did endure was the attempt to gain management control over the shop floor by incorporating the foreman more clearly into management. Earlier in this chapter management's attempt to by-pass the moulder as foreman was discussed; his growing involvement with management led the society to amend its rules in the 1950s, forcing foremen who held office to resign from that position in the union.[60]

Yet if the results of scientific management were ambiguous for the white worker, they were to have greater long-term significance for the black worker. Organized resistance among black metal workers in the 1940s was mentioned in Chapter 3: the crucial point is that it was easily crushed. Capital, writes Bozzoli, was therefore in a position to impose profitability requirements upon black workers in an unrivalled fashion, possessing a freedom of action which even the most active practitioners of Fordism and scientific management in European or American countries were unable to achieve.[61] Racism, as this quotation from a foundry manager addressing his colleagues indicates, was to give management illusions of control reminiscent of Charlie Chaplin's *Modern Times*:

> In the past one of my favourite sayings has been that the only way to bring a native into industry was to put him on a conveyer belt, where if he stopped working for a moment something red-hot fell on his foot.[62]

The element of scientific management most attractive to management was the idea that the job could be reduced to a repetitive basis, and that with training and scientific selection productivity could be increased. The rapid growth of black metal workers in expanding repetition foundries made scientific management seem the ideal solution. In a speech to the Institute of Production Engineers in 1947, Dr de Beer condemned the inefficient use of black labour in the past, calling for its more efficient use in repetition work. Before the war, he said, 'the native was regarded as nothing more than the man servant of white labour and a result of this condition was general suffering, and inefficiency in the use of native labour'. But, he continued, experience had shown that 'the native was excellent in jobs of a repetitive nature' and he considered that the method of doing many jobs could be very much simplified so as to increase the scope of native work'.[63] Similarly, Stanton of Dunlop discussed the results of experiments made with 300

Africans who were placed in semi-skilled repetitive work during the Second World War. Condemning the attitude 'that the native was essentially a hewer of wood and drawer of water', he argued that with scientific selection and training, production could be increased enormously.[64] However, the crucial finding of the Dunlop research was that it was the high labour turnover resulting from migratory labour that caused the low productivity:

> Whether productivity would increase further will depend on whether the average length of service can be lengthened. A higher proportion of Africans are staying longer and are thus the nucleus of a permanent industrial native population.[65]

Echoing the Dunlop findings, Dr Eiselen, Secretary for Native Affairs, called for a move away from

> our belief in the existence of the native as an interchangeable unit of a large undifferentiated mass of individuals . . . it is time for us to realise that there is no such thing as a drab, uniform stream of labour which can be turned into any channel to serve any purpose. It should be patent to all that this stream is made up of an untold number of individual aptitudes, which can, by skilful canalization, be turned to good account.[66]

Dr Eiselen saw in the newly-formed labour bureaux 'the efficient machinery for selective direction of the labour stream into appropriate channels of occupation'.

An important effect of the growing popularization of Taylorism in managerial circles was the legitimization of scientific management as an ideology. Bendix, writing of scientific management in the United States, concludes that employers did not regard Taylor's methods as an effective answer to the challenge of trade unions. The social philosophy rather than the techniques of scientific management, he said, became a part of prevailing ideology.[67] Maier takes Bendix's argument much further, showing how Taylorism was most strongly embraced in those nations faced with a political crisis.[68] Discussing its popularity in post-war Italy and Germany and the early Soviet Union, he says all these social movements shared 'in the attempt to transcend immediate political institutions by mobilizing scientism in the projection of a Utopian image of a harmonious society where "politics" becomes superfluous'.[69] Elsewhere it has been shown how management, faced by the political crisis of the 1940s, in particular the growth of black labour, turned increasingly to harness the wider intellectual resources of the social scientific community.[70] The growth of the scientific study of 'personal problems' is the clearest example of this.

Personnel management did not evolve chronologically out of scientific mangement; it is a development of the same principles in the human field. I.H.B. White, the founder (in 1944) of the Institute of Personnel Management in South Africa, demonstrated the scientific basis of personnel management when she discussed the origins of personnel management in Britain at a meeting of managers in Johannesburg in 1946. Describing the transformation of the Institute of Welfare Workers in Great Britain in 1909 to the Institute of Labour Management, she said:

> Members were engaged in social welfare work in industry and in alleviating the lot of the worker. As industry moved away from the paternal conception to the more scientific one, the institute changed its name to the Institute of Labour Management and it will shortly change again to the Institute of Personnel Management.[71]

Thus to try (as Bozzoli does) to explain the difference between scientific management and personnel management at the level of two fractions of capital — imperial, mining, monopoly capitalism as the propagator of scientific management; local, national, competitive capital as the propagator of liberal personnel management — is to miss the point.[72] The essential similarity between these two strategies was made clear in a speech given in 1948 to the Institute of Production Engineers. Arguing for a closer relationship between personnel management and production engineering the speaker said:

> It should be stated that no clear line of cleavage can be established between what are production procedures and what are matters of personnel relations. Work simplification, time and motion study, the establishment of rates, and the incentive method of payment, personnel services (health, safety, feeding, sanitation, also lighting and ventilation) all have influence upon production per unit of time and per unit of cost.[73]

The speaker went on to remind the employers of what she called the utilitarian advantage of the scientific study of personnel problems: 'In brief it can overcome the sinister danger of hostility to management'. It is clear from the syllabus proposed that time and motion study performed a central role in personnel management at this time. Arguing for the need for workers' committees to 'help to maintain an increased productive efficiency' she concludes by accepting Taylor's principles of work design with personnel departments as 'the maintenance group for the human machinery'.[74]

> Mass production, mechanization (jobs of a repetitive and monotonous nature) and the assembly line had tended to reduce workers to a cog-in-the-wheel status, causing a complex amount of human discontent. This can be compensated for to some extent in modern industry through fuller attention to the human beings.[75]

So what was the significance of Taylorism? Burawoy sees its significance precisely in its limited capacity to enhance capitalist control over the labour process, thus necessitating the transition to a new type of labour process inaugurated by the scientific/technical revolution. Was Taylorism, he says, an expression of the transition from a labour process that had developed its greatest potential in a detailed division of labour, to a labour process that incorporated 'capitalist control' within the very form of technology? Distinguishing technology from simple mechanization, Edwards develops this point further in what he calls technical control:

> Technical control involved designing machinery and planning the flow of work to minimize the problem of transforming labour power into labour, as well as to maximize the purely physically based possibilities for achieving efficiency . . . . Technical control is structural in the sense that it is embedded in the technical structure or organization of production.[76]

The foundations of this new form of technical control in South African foundries were laid in the Board of Trade and Industries report in 1948 on foundry production.[77] The report begins by drawing attention to the uneven development of foundry production, distinguishing between production foundries (some of which it says are based on the conveyor system) and jobbing production (para. 13). Until recently, the report observes, both types of production were carried out in a common foundry but 'the position has since changed completely, and the large bulk of quantity production now takes place in relatively few concerns with plants which have been suitably designed, and the remaining concerns find it increasingly difficult to compete with these establishments for any manufacturing on an appreciable scale'. (Para. 16.) The success of quantity foundry production, the report emphasized:

> depends to a great extent upon the accurate synchronization of all material supplies and operators with the speed of the main conveyor . . . . Once the production flow has been suitably adjusted the resulting output is practically consistent with the speed of the conveyor and a large productive capacity is possible with a comparatively small labour force. [Para. 23.]

Efficient production is embedded in three principles: convert every suitable operation into the repetitive; substitute mechanical means for manual labour wherever practicable; and retain maximum capacity through all working periods. (Para. 23.) The report then emphasizes the importance of management extending control over production to 'avoid loss of efficiency as a result of idle time during working periods'. (Para. 26.) For these new production foundries the greater complexity of organizing production raises the costs of disruption and control failure,

> since the concerns engaged in quantity production would be involved in very heavy losses if all unsatisfactory production features were not discovered and rectified at the earliest possible stage of manufacture. Adequate quality control is an essential part of the organization in these plants, and the effectiveness of these control measures can be judged by the consistently good quality which is maintained for relatively high outputs in these cases. [Para. 31.]

An earlier Board of Trade and Industries report (1945, report 282) had taken further the significance of technical control:

> Time wages are favoured by conditions of production which are not uniform, and a product or service which is difficult to measure, or the quality of which is a dominant consideration . . . . Standardized conditions of production and product, on the other hand, favoured the output basis of payment. But even in very highly organized establishments, such as automobile plants, where repetitive work predominates, piece work may be dispensed with because strict supervision and 'production control' make such added incentives unnecessary.

In such plants each worker must conform to the *rhythm of output* and the slacker is soon revealed and his services dispensed with.[78]

Thus Taylor's work was to be superseded by the flow method of production:

> The flow method of production is the mode of production most perfectly adapted to the demands of the economy of time in monopoly capitalism. The entirety of the workshop or factory is integrated into one continuous process in the service of the rule of speed . . . this continuity is now implemented by machine, a conveyor belt or other transfer mechanism, subjecting to the set speed the action of all production machinery and the human labour serving it.[79]

The introduction of science into labour — scientific management — in South African foundries was only partially successful. It was resisted where moulders were organized and quickly surpassed by the flow method of production when mass production was introduced. It was most successful where workers — such as black workers — were weakest and management was free to introduce repetitive assembly line work along Fordist lines. How did iron moulders respond to these new technological innovations introduced in the post-Second World War period? This will be examined in the next chapter.

Notes

1   Accession No.1008, Executive Committee 17.3.1947.
2   *Ibid*.
3   A.G. Thomson, *The Years of Crisis* (Johannesburg, 1946) p.6.
4   SEIFSA, *Organization and Structure of the Metal Industries of South Africa* (1964), pp.33-34.
5   The Industrial Employers' Association, 'Memo on its formation, aims and functions', p.7, in P. Tobiansky, 'SEIFSA and the industry it represents', B.A. Honours thesis, University of the Witwatersrand, 1980.
6   *Ibid*., p.54.
7   *Engineer and Foundryman*, December 1944, pp.63-7. See also 'The premium bonus system', January 1945, 'The wage incentive system', December, 1945.
8   SEIFSA, *Organization and Structure*, p.54.
9   *Ibid*., Exco., 12.12.46.
10   *Ibid*., 12.12.46.

11 *Ibid.*, 12.12.46.
12 *Ibid.*, 12.12.46.
13 *Ibid.*, 17.3.47.
14 *Ibid.*, 20.4.47.
15 *Ibid.*, 10.7.47.
16 W.E. Hold, 'Some notes on the application of industrial time and motion studies', *Engineer and Foundryman*, May 1939, and June 1939.
17 Dr H.N. Berliner, 'Mass production in South Africa: a study of scientific management', *Engineer and Foundryman*, May 1944.
18 H.H. Fraser, 'Incentive payment in scientific management', *Engineer and Foundryman*, May 1944.
19 Richard B. Spiro, *Rationalization of South African Industry* (Knox Publishing Company, Durban, September 1944.)
20 Board of Trade and Industries Report No.282, 1945, para. 226.
21 Board of Trade and Industries Report No.311, para. 33.
22 *Ibid.*, para. 33 and para. 37.
23 *Ibid.*, para. 38.
24 A. Sohn-Rethel, *Intellectual and Manual Labour, a Critique of Epistomology* (Macmillan, London, 1978), p.149.
25 *Engineer and Foundryman*, May 1944, p.110. 'Soldiering will cease', he proclaimed, 'because the object for soldiering will no longer exist. The great increase in wages which accompanies this type of management will largely eliminate the wage question as a source of dispute.' Taylor, *Scientific Management* (New York and London, 1947), p.143.
26 *Engineer and Foundryman*, August 1946, p.35.
27 See Richard Edwards, *Contesting Terrain: the transformation of the workplace in the twentieth century* (Basic Books, New York, 1979), for a discussion of this argument in the American context.
28 'The premium bonus system', *Engineer and Foundryman*, January 1945; see also the complicated mathematical formula in the Bedaux system presented in the May 1944 edition of *Engineer and Foundryman*.
29 IMS organizer's report, 7th Biennial Conference, 1947.
30 *Ibid.*
31 *Ibid.*
32 Paine (Works Manager), 'Vecor and its organization', *Engineer and Foundryman*, December 1948.
33 Evidence for the existence of this custom can be found in the records of the union's minutes. See, for example, the letter to all members in 1929 reminding them of this custom. Exco, 30.8.29.
34 IMS Records, 5th Biennial Conference, 1943.
35 Foremanship as a managerial function was being actively promoted at the time. For example, in 1943, the *Engineer and Foundryman* wrote:
    'Foremanship development aims at increasing production and

industrial relations by including foremanship with management but not omitting the foreman's special relationship with his men'. February, 1943, p.745.

36 IMS Records, 7th Biennial Conference 1947.
37 *Ibid.*, Exco, 22.3.1949.
38 *Ibid.*
39 *Ibid.*, 16.5.1949.
40 *Ibid.*, 12.7.1949.
41 *Ibid.*, 12.7.1949.
42 *Ibid.*, 30.8.1949.
43 *Ibid.*, 6.9.1949.
44 *Ibid.*, 20.10.1947.
45 *Ibid.*, 8.3.1950.
46 *Ibid.*, 1.3.1950.
47 *Ibid.*, 5.2.1950.
48 Interview with Arthur Lenthall, assistant superintendent of the foundry 1947 to 1971, on 7 March 1980.
49 Interview with Bob Thorpe, Van der Bijl Park, 7 March 1980.
50 *Ibid.*
51 IMS Records, Exco, 16.11.1951.
52 *Ibid.*
53 *Ibid.*, 9th Biennial Conference, 1951.
54 Organizer's report, Exco, 6.7.1951.
55 See Part III of this study for further discussion of the bureacratization of the IMS.
56 Interview with Crawford Brandt, Vecor, 22.2.1980.
57 *Ibid.*
58 *Op.cit.*, 7th Biennial Conference, 1947.
59 South Africa: Industrial Tribunal on Wage Incentives Report, 1960, p.22, mimeo.
60 IMS Rules 10 and 14.
61 B. Bozzoli, 'Managerialism and the mode of production in South Africa', *South African Labour Bulletin*, III, 8 (October 1977), p.13.
62 K. Brecknell, 'A comparison of the economics of production foundries and engineering establishments in South Africa and England as at January 1946', *Engineer and Foundryman*, April 1946.
63 Dr de Beer, *Engineer and Foundryman*, May 1947, p.61.
64 E.W. Stanton, *Engineer and Foundryman*, July, 1948, p.39.
65 *Ibid.*, p.45.
66 *Engineer and Foundryman*, March 1952, p.52.
67 R. Bendix, *Work and Authority* (University of California, 1974), p.281.
68 Quoted in Burawoy, 'Towards a Marxist theory of the capitalist labour process', *Politics and Society*, XIII,1 (1978), pp.279-80.

69 *Ibid.*, p.281.
70 E. Webster, 'Servants of apartheid? A survey of social research into industry in South Africa', *Africa Perspective*, 14, 1980.
71 I.H.B. White, *Engineer and Foundryman*, February 1946.
72 B. Bozzoli writes: 'While scientific management fulfilled the needs of the monopoly repressive mining fraction, with its migrant labour force, different ideological and practical solutions were required to satisfy the needs of national capital with its (non-migratory) black working class' (pp.129-30). Having structured her argument around this misleading distinction, she then correctly concludes that these two strategies did not evolve chronologically from each other but 'evolved' and are 'still evolving' together. 'Managerialism', p.41.
73 N. Lester, 'Personnel management and its relationship to production engineering', *Engineer and Foundryman*, March 1948.
74 See H. Braverman, *Labour and Monopoly Capital. The degradation of work in the twentieth century* (Monthly Review Press, New York and London, 1974), p.87.
75 Lester, 'Personnel management', p.63.
76 Edwards, *Contested Terrain*, p.112. See Chapter 10 for further discussion of types of control.
77 Board of Trade and Industries, No.311, 1948.
78 Board of Trade and Industries, No.282, para. 220.
79 Sohn-Rethel, *Intellectual and Manual Labour*, p.161.

CHAPTER 5

From Craft to Colour: the IMS and Job Protection, 1944 — 1968

The rapid growth of mass production during the Second World War had placed the skilled moulders on the defensive in the foundry. To retain control over the moulding labour process, the IMS opened its membership to production moulders in 1944. Unable to protect all their jobs through skill alone, the moulders were now forced to use their position on the Industrial Council to reserve jobs for some union members. This chapter traces how under the impact of accelerating technological change and growing numbers of African operators, the engineering craft unions increasingly redefined demarcation along lines of race rather than skill. The age-old form of craft protection — the closed shop — now appeared in racial guise; *craft* and *colour* coincided.

The Impediments to Accumulation

In his presidential address to the South African Federation of Engineering and Metallurgical Associations in January, 1946, J.M. Osborne observed that:

> South Africa has undergone an industrial revolution during the past five years when the need to produce was so paramount that all the ingenuity and skill of management and workers in the engineering and metal industries were employed to meet not only the immediate needs of the country, but to contribute to the general commonwealth pool . . . . We have emerged from the war having gained much experience. We have learnt the lesson that costs of production are chiefly affected by volume and in order that our production may be economic, it is necessary to concentrate on those lines for which an adequate market exists, either in this country or near its boundaries.[1]

Improved communications and South Africa's rich resources, Osborne believed, made local production by foreign investors increasingly likely.[2] His successor, Dr. H.J. van der Byl, was more cautiously to stress that both the small size of the market and the 'slip-shod and inefficient manner' in which some branches of the industry had been developed were serious problems.[3]

W.F. Boustred of SEIFSA also stressed the restrictions on capital accumulation created by the size of the South African market, and the fact that it made mass production difficult;[4] while Dr S.P. du Toit Viljoen, chairman of the Industrial Tribunal, summarized a survey undertaken by his department which extended the argument:

> As yet a number of factors militate against the large-scale application of automated equipment in the metal industries of the Union. These are: 1) the high capital cost of installation of automation plants; 2) the specialized nature of such plants, in relation to the end product; 3) the inflexibility of such plants to meet quick and intermittent changes caused by variations in demand patterns and short runs; 4) the size of the domestic market and its absorption capacity.[5]

It is against this background that we need to understand the two major reports in which the Board of Industries laid the basis for the developmental strategy of capital and the state after the Second World War.[6] In this case the major impediment to accumulation was not simply a result of the accident of size, but bore directly upon working class strategies and struggles. It rested upon what they called South Africa's 'peculiar wage structure', i.e. the existence of skilled wage rates which were high in relation to both skilled rates elsewhere and the average productivity of labour. Thus, Report 282 argued that 'whereas in the western world the spread between the highest and lowest rates of wages is usually about 30 percent and seldom more than 50 percent, in the Union it is several hundred percent'.[7] Furthermore, the report held, to the peculiar wage structure there corresponded a peculiar labour structure which was itself tied up with the problem of the small market:

> In the modern manufacturing process organization and technique are combined to break up the differentiated work of the artisan into simplified processes, each of which can be transferred to an operative, with only a few mechanical movements to perform. [But] . . . South Africa's industries have been slow to make the fullest possible use of

operative labour. This is especially true of the metal industries which employ about one third of the skilled mechanic labour force in the country . . . . Partly, [this] . . . has been due to trade union regulation, which restricts an operative's work to one specific task, rather than to the functions included in a specific operative class, and the South African market has generally been too small to allow such an excessive specialization.[8]

Trade unions, the report continued, made this process of reclassification of jobs 'both slow and uncertain', because 'the bargaining powers of the respective parties, rather than the requirements of developing a manufacturing industry in the Union, have been the determining factor'.[9] The strength of the white working and artisanal classes was thus seen to be at the root of the problem.

Not surprisingly, the report saw this new 'operative' labour as coming from within the ranks of the growing African working class, suggesting that 'there can be no doubt that the native is well suited to perform a good deal of work of the semi-automatic character requiring a relatively low degree of skill . . . provided the processes are suitably sub-divided and the work simplified'.[10] At the same time the report was acutely aware of the sociological and political implications of this attempt at greater use of black labour:

> Racial and class differences will make a homogeneous proletariat which will eventually lose all contact with its former communal rural relations which had previously given their lives a content and meaning. The detribalization of a large number of natives congregated in masses in large industrial centres is a matter which no government can view with equanimity. Unless handled with great foresight and skill these masses of detribalized natives can very easily develop into a destructive rather than a constructive factor in industry.[11]

The broad solution to most of these problems offered by the reports was that of 'rationalization'. This they defined as the method of 'reorganizing an industry in order to eliminate sub-marginal firms and to concentrate production in those establishments which can produce most effectively, thus effecting a reduction of unit costs for industry as a whole'.[12] Rationalization would make possible the development of a local engineering industry capable of surviving in the face of international competition. This process was seen as involving two main aspects. The first concerned the technical and human reorganization of production through scientific management.[13] This involved such factors as the use of modern technology,[14] scientific lay-out,[15] standardization of production,[16] and, above all, scientific research into industry.[17]   The perceived need for the application of science to industry had already been the concern of a number of industrialists in the 1930s such as Bosman[18] and De Villiers[19] and was now to lead to the establishment of the Council for Scientific and Industrial Research (CSIR) in 1946.

The second aspect of rationalization was the need to concentrate and centralize production.[20] Although foundry production continued to be characterized by the juxtaposition of jobbing (usually in small foundries) and mass production, the process of concentration and centralization was already far advanced by 1953, with 4,8 percent of the engineering establishments producing 50 percent of the output.[21]

Both of these aspects of 'rationalization' were to have profound effects on black, white, and coloured workers in the engineering industry in general, and in foundries in particular, not all of which can be examined here. This chapter will focus only on the attempt to increase productivity through technological innovation — and the responses which skilled, mainly white iron moulders made to these attempts through the IMS.

Technological Innovation and Response, 1944 – 1955

After the First World War members of the IMS had been increasingly threatened by a double-edged process of craft dilution/fragmentation and deskilling. One edge of this process was mechanized methods which made some of the artisan skills redundant; the other was the introduction of less skilled workers (coloureds, blacks, and Afrikaners) who could perform part of the artisan's job, thereby undermining his skill status. The mechanisms through which the society had maintained control over the job had been two-fold — the closed shop and the apprenticeship system — while a key variable shaping resistance to dilution was the strength of shop floor organization in particular foundries.[22] But now, faced by growing pressure to move the industry on to a mass production basis, the society chose strategically to confront mechanization and craft dilution in a different way — by opening up the society to those who were not strictly craftsmen, many of them coloureds from the coastal towns. In 1936 it was opened to non-artisan production moulders in Durban Falkirk, and in 1944 to production moulders throughout South Africa.

This 'dilution' of the craft nature of moulding was to reduce the significance of the apprenticeship system, and to place the closed shop at the centre of the iron moulders' defensive strategy. In the early years of the society, the closed shop had been informal, enforced by the shop stewards and IMS members at particular foundries. After the establishment of an engineering industrial council in the Transvaal in 1927 the society was to debate continually whether the 'closed shop' should be formally included in the agreement with employers,[23] and when a national agreement was finally drawn up in 1944, it contained a closed shop provision (Section 20).[24] However, members were to complain at the 1945 Biennial Conference that it had proved ineffective

> due to there being a period of six months during which persons may not be members of a recognized trade union while in the employ of a firm. This enabled the discharging by a firm of members of a society in order to provide work for non-members and due to this deficiency the employers were able to slave-drive and demand certain outputs.[25]

By the time the seventh biennial conference took place in 1947, the period for which moulders could not be members of the IMS had been reduced to three months. However, with the growing number of production moulders joining the society, the magnitude of the problem facing it had changed considerably. The secretary said:

> it is now absolutely vital that all production moulders be made to join the society. The society had to organize completely and effectively the production moulder and instil upon him that if he permitted men who were not members of the society to start working alongside of him, whereas members who had worked alongside of him, were fired, it was only a matter of time before he would be replaced by a non-member from the streets.[26]

The society was clearly concerned that other 'craft unions' — such as the engine-drivers and the Amalgamated Engineering Union — seemed less committed to the closed shop principle. In the IMS, by contrast: 'We had forced the position in the Transvaal through strength of organization. Our principle of the closed shop, where we take the line that we do not work with a non-member, is our greatest strength.'[27]

Indeed, by 1949 it was recorded at the biennial conference that *only* the IMS had a specific provision confining specialized work to its members; the other Mechanics Union Joint Executive unions had agreed to grant exemptions as long as standard rates were paid.[28]

The logic of this 'closed shop' strategy was now to be extended even further, to the point where the IMS actually considered transforming itself from a 'craft' to an 'industrial' union. In 1951 the biennial conference suggested 'closing the foundry' by enrolling *all* remaining labour as members of a General Union shop. Referring to the growth and strength of Afrikaner workers, one speaker said:

> You must realize that there is a racial group making big strides in the industry and organizing all and sundry into its organization. All foundry workers should be enrolled into the organization — pattern makers and sand slingers and operators, sand conditioning plant employees . . . . The Mechanics Union, that is the individual unions in the mechanics group, outside of ourselves, were losing ground rapidly. The time had come that all foundry workers should be enrolled into the organization.[29]

However, this strategy was not to prevail: at a special conference held a year later it was decided not to proceed with the transformation of the union into an industrial union as the time was 'not opportune'. The failure of the IMS to follow through its resolution in 1951 to 'close the foundry', left a substantial number of white, mostly Afrikaner, semi-skilled and unskilled workers outside of the society, to be mobilized by the Yster en Staal. The IMS remained an exclusive and sectional white union with a diminishing bargaining power on the factory floor, organizing an ever-smaller proportion of the work force as the process of mechanization and job fragmentation intensified. The basis for this decision by the IMS not to widen its base in the foundry, choosing instead to confine its 'resistance' to the retention of 'craft' privileges in the face of new technology, must be sought in the more specific bargaining that took place between employers and moulders over the restructuring of the labour process.

The early apartheid period was characterized by a rapid increase in expenditure on new technology and machinery in foundries. From 1956 to 1960 expenditure on machinery increased by 139 percent with wages (63 percent) and employment (32 percent) increasing at a slower rate. As these figures suggest, a widespread reorganization of the labour process was taking place.[30] Two central technological innovations were introduced into the foundry during this period, both of which undermined the skilled worker: the shell moulding process and the CO_2 process. 'What the shell moulding process did for production', said John Steele, editor of the *Foundry Welding and Production Journal*, 'the CO_2 process did for jobbing. It took the skill out of the hands of the moulder. It became a push button operation.'[31]

The shell moulding process was invented by Johannes Croning, a German engineer, during the Second World War. The invention involved the chemical reaction of sulphur with a bituminous substance enabling component parts of aircraft to be cast to such a fine tolerance that no subsequent machining was necessary.[32] It was claimed by the allies as a war prize and introduced into South Africa in 1954 by a patent firm known as Polygram Shell Moulding Company.[33] Rely Precision, East Rand Engineering Company, James Barlow (now Ferrovorm), Denver Metals and Eclipse Engineering were the first to use the process.[34]

Members of the IMS were quick to realize the implications of the new process. In November 1953 the chairman of the Johannesburg Branch Executive Committee reported that it was common talk in the East Rand Engineering Company foundry that a white fettler (a non-moulder) would be employed on this new process. 'The moulders', he said, 'held the view that it was moulding and there might be trouble if the firm persisted and brought the mould into the shop. There had been suggestions of kicking the mould to pieces.'[35] The chairman had contacted the firm trying to persuade them to use a chemist on the mould while they were experimenting, but he said the firm was adamant in using a white fettler.

In January 1953, the general secretary of IMS made a report to the National Executive Committee (the NEC, previously known as Exco), on the shell moulding process and the likelihood of employers wanting to use non-union labour on this process. It was agreed that members of the NEC should see a demonstration of this process.[36] In December 1954 the society reported that a delegation, consisting of employers and unions, had visited African Malleable Foundries, ISCOR, Light Castings and James Barlow to investigate the new process.[37] In addition a letter was sent to the Amalgamated Union of Foundry Workers of Great Britain (AUFW of GB) requesting information about the type of employee and wage rates for this process. AUFW of GB advised that the process was in an early stage of production in Britain and as yet there was no control over wages or over who would do the work.[38]

At their biennial conference in Durban in December 1953 the IMS discussed the introduction of the shell moulding process. The secretary said it was quite evident that the employers were going to make a concerted move to have this work scheduled as labourers' work. A sample of the shell mould biscuit was passed round the conference room for inspection. The secretary had obtained a copy of a report of the United Kingdom Scientific Mission to the United States of America which outlined what management saw as the advantages of the process. The report mentioned that the new process increased the rate of mould production, did not require any skill, and could be readily mechanized by the use of automatic shell moulding machines.[39] The NEC was instructed to watch the position carefully as the IMS was determined to 'resist the employers' attempt to have labourers and natives produce castings by this method'.[40]

The IMS was able to resist the employers' attempt to use the shell moulding process to dilute the trade by obtaining a technical schedule in the industrial council agreement in 1955 for shell moulding in which only the closing of the biscuits (i.e. the moulds), backing up, investing, placing of plates in the oven, removing the plates from the ovens and turning of boxes became labourers' work. The rest of the process was retained at production moulding rates (3*s* 6*d* per hour) and protected by the closed shop.[41] At the 1955 conference, the president described the threat facing the moulders at some length, making explicit the fear that the new processes would be handled by blacks:

> It is strange that troubles do not come singly and you have heard the efforts of the employers in our own foundry industries to dilute the trade, not by giving the work of the moulder to the production moulder, but to delete both the moulder and the production moulder's work by giving what operations we have always regarded as moulders' and production moulders' work, to the natives at labourers' rates of pay, furthering the threat to our standard, and closing still further avenues of potential employment for our sons and daughters. During the past year there has been a concerted effort by employers to have us believe shell moulding work is natives' work. The tempo of the introduction of the native into industry, replacing the European and the coloured, has increased at an alarming rate over the past three to four years. The process of mechanization today and the new processes being introduced are to a large extent removing the necessity of the skill of ten to fifteen years ago. I venture to suggest that it will not be a long time before we reach

the press-button stage. The harnessing of the electronic brain to mechanical muscles is just around the corner. The way things are going on the basis of skill involved, the native will be pressing the button. The employer's argument that no skill is involved is the gravest danger facing the workers who have attained reasonable standards and wages.

He concluded by referring to the threat of automation to the skilled worker in Britain and the United States, but noted — as the Board of Industries had noted in a different context — the crucial difference. 'If their problem is great when their labourer receives at least 85 percent of the wages paid to the skilled worker, how much greater is our problem when our labourers, the native, received about one eighth of the pay of a skilled worker.'[42]

The other innovation — the CO_2 process — was introduced in 1954 to South Africa by Bob Cross, the founder in South Africa of FOSECO, a multi-national company providing technical knowledge to engineering firms.[43] Under the old process the moulder required a range of moulding tools to top the hinges, such as the sleeker and a hammer to pack the sand and finish off the weak sand. This new process acted as a bonding agent, binding sand at an 80-100 percent faster rate than normal.[44] 'It cut down my skill quite a bit', said L.W. Botes, a journeyman moulder nearing retiring age, 'but I didn't object because it made the job easier. It was a tiresome job. You had to prepare the hooks. The new process took hard work off my shoulders.'[45] Cross described the advantage to employers of this new innovation in a lecture to the Institute of Foundrymen in 1955:

> Due to the high flowability of sands bonded with this material, cores in moulds can be prepared more rapidly and with less effort after a certain amount of experience has been gained. It would also appear that cores and moulds can be prepared by semi-skilled labour since there is no longer any need, as with conventional coarse sand, to sprig the core carefully, varying the degree of packing, etc. and this naturally leads to rapidity in core making.[46]

Again the IMS was able to resist successfully the employers' attempts to classify the new process as non-artisan work. In October 1955 the minutes record a letter from the South African Railways workshop in Durban informing the NEC that management intended having first-class core makers on artisan cores with the introduction of the CO_2 system. The minutes conclude:

It was argued after discussion that the general secretary advised the Durban branch and all railway branches that the CO_2 system is not a method of making cores or moulds. It is purely a process for drying cores or moulds by the action of a gas on ingredients with sand and that all the principles of moulding, ramming, draining, etc. are still involved and it is still journeymen's work. In other words by using the gas drying process we cannot accept that the job which is a journeyman's work, can now be allocated to first-class core makers or any other type of labour.[47]

At the biennial conference in December, B. Plunkett, a veteran of the 1934 railway strike on 'dilution' in the S.A.R. foundry, said: 'I must warn railway delegates that CO_2 is the danger and we must resist dilution. Just because of the introduction of CO_2 it does not mean that it is semi-skilled work.'[48] He then read from the agreement and pointed out that work could not be allocated unless mutually agreed upon by the moulders' representatives and the employers. The danger of work being given to Africans or semi-skilled men just because of a new process was thus prevented, he said.[49]

Thus it was in return for the maintenance of 'craft' principles, which meant continued protection against both black and white semi-skilled workers, that the union leadership accommodated to technological change, bargaining with management in the Industrial Council over what jobs would be confined to moulders. Provided employers were prepared to concede moulding jobs to members of the society, the IMS saw no fundamental reason for widening its base, and becoming an industrial union.

This had far reaching effects on the nature and *modus operandi* of the union. For example, through this process of accommodation, the leadership of the IMS came increasingly to rely on Industrial Council agents to police the agreement. The Johannesburg BEC minutes make clear, for example, that the Industrial Council agent came to usurp the shop steward's function, by negotiating directly with management over alleged breaches of the agreement; in one case, the Industrial Council agent had been called in to investigate the underpayment of a moulder at Reef Engineering,[50] while the firm of Besaan and Du Plessis was using non-union labour on production moulding work and the Industrial Council agent had been asked to investigate.[51] Similarly the Industrial Council investigated the Pretoria Iron and Brass Foundry because it was allegedly using 'native' labour for the making of cores and moulds.

This decline in the role of the shop steward on the shop floor is also reflected in the increasing use of the stop order system, rather than the shop steward himself, to obtain union dues. Thus in 1952 the Vecor shop steward was removed because of 'irregularities' in the collection of subscriptions. It was, he said in his defence, difficult to collect subscriptions on a three shift system.[52] A month later it was recorded that the stop order system had now been established at Vecor.[53] This was to lead to a growing number of foundries opting for the stop order system, including African Malleable Foundries,[54] Smith and Welsted,[55] Standard Brass,[56] Scaw Metals,[57] Barratt & Pillons,[58] H. & M. Foundry,[59] Stewart and Lloyds[60] and Dunswart.[61] By 1964 the secretary reported that the stop order system was now widespread in the industry.[62] Whether the decline of shop floor activities can be said to have caused the introduction of the stop order system is difficult to say. What is clear is that by the end of the decade, when management began to concede 'check-off' facilities, this method of dues collection seemed the obvious solution.[63]

This decline in the significance of the shop steward in the union was accompanied by allegations of an increasing remoteness of the officials from the rank and file members. It was felt by some members that since the appointment of a full-time organizer in 1944 the leadership of the IMS had become excessively bureaucratic. In 1951 the veteran shop steward Naysmith was strongly critical of the secretary for being on too many committees. At the same meeting it was reported that the employers' representative on the Industrial Council had 'accused head office officials of putting forward demands and views which were not the demands and views of the rank-and-file membership'.[64]

In spite of these changes, this was nevertheless an attractive style of unionism, for it was increasingly effective in winning, as the secretary said at the 1960 meeting, 'a very high degree of service to the membership'.[65] It is true that officials were against the use of the strike weapon, except in order to pressurize management in negotiations, and then strictly according to the procedure laid down in the Act.[66] But the fact of the matter is that they were able, by this tactic, to win considerable benefits. The leadership came to conceive of trade unions as service organizations. When faced by criticism at the 1960 meeting, and by the suggestion that Yster en Staal was getting a foothold among society members, the sehretary said that:

We were living in times of political affiliation and he personally did not believe that it would make any difference if members, for political reasons, were going to join Yster en Staal. They would do so in any case. The point is that what we have got to be sure of, is in our conscience that we know full well that we are catering for the membership and giving a very high degree of service to the membership. We have no fear in saying that the service rendered to the membership by this office was better than the service rendered by any other trade union in the mechanics group. Everything was done for the member.[67]

Indeed it was, and this was due to the far-sighted administrative leadership given by the secretary after he took office in 1943. His central objective was to build up the benefits of the union, beginning in 1947 with the establishment of the South African Trade Union Building Society (SATUBS).[68] By 1951 the union had established a building society fund, an insurance company, a pension fund, death benefits and an idle benefit. As Jock Naysmith said in his retirement speech:

> The rank-and-file do not realize the conditions, work and thought which has been put into the society by the executive committee and officials. We have always been blessed with able officials and the rank-and-file membership had conditions handed to them virtually on a plate, without any sacrifice on their own part.[69]

Provided the union could retain its closed shop in the Industrial Council and win substantial benefits, it seemed as if the IMS was prepared to accept craft dilution in return for what can best be described as benefit unionism.

From Closed Shop to De Facto Job Reservation, 1955 – 1968

Even in the early apartheid period the IMS had found it increasingly necessary to give exemptions to employers to employ non-union labour on moulding and production moulding work. This was either because there were no society members available[70] or because journeymen refused to do what they believed was 'diluted' machine moulding.[71] Of course the society tried to avoid giving exemptions. In one case the NEC resolved that 'any moulder selected by the management to work a moulding machine must work it' and that failure to accept this instruction would give the firm the right to dismiss a moulder. Furthermore, any moulder dismissed for refusing to work a moulding machine would be expelled from the society and prevented from working in any other foundry in South Africa.[72]

However, by the end of this period, the society was fighting a losing battle — by 1969 at least 13 percent of the production moulders were Africans who had been given exemptions and by 1971 the figure was 33 percent. The initial 'craft protection' strategy was no longer appropriate and new responses emerged. It was out of the complex interaction between state policy, employer strategy and iron moulder reaction that a more racially-explicit form of protection for iron moulders emerged.

Table 6: Racial Composition of Production Moulders and Core Makers, 1969-1971

Year	White	Coloured	Asian	Black	%Black
1969	1 121	175	0	162	13
1971	705	437	18	380	33

Source: Manpower Surveys Nos. 8 and 9, Department of Labour.

The case of the Union Steel Company illustrates the pattern of change taking place at this time. After hearing a report that Union Steel was employing Africans and coloureds at the moulding grade, the society investigated. It was told by management that members of the IMS were not available — but it soon became clear that Union Steel was using non-union labour to intensify production. These workers were paid at the basic rates, on an anomalous bonus system, working seven days a week.[73] Having got management to agree to more acceptable working conditions, the IMS then undertook to find qualified moulders; but six months later the IMS granted Union Steel an exemption, since no moulders were available.[74] This example illustrated two different but related points. On one level the employers were correct in claiming that there was a shortage of moulders. And yet, 'African advancement' concealed a process of cheapening of labour power and the intensification of exploitation with which old conceptions of craft-diluted unionism could not cope. As Crompton said:

. . . the whites cannot get a job in this industry because the employers are running it cheaper now than they have ever done in their lives. They are running it on basic rates not on premium rates. Before they came in [coloureds and Africans] the rate of pay in this particular industry was nearer R1.50 an hour than R1.15 an hour. Now it is nearer R1.15 than it is R1.50. But make no mistake about it, we are becoming more unrepresentative of the workers in the industry every year, and to close our eyes to the fact that Africans cannot, and will not be permitted to belong to our unions, is something we cannot tolerate. We also cannot open the floodgate to this unorganized herd, that will bring our standards right back to 200 years ago![75]

It was this process of job dilution that the state strategy of racially defined job reservation purported to resolve through Section 77 of the Industrial Conciliation Act introduced in 1956. The 'rate for the job', a Department of Labour pamphlet argued, no longer served the purpose of protecting the skilled worker:

The skill of the old type of journeyman . . . is no longer necessary in modern methods of manufacture and the journeyman is replaced by the operative . . . (usually coupled with a revision of wage scale) . . . on a level unacceptable to white employees. The numerous complaints received by the Minister of Labour in his department in recent years concerning the ousting, directly or indirectly, of white workers by non-whites from classes of work which had traditionally been performed by whites, revealed that appropriate action was essential before the evil had become too deep-rooted.[76]

It was at this time that two attempts were made to introduce statutory protection for white workers, in the form of job reservation through the Industrial Conciliation Act, in the engineering industry. It was a time of recession in the industry, when unemployment was growing and large numbers of firms were working on short time.[77] In March 1958 the Amalgamated Engineering Union noted that there was growing unemployment amongst its semi-skilled members, and a year later claimed that dismissals were also accompanied by a tendency to get the job done 'cheaper than ever and trying to allow more and more work to be done by native labour'.[78] Employers in the engineering industry had been warned as early as October 1956 of the importance, in times of recession, of retaining for white workers those occupations which had traditionally 'been theirs'.[79]

The first job reservation determination in the industry was made in July 1958 (Determination No.3) reserving for whites 15 categories of work in a section of the engineering industry concerned with the manufacture of door and window metal surrounds, Cliscoe windows and airtight louvres.[80] Yster en Staal had applied for this determination because, as its secretary Van den Berg said, the Industrial Council was not prepared to 'stop the gradual taking over by non-Europeans of jobs done by Europeans'. As far as he was concerned there would have been no need to call on the state if the employers had agreed to retain these jobs in white hands.[81] According to the Department of Labour, 'two leading firms who employed white persons on the manufacture of both windows and surrounds, threatened to replace the whites employed by them with Bantu labour because of the competition experienced from firms who employed Bantu [at lower wages than were paid to the whites] on such manufacturing. About 90 white persons at the two firms concerned would have lost their work in this manner.' After investigation by the Industrial Tribunal, it was 'found that a number of white persons employed . . . had already been replaced and that further replacements would take place unless the work was reserved for white persons'.[82]

In 1959 Yster en Staal applied to the Industrial Tribunal for a second job reservation determination (No.7) covering the manufacture of domestic appliances, claiming that employers who had been using whites in certain lowly paid operative jobs were finding it difficult to compete successfully on the open market, and that in consequence a trend of displacement by non-whites was developing. The application was successful and in introducing the determination, the Minister of Labour confirmed that one of the biggest employers of white labour in the industry had found it difficult to compete with others who were employing non-whites at lower rates of pay, and was considering displacing about 400 whites by non-whites.[83]

However, statutory 'job reservation' did not survive in this industry. Employers were strongly opposed to Yster en Staal's application — arguing, in the Industrial Council, that 'you either negotiate or you go to the government for assistance, but surely you don't do both!'[84] The employers asked the unions whether they were prepared to 'join with them in approaching the Minister of Labour and asking him to lay off the metal industries in respect of job reservation and leave the industry to fight its own battles, as it had done for over thirty years'.[85] The IMS, however, clearly saw job reservation as a useful threat to hold over employers if they did not concede to their demands, although Crompton undertook not to apply for job reservation during the normal currency of an agreement without first acquainting the employers with the matters that were troubling them, while others emphasized that they would not appeal to the Minister for a determination if employers ceased to fragment jobs.[86]

The outcome of these negotiations was that the Industrial Council agreement began to prescribe considerably higher wages in the categories of work that had previously been reserved for whites in Determinations 3 and 7,[87] thus, in the words of the Minister of Labour, rendering 'the employment of cheap non-white labour in these occupations impossible'. Because the principle of 'the rate for the job' on its own paid insufficient attention to the white man, he said, this rate must be fixed at a sufficiently high level to enable a European to live on it. 'The white man, with his superior knowledge, must be able to retain that work against the non-white, with his inferior civilization.' Determinations 3 and 7 were consequently suspended for the currency of the Industrial Council agreement.[88] Employers were no longer prevented from employing non-white labour by law, but now they would have to employ it at 'white rates'. This solution, the minister felt, should be tried in all industries: when a complaint about non-white competition was received, the employer would be notified, he said. If he agreed to raise the wages to a level considered adequate for whites, no further action would be taken. If he did not, the matter must be referred to the Industrial Tribunal for investigation.

In the light of this, it is misleading to argue, as Davies does, that because job determinations only affected five percent of the total white work force 'they were marginal to maintaining the racist division of labour'.[89] While he is right in concluding that job reservations did not bring about 'a class structure fundamentally different in its broad composition to that which would otherwise have been brought into existence at that particular stage of capitalist development',[90] to focus on determinations is to miss the crucial point. It was the *threat* of job reservation that allowed the unions to negotiate jobs at a higher rate than would otherwise have been the case. The logic of this strategy was that in later years, as we shall see, trade union membership itself became a form of job reservation within the Industrial Council system. Thus we shall show how in 1968, in return for downgrading a number of rates to allow blacks in, the agreement entrenched guarantees that only those eligible for trade union membership would be employed in the top categories A – D. It was, as Crompton was to remark, a form of closed shop and *also* a form of job reservation.[91]

An analysis of the response of the IMS to the Nationalist

government from the early 1950s reveals how its 'mixed' (white and coloured) character led the union and others of its type to pursue a middle course between the 'left' and 'right' wings of the union movement as a whole; and how the isolation engendered by this strategy presented grave problems. On one hand the IMS did not conceive of itself as being political: it, along with other 'craft diluted' unions, had withdrawn from the more left-wing Trades and Labour Council in 1950 to form the short-lived South African Federation of Trade Unions. This move had been precipitated when the council had appointed a sub-committee to investigate the possibility of providing for the parallel organization of African unions. The chairman explained that

> the IMS was a non-political body and they could not jeopardize their membership by taking part in a political struggle. They had withdrawn, as the so-called right wing, i.e. mechanics, as they were not prepared to defend people who were named as communists, and were in fact communists, as did the left (i.e. Sachs).[92]

When the Trades and Labour Council asked the IMS to support their resolution opposing the recommendations of the Botha Commission in 1951, the NEC felt that the resolution had been 'framed in the usual Sachs phraseology' and that 'the trade union movement would be better served by precise and directed criticism of the various recommendations which the trade union movement must, of necessity, oppose rather than a torrent of general abuse'.[93]

At the same meeting, however, it was reported that an IMS stalwart, Plunkett, had himself been named under the recently promulgated Suppression of Communism Act. In this case, it was agreed to assist Plunkett in having him 'unnamed' as 'he had given a lifetime of service to the trade union movement and the IMS in particular'.[94] The IMS approached the minister to have the Act amended to 'give protection to union officials and have removed from the bill the right of the minister to declare a person a communist, and, at the same time, to deprive such a person of trial by a court'. The minister refused, it was said, as state security was involved.[95] The IMS then joined the Mechanics Union Joint Executive in putting forward a resolution to amend the Act at a special conference of the South African Federation of Trade Unions: in the end the resolution was defeated by the Coordinating Council of South African Trade Unions — the right, predominantly Afrikaner wing of the labour movement

— with a suggestion that the Federation was 'being soft on Communism'. Furthermore, Van den Berg of Yster en Staal was critical of the IMS for not being prepared to confine their delegation in principle to whites. The IMS replied in its defence that 'our coloured membership enjoys the same rights, benefits and privileges, voting powers and wages as enjoyed by the European section of our membership'.[96]

The ambiguous strategy of the IMS in particular and the 'craft diluted' unions in general rested on a defence of the status quo. As has been shown, both racially mixed unions and the Industrial Council were defeated. The contradictory nature of the strategy became clear in the mid-1950s, with the promulgation of the new Industrial Conciliation Bill, which aimed to separate mixed unions on racial grounds. By this time, the South African Federation of Trade Unions had collapsed and been absorbed, together with the more conservative wing of the Trades and Labour Council, into the newly formed Trade Union Council of South Africa (TUCSA). The craft unions were now back in the mainstream of union activity, and found support for their ambiguous 'mixed' but not fully 'multiracial' policy in TUCSA. Opening the IMS biennial conference in 1955, Thomas Rutherford, president of TUCSA, outlined the nature of TUCSA's opposition to the proposed bill. It was not, he said, that TUCSA 'wished to retain native workers in our ranks' — this was prohibited by law anyway. It was in fact the coloured workers who were of concern to them: 'The non-white workers we are concerned with are those who have been members of our organization for more than half a century, and have worked beside us in the occupation for even longer than that.' Directly linked to the strategy of retaining the mixed unions, Rutherford said, was TUCSA's defence of the closed shop principle. 'TUCSA had offered', he said, 'to accept the apartheid provision of the bill in regard to separate branches and meetings, subject to the sections providing for the splintering of (our) mixed unions and the division of our assets being withdrawn.' TUCSA had, in fact, initially tried to persuade the minister to withhold the bill altogether for one or two years and enact Section 77 (under which job reservation was guaranteed) under separate legislation. 'If', the TUCSA delegation to the minister said, 'after the period of one year the minister was proving to the trade unions that he could and was applying the powers conferred under Section 77 . . . then the trade union movement were prepared to accept the bill as now drafted.'[97] Clearly the issue at stake was

TUCSA's disbelief that the government would in fact use Section 77 to protect white workers:

> We have been repeatedly assured — despite our outspokenness — that there will be no hesitation in applying Section 77 to protect the present standards of the workers against the interracial competition that it is acknowledged will occur in due course. Why thus the repeated warnings by the minister that only by his own efforts and not the protection of his white skin, can the white worker hope to retain his status in industry? Is all that really necessary if the law is going to afford the white worker his unalienable right to any job he wishes to have especially reserved for him? And why the need to consult the Minister of Economic Affairs? Either the job is to be reserved for the protection of the white man's standards, irrespective of any other economic considerations, or else primarily economic and not racial considerations will determine the issue. We believe the latter must be the case, hence our contemptuous rejection of the fairy tale entitled 'safeguard against interracial competition'.[98]

In 1956 the Industrial Conciliation Act was passed, and contained a provision which provided a loophole for the 'mixed unions': Section 8(3A) allowed racially separate union *branches* (i.e. not parallel *unions*), to be formed. The IMS decided to apply for exemption, arguing that they were 100 percent organized among moulders, white and coloured, and that 'unless the coloured production moulder workers were organized, they were likely to be a danger to the living and working conditions of our members built up by the society over a period of forty years'. Coloured moulders employed at Falkirk were then organized into a separate branch known as Durban (Falkirk),[99] although the society made it clear that it felt whites should play the dominant role:

> Our Falkirk Durban branch has always had a fair proportion of white moulders and a proportion of coloureds, yet the branch has always seen fit to elect white members as branch officers. It is, however, our continued belief that the minority of white members, the leaders of coloured moulders — our watchdog in the foundry — are essential in the preservation of the working conditions of the moulder. We have only one branch in the Cape — the society has always had white officials representing the branch in all bodies. In the Transvaal area membership is exclusively white.

They concluded this application for exemption to the minister by pointing out that of the 2 292 moulders only 103 — five percent — were coloured.

After discussion with the minister, the society decided to establish a separate branch, called Durban No.1 Branch, for coloureds at Falkirk and a separate branch for whites. It was agreed 'that it was in the best interests of the coloured membership that the present white Falkirk membership should have their own branch within Falkirk as in this way they would continue to assist in the Pricing Committee and have interviews with management at Falkirk'.[100]

With regard to the Cape, the Department of Labour said they should make an attempt to separate the branches racially but gave them an exemption on the grounds that it was uneconomic to separate 73 whites from 19 coloureds.[101] In fact in 1962 the white Falkirk branch was to be disbanded and in 1963, after continual annual applications from the Cape branch, the Department of Labour gave them a permanent exemption.

In deciding to apply for an exemption, rather than creating a separate union for coloureds (as the AEU did in 1961, when they created the Engineering and Industrial Workers' Union)[102] the IMS was pursuing a consistent policy. They retained one union for all coloured and white moulders, creating a separate branch in Durban for coloureds in order to comply with the new Act. How did the coloured membership respond to this decision to create a separate branch for them? There was anxiety and later dissatisfaction with the IMS, and a feeling that the union was white-dominated. A lengthy dispute arose when M. Keshwar, secretary of the Durban No.1 Branch, unconstitutionally signed on four coloured production moulders from the Transvaal as members of the Durban No.1 Branch. The NEC suspended the secretary, but, finding that no-one else was prepared to accept nomination, was forced to instruct Keshwar to continue. The NEC argued that the Department of Labour would not permit the IMS to form a separate branch for coloureds in the Transvaal. By signing on Transvaal coloureds to Durban No.1 Branch Keshwar was hoping to give an opening to those coloureds who wanted to go to the Transvaal to work. The NEC was eventually able to bring the Durban No.1 Branch into line by stressing the fact that the moulders had a closed shop, and that they were the only union that had retained the operation of semi-automatic and automatic machines as a rate A machine job — 'in all other sections of the industry the agreement provides that automatic and semi-automatic machines be operated at the rate E and the work is performed by Bantu' — and 'that any successful splitting of moulders must weaken our trade union and weaken our bargaining position when having to face the employers'.[103]

In 1962 TUCSA amended its constitution to allow African unions to affiliate and the following year set up an African Affairs section, establishing the African Sheet Metal Workers Union — later the Engineering Industrial Workers Union — as TUCSA's first African 'parallel' union. This section of engineering was selected because 'in this particular section the concentration of blacks was very high; job fragmentation was greater in this section because of mechanization and consequently a lot of blacks were being employed illegally'.[104] Little progress was made, E. Tyacke (a TUCSA official at the time) suggests, because on the instructions of the engineering unions they operated through the Industrial Council. Furthermore, at this stage the 'craft' engineering unions felt they still had control over their jobs, and were not sufficiently threatened by blacks to promote these parallel unions. In fact when the issue of African admission to TUCSA was debated in 1962 the Amalgamated Engineering Union, the Motor Industry Employees Union and the Iron Moulders' Society of South Africa opposed the admission of blacks. McCann of the AEU asked 'what could they do for their African friends by bringing them into the council as affiliates that they could not do by liaison? . . . He believed that in time they would convince the membership that the workers should all be united, irrespective of colour, but he did not think the time had arrived as yet.'[105] Crompton, for the IMS, argued in the interests of mixed unionism and the rate for the job, asserting that since Africans were not permitted to join an established union he could not support the creation of separate unions for Africans: their unions might undercut the established standards of the unionized whites and coloureds by breaching the rate for the job.[106] Again in 1966 Crompton was to oppose parallel unions for Africans, arguing for the need to maintain one organization for all moulders. He said, 'We believe that if a man is a moulder, or production moulder, his rightful home is in his craft union. We disagree with the government belief that there should be no Africans in registered trade unions. Any belief that the Africans should be organized into parallel organizations and form two Iron Moulders' Societies . . . is impractical. We believe that this thinking can only lead to division at the bargaining table with the employer.'[107] Africans could use the staff and facilities of TUCSA but 'at this stage it will be dangerous to continue with the present constitution of TUCSA'. However, the IMS was not one of the unions which left TUCSA between 1968 and 1969 over the African membership issue, choosing instead to stay in the organization and supporting TUCSA's decision to exclude Africans in 1969.

The IMS strategy rested on its capacity to maintain control over the moulding jobs and establish agreements that protected these jobs in the Industrial Council. The ravages of mechanization and technological change were, in the second half of the decade, finally to undermine this strategy. Between 1964 and 1968 there was a further explosion of capital investment of 141 percent in base metals which, when compared with an increase in wages of 52 percent and in employment of 18 percent, suggests that a new reorganization of the labour process was under way, based on the introduction of yet more new machinery and the further relative extrusion of workers. By 1970 the value of machinery was 2,7 times higher than the value of wages. The base metal industry was now second only to the chemical industry in terms of capital intensity.[108] At its 1967 conference TUCSA delegates called for a government commission on automation. The Minister of Labour rejected TUCSA's proposal on the grounds that in this period of 'unparalleled growth' there was no evidence of job displacement.[109] The proposer of the motion, Tom Murray, clearly felt otherwise as indicated in another speech:

> With the widening gap between skilled and unskilled wages, coupled with the decline in prices of single purpose machines which work automatically, requiring only starting, loading, unloading and stopping, there is an obvious incentive to the industrialist to dilute his skilled labour by investing in this type of equipment. The pace towards even more advanced mechanization of South Africa's industries is therefore accelerating.[110]

Looking into the future, he said:

> only the blind . . . will fail to see the Republic's greatest problem in the future is, what is to become of the mass of unskilled and semi-skilled African workers in the age of cybernetics if the American experience is anything to go by? The African, uneducated, or at best poorly educated, will be the first to be displaced by automation and will be the most difficult to re-integrate into the economy.[111]

The Industrial Council negotiations of this time reflect the increasing tempo of technological change. The employers demanded the

telescoping of grades (reducing the number of grades) and the concomitant down-grading of work in wage terms. At the Foundry Group
meeting of the Industrial Council employers proposed fragmenting
and down-grading the semi-automatic and automatic moulding
machines and core making machines to grade E, and the manually
operated moulding machines and core making machines to grade B
(grade E being below the rate proposed by employers for 'white'
jobs).[112] Crompton opposed this process desperately, eventually
threatening to call for statutory job reservation. Arguing forcibly that
white workers should benefit from new technology he said:

> Because a machine becomes more sophisticated, because some of the
> hard work is taken out of the job by a more versatile machine, because a
> machine becomes semi-automatic or — for that matter — automatic,
> our employers now contend that the worker must not benefit by the less
> arduous nature of the work . . . . The job must now go to the Bantu
> and this attitude, in the face of more productivity, greater profits, and
> the added advantage of the moulder being able to take charge of two
> machines — whereas the old type of machine required the moulder's full
> time and attention. The moulder now has to possess the stamina of a
> gorilla, plus the speed of a finely drawn racehorse . . . . We are not
> prepared to legislate ourselves out of existence. We are not prepared to
> go along with the idea that with the advent of greater mechanization the
> Bantu will remain the only survivors, with few exceptions . . . . Some
> of our foundries are exporting their entire output to overseas countries,
> and one of the prime movers in this 'fragmentation' is a firm that exports
> up to 65 percent of its total production . . . . Some employers, due to
> their being able to exploit the ever increasing introduction of black
> unorganized labour into the industry, have now reached a position that
> they believe they can ignore the voice of organized labour, and not miss
> its presence in the workshop . . . . We believe that the time has been
> reached for the workers, i.e. our members, to demonstrate that this
> country will not become a second Hong Kong. Unless our members are
> to have reserved for them the right to be the producers of castings,
> irrespective of method of production . . . we shall have to resort to job
> reservation.[113]

The outcome of protracted negotiations was that the union accepted
wage increases, lump sum payments and entrenched guarantees that
only those eligible for trade union membership would be employed in
the top categories of A to D. In return the number of rates was
telescoped from sixteen to twelve and down-grading took place.[114] As

Harris, SEIFSA labour officer, put it, 'The job reservation clause was a *quid pro quo* for fragmentation.'[115] It had an advantage over statutory job reservation for union members — for the unions could negotiate the wage rates for the work involved and could reserve both the value and the concrete aspects of the job. It also helped restore the principle of preferential advancement since reservation of work categories meant union members had to get preference when an opening was created. It would tend to concentrate members in the highest wage rungs again.

At the same time as *de facto* job reservation was introduced into the engineering industry, most of the 'craft' unions resigned from TUCSA, despite TUCSA's decision to exclude Africans. This was no coincidence. By presenting a common demand for *de facto* job reservation the engineering unions had at last come to accommodate the demands of the previously more right-wing white industrial workers in Yster en Staal around a common strategy. The process of mechanization and job fragmentation since 1944 had turned the vast bulk of white wage earners into either supervisory and white collar workers, or semi-skilled machine operators with no other bargaining power than their colour. The very necessity of formalizing their protection by resort to colour was a measure of their defeat. If they saw it as a victory, it was clearly a pyrrhic victory as the subsequent decade so clearly revealed. By mobilizing around colour, the engineering unions were to strengthen capital's resolve to restructure the racial division of labour, and to remove the remaining impediments to capital accumulation presented by white privilege. Capital was to achieve its objective ten years later when, in the 1978 Industrial Council agreement for the engineering industry, 'job reservation' was removed. The analysis of the implications of the restructuring of the racial division of labour in the 1970s will be dealt with in Part II.

Notes

1   J.M. Osborne, presidential address at the 3rd AGM of the South African Federation of Engineering and Metallurgical Associations in Johannesburg, 22 April 1946, SAF & EMA Annual Report, 1946.

2   While such links were established after the Second World War at an increasing pace, particularly with the UK, they tended to be in the field of technology and skilled personnel rather than foreign capital. The amount of foreign capital in all engineering was only 3,3 percent by 1969,

suggesting that the engineering industry was financing its capital resources from within South Africa. See A.J. Norval, *A Quarter of a Century of Industrial Progress in South Africa* (Johannesburg 1962), table XV. For further information on the proportion of foreign investment, see G. Bloch, 'The development of manufacturing industry in South Africa, 1939 – 1969', University of Cape Town MA thesis, 1980. Bloch argues, against the common conception, that 'foreign investment has not really been important because of any quantitative contribution . . . South Africa has . . . had an exceptionally high rate of domestic savings'. (p.142.)

3   Dr H.J. van der Byl at the 4th AGM of SAF & EMA in Johannesburg, 21. 1.1947.

4   W.F. Boustred, 13th AGM of Steel and Engineering Industries Federation of South Africa (SEIFSA), 18.10.1956.

5   Automation Conference convened by the Minister of Labour on 31 October 1956, Industrial Tribunal Collection, ISCOR Library, 1957.

6   Board of Trade and Industries Report No.282 into the manufacturing industry in South Africa, 1945; and Report No.286, into the iron, steel and engineering industries in South Africa, 1946.

7   *Ibid.*, Report No. 282, para. 120.

8   *Ibid.*, para. 121.

9   *Ibid.*, para. 131.

10   *Ibid.*, para. 134.

11   *Ibid.*, para. 135.

12   *Ibid.*, para. 194. The rationalization movement was to emerge as a major issue in the post-war debate on economic development. See Richard B. Spiro, *Rationalization of South African Industry* (Durban, 1944).

13   *Ibid.*, Report No.282.

14   *Ibid.*, para. 197.

15   *Ibid.*, para. 199. The Institute of Production Engineering was established in 1946 and the first work study symposium held in South Africa was in 1953 at Escom. Collected papers of the Work Study Symposium, 1953, Pamphlet No. 4578, Gubbins Library, University of the Witwatersrand.

16   *Ibid.*, Report No.282, para. 202.

17   *Ibid.*, para. 207.

18   See V. Bosman, 'The value of scientific research in industry and the establishment of an Institute for Scientific and Industrial Research', unpublished MS, February 1930, 040, No.18057, Gubbins Library, University of the Witwatersrand.

19   F.J. de Villiers, 'The application of science to industry in South Africa with special reference to industrial research', unpublished lecture, 1936.

20   Board of Trade and Industries Report No.282, para. 235.

21   Commission of Enquiry into the policy relating to the protection of

industries (Du Toit Viljoen Commission), UG 36/1958, para.236.

22 See Chapters 2 and 3 of this study.

23 See, for example, the debates around the issue at the 4th Biennial Conference in 1941 which was to lead to employers temporarily conceding a closed shop in return for the IMS agreeing to emergency labour.

24 Government Gazette No.3361, 23.6.1944.

25 6th Biennial Conference of the IMS, December 1945, F.

26 7th Biennial Conference of the IMS, December 1947, F.

27 *Ibid.*

28 8th Biennial Conference of the IMS, December 1949, F. When it was formed in 1927, the Mechanics Union Joint Executive (MUJE) consisted of the Amalgamated Engineering Union (AEU), the IMS, the South African Boilermakers Society (SABS) and the South African Electrical Workers Association (SAEWA). M.B. Jankleson, 'The operating of the industrial council system in South Africa', MBA thesis, University of the Witwatersrand School of Business, p.152.

29 9th Biennial Conference of the IMS, December 1951, F. The reference to a 'racial group' was to the largely Afrikaans speaking Yster en Staal, formed in 1936 in ISCOR as a breakaway from the South African Boilermakers' Society because this craft union neglected its non-craft members.

30 D. Innes, 'The state, post-war manufacturing and class struggle', mimeo, 1978.

31 Interview with John Steele, managing editor of *Foundry, Welding and Production Journal*, March 1980.

32 *Ibid.*

33 Application for a patent by Polygram Shell Moulding Company, 'Moulding composition for making shell-like foundry moulds', 16 October 1954. The Registrar, Patent Office, Pretoria, No.3518.

34 Interview with John Steele.

35 Records of the IMS, accession No.1, AH1008/C (hereafter C) containing minutes of the Branch Executive Committee (BEC) and National Executive Committee (NEC); Johannesburg BEC, 11.11.1953.

36 NEC, 10.1.1953, C.30.

37 NEC, 11.12.1954, C.

38 NEC, 1.8.1953, C.

39 10th Biennial Conference, December 1955, F.

40 *Ibid.*

41 Government Gazette, 3.6.1955, Ref. No.1138.

42 11th Biennial Conference, December 1955, F.

43 Interview with Bob Cross, managing director of FOSECO, March 1980, Alberton.

44 *Ibid.*; interview with L.W. Botes, a journeyman moulder since 1939, March 1980, Benoni.

45 *Ibid.*
46 B. Cross, 'The CO_2 Process', *Engineer and Foundryman*, April 1955, p.52.
47 NEC, 1.10.1955, C.
48 11th Biennial Conference, December 1955, F.
49 *Ibid.*
50 Johannesburg BEC, 14.12.1958, C.
51 *Ibid.*
52 NEC, 1.11.1952, C.
53 NEC, 6.12.1952, C.
54 Johannesburg BEC, 24.6.1954, C.
55 Johannesburg BEC, 16.5.1956, C.
56 Johannesburg BEC, 1.2.1956, C.
57 Johannesburg BEC, 1.2.1956, C.
58 Johannesburg BEC, 23.11.1962, C.
59 Johannesburg BEC, 28.11.1962, C.
60 Johannesburg BEC, 3.10.1962, C.
61 Johannesburg BEC, 19.6.1963, C.
62 NEC, 16.3.1964, C.
63 Johannesburg BEC, 4.3.1962, C. Interview with Ben Harris, national organizer of IMS, August, 1981.
64 NEC, 14.2.1951, C.26.
65 NEC Special Meeting, 7.5.1960, C.
66 This is illustrated by the 1952 dispute in the Industrial Council, in which the IMS was strongly critical of certain branches of the AEU for going out on strike before the procedure was followed and insisted on the correct procedure, *ibid.*; NEC, 20.2.1952, C.28.
67 *Ibid.*; NEC Special Meeting, 7.5.1960, C.
68 Interview with Cliff Crompton, Secretary of the IMS from 1943 to 1974, March 1980, Germiston.
69 NEC, 26.2.1952, C.28.
70 As in the case of the Kroonstad Industrial Foundry in 1951; see NEC, 21.2.1951, C.26.
71 As in the case of Wright Boag in 1952; see NEC, 25.6.1952, C.29.
72 *Ibid.*
73 NEC, 17.12.1969, C.
74 NEC, 18.7.1970, C.
75 C. Crompton, quoted in 'Africans in trade unions', p.30; 9th Biennial Conference, December 1951, F.
76 Department of Labour, *Job Reservation: Its Background, Motivation and Application* (Government printer, Pretoria, 1960), p.15.
77 South African Institute of Race Relations, *Survey of Race Relations 1958-1959* (Johannesburg, 1959), pp.197-199.

78 AEU Journal, March, 1958, National Organizers Report; AEU Journal, April 1959, p.86.
79 South African Institute of Race Relations, *Survey of Race Relations 1956-1957* (Johannesburg, 1957), p.153.
80 South African Institute of Race Relations, *Survey of Race Relations 1961* (Johannesburg, 1961), p.191.
81 Records of the NEC of the Industrial Council for the engineering industry reproduced in the minutes of the 13th Biennial Conference in December 1959, p.70.
82 Department of Labour, *Job Reservation*, p.15.
83 South African Institute of Race Relations, *Survey of Race Relations, 1959-60* (Johannesburg, 1960), p.177.
84 Records of the NEC of the Industrial Council, p.60.
85 *Ibid*, p.63.
86 *Ibid.*, p.57.
87 *Survey of Race Relations, 1961*, p.193.
88 *Ibid.*, p.193.
89 R. Davies, *Capital, State and White Labour in South Africa, 1900-1960* (Brighton, 1979), pp.349-50.
90 *Ibid.*, p.350.
91 C. Crompton, quoted in 'Africans in trade unions', p.30.
92 9th Biennial Conference, December 1951, F.
93 NEC, 21.1.1951, C.26.
94 *Ibid*.
95 NEC Special Conference, 1952, C.29.
96 Report of a special conference held to discuss the Suppresssion of Communism Act, reported at the NEC Special Conference, 1952, *ibid*.
97 11th Biennial Conference, December 1955, F.
98 NEC, 26.12.1955, C.
99 13th Biennial Conference, December 1959, F.
100 NEC, 30.8.1958, C.
101 NEC, 16.7.1960, C.
102 NEC, 12.8.1961, C.
103 NEC, 23.1.1968, C.
104 Interview with Eric Tyacke, official of the African Affairs Section of TUCSA from 1963 until its dissolution in 1967, December, 1980, Johannesburg.
105 Quoted from A. Sitas, 'Disorganizing the unorganized: registered unions and the black worker, 1962-1980', unpublished mimeo.
106 *Ibid*.
107 12th Annual Conference of TUCSA, December 1966, p.188. Sitas refers to the practice of separate racial branches, with a white NEC, as 'parallelism within one union', *ibid*.

108 D. Innes, 'The state, post-war manufacturing and class struggle'.
109 13th Annual Conference of TUCSA, 1967, p.45.
110 Speech delivered to the Conference on the Impact of Automation on the Productivity of South Africa, South African Council of Automation and Computation, September 1965.
111 *Ibid.*, p.60.
112 NEC, 5.8.1967, C.
113 *Ibid.*
114 Government Gazette, RN 632, 19.4.1968.
115 Interview conducted by R. Le Grange with D. Harris, Labour Officer, SEIFSA, Johannesburg, June 1979.

PART 2

The Crisis of Control
in the Labour Process

The conclusion to be drawn from Part I of this study is that craft workers resisted the process of deskilling and thus retained considerable control over the supply of labour at the level of the firm and the industry. Craft workers attempted to maintain the exclusivity of the trade well after technological change had rendered craft skill redundant by contesting the definition of skill. Colour and craft coincided, and the vulnerability created by the challenge from cheaper non-union black labour gave craft exclusivity a racial form. Craft workers, with institutional leverage in the industrial relations system, relied on this privileged access to entrench the exclusivity inherent within craft unions along lines similar to those described by Penn and discussed in Chapter 1. The result was the survival of a higher number of 'craft' jobs than the deskilling thesis would appear to indicate. This, it is suggested in Part II, was to contribute to a crisis of control in work relations in the 1970s.

In the early days of small-scale foundry production in South Africa employers were able to exercise authority directly on the shop floor, through the entrepreneur himself or through the craftsmen. During this phase, craft workers exercised a significant degree of control over the job through the closed shop and the apprenticeship system. In some respects these craft workers acted as the foremen in hierarchical control; for example, it was customary in early foundry production for craftsmen to hire their own 'helpers'. But employers were able to break the control of the craftsmen by job fragmentation and deskilling, introducing what in Chapter 1 we called 'technical control'. By the end of the 1960s a growing number of craftsmen had been transformed into supervisors performing a control function in the workplace.

As a consequence of this abdication of managerial authority to the supervisor, industrial relations had been a neglected managerial function in the foundry in the pre-Wiehahn period. According to a survey conducted in 1971 and in 1980, only one quarter to one third of the foundries employed a full-time personnel officer.[1] Management relied on South Africa's dualistic industrial relations structure (discussed in Part I), a legalistic formal guarantee of certain industrial rights to non-Africans through the Industrial Council, and a unilateral system of control for African workers resting on the white supervisor and 'his' boss-boy or *induna*. ('My eyes, ears and hands', said one supervisor.) In terms of this industrial relations system Africans were denied participation in recognized trade unions; more specifically, they were excluded from the definition of employees in the Act and played no direct part in collective bargaining. Because of problems of communication between black and white the supervisor was often a figurehead with real control being exercised by the *induna*. As Alverson observed: 'To the *induna* falls the charge of making the organization and its policy and directives intelligible to Africans who work on the line.'[2] It was, in addition, the *induna* who actually selected the worker, introduced him to the company with a short talk, and told him what to do. Backed by the white supervisor and the system of *impimpis* (informers) the *induna* exercised, from all accounts, a form of despotic control.

This despotic regime was to trigger off a crisis of control in work relations. The crisis was in part the result of the growth in the size of the firm that accompanied the transition to monopoly capitalism in the 1960s, discussed in Chapter 6. It emerged from the contradiction between the firm's increasing need for control on the one hand and its diminishing ability to maintain control on the other. Increased control was a concomitant of the firm's continuing growth. Yet just when the firm was experiencing a qualitative leap in the need for control, its traditional means — hierarchical control — became less effective as a method of managing the growing workforce. The racial nature of this control was to become the focus of a systematic offensive in the 1970s by capital on the one hand and the emerging black labour movement on the other.

The employer's need to increase control over a larger and more distant workforce necessitated an intensification in the discipline and harshness of the foreman's rule. Furthermore, with the establishment of the National Productivity Institute (NPI) in 1967 and the publication of the Reynders Report five years later, the need to increase the productivity of labour had become a driving concern of capital.[3] The chairman of the Productivity Committee of the South African

Federated Chamber of Industries (FCI) was to report in May 1973 that South Africa's labour productivity over the period 1968 to 1971 was low by international standards.[4] The speaker concluded that 'the industrial engineer should be the key person responsible for the implementation of productivity decisions.'[5] As the Foundry Productivity Survey noted later that year: 'Higher productivity is necessary in view of the increasing demand and to be competitive on overseas markets.'[6]

These growing pressures were to erupt in a wave of factory and township based conflict in the 1970s. The mass strikes in January and February 1973 in Durban dramatically highlighted the crisis of control in work relations, when an estimated 100 000 workers broke a decade of 'industrial peace' and took to the streets with a demand for wage increases. Part II of this study deals with the emergence of this challenge and the response of management and the established unions to it.

Notes

1 See Table 9, E. Webster, 'The labour process and forms of workplace organization in South African foundries', Ph.D thesis, University of the Witwatersrand, 1983.

2 Hoyt Alverson, 'Africans in South African industry: the human dimension', in C. Morse and C. Orpen, *Contemporary South Africa* (Juta, Cape Town, 1975), p.285.

3 Personal communication with Dr. Jan Visser, executive director of the National Productivity Institute, Pretoria, April 1980; Report of the Commission of Inquiry into the Export Trade of the Republic of South Africa (Reynders Report), p.380, para.4: 'It appears that if the high growth rate is to be maintained, the emphasis will have to shift from further input to improving productivity performance to be brought about, inter alia, by better management and better quality of the non-white labour force.'

4 These figures were quoted in the Report of the Chairman of the Productivity Committee, May 1973, South African Federated Chamber of Industries, 10.4.1973. Supplied by J.L.W. de Jager, SAFCI, 28.1.1980.

5 *Ibid.*, p.4: this was to lead to an investigation by the NPI into the demand for industrial engineers. The nature of their role in increasing productivity was made clear by the president of the FCI in an address to the Afrikaanse Handelsinstituut on 9 May 1979: 'Industrial engineering is a most fascinating side of manufacturing. One has to continuously ask oneself

why an operation is being carried out in the manner in which it is being currently performed. To study what each and every employee in a unit is actually doing. Is the operation designed in a manner which enables the operator to work efficiently? Can the overall manufacturing technique be simplified and maybe deskilled?' Address by Mr H.C. Morecombe to the AHI, 9.5.1979.

6　　National Productivity Institute survey, *Productivity of the Iron Foundry Industry in South Africa, 1973* (NPI, Pretoria, 1973), p.4.

CHAPTER 6

Managerial Resistance to Black Unions, 1973 — 1977

In the early 1970s African workers began to organize into trade unions, and thus to challenge the dualistic structure of industrial relations. This chapter is concerned with management's resistance to these early attempts to organize. By 1977, however, management and the state had been forced to recognize and negotiate with the new unions.

It is possible to identify three phases in the growth of a trade union. During the initial phase of *recruitment*, the task of the union is to get members to join. During the second phase the problem is that of *winning recognition from management*. During the third phase, the union attempts to *negotiate and maintain an agreement* that ensures workers' rights in the factories.[1]

The problem facing an emerging union is how to move from phase one to phase three, or, as Flanders puts it, how to convert temporary movement into permanent organization.[2] In the early period of mobilization membership is loose; to sustain the impetus the union leaders must acquire sanctions to maintain continuous membership. The crucial phase of conversion takes place with recognition from employers so that the union is able to build up enduring relations with management in the form of collective bargaining.

A central problem in the development of black trade unions in South Africa has been the rupturing of the process of maturation by the failure to win management recognition, as well as by state hostility and registered trade union indifference. Before the 1970s there had been three major thrusts towards African unionization in South Africa's labour history — in the 1920s; during World War II; and in the 1950s and early 1960s. Each wave of unionization was followed by repressive legislation: the state's response in the 1920s was the Industrial Conciliation Act, excluding Africans from formal collective bargaining, and the Native Administration Act with its 'racial hostility' clause; the unions of the 1940s were countered by anti-strike legislation during the war, the Suppression of Communism Act, and the Bantu (Settlement of Disputes) Act; while the unions of the 1960s were hit early in the decade by the Unlawful Organizations Act and the General Laws Amendment Act. What seems to have happened in South Africa is that at each stage in the emergence of embryonic African trade unions, the process of maturation has been ruptured at a crucial point, and the unions have been unable to convert from a temporary movement into a permanent organization. The state, faced by the organization of African workers, chose repression rather than incorporation.[3]

In the wake of the crushing of worker organization in the early 1960s, the South African economy grew as never before. By 1976 an exceptionally high degree of concentration of economic power — a system of monopoly capitalism — existed.[4] (See Table 6). The most useful way of understanding the profound structural change in the post-Sharpeville economy is through the concept of capital restructuring. This concept, according to Bloch, points to the process of rupture and reconsolidation involved in the transition from one phase of development to another.[5] For Bloch this transition involves a change from the competitive stage of capitalism to the higher stage of monopoly capitalism. While restructuring is a response to a crisis it 'is both the signal, and the means of overcoming the limitations or the development of particular forms of accumulation.'[6] Holloway and Picciottio argue:

> It is clear that what is involved is a process of struggle primarily between capital and labour but, flowing on from that, also between different capitals and fractions of the capitalist class . . . . [It] is not just an economic struggle but a struggle aimed at the reorganization of the whole complex of social relations of production.[7]

The process which saw the consolidation of monopoly capitalism in South Africa also led to a corresponding growth of the black working class, bringing black workers firmly to the centre of the industrial stage. In particular it led to the growth of the semi-skilled black worker — the organizational base for the industrial unions. A relatively homogeneous workforce was created that was technologically linked within the labour process. The combination, suggests Edwards, proved to be exceptionally favourable to building unions.[8] As Hemson writes:

With the growth of monopoly capitalism and the concentration of

Table 6. Firms, Employment, Output and Assets by Size of Firm in Basic Metal

Percentage of Total Co.s	Number of Co.s	Percentage Employees	Percentage Output	Percentage Assets
5	6	70,68	73,48	92,49
10	12	77,76	82,97	95,83
15	19	82,88	88,19	97,38
20	25	87,02	91,30	98,03
25	31	89,32	93,35	98,05
30	38	91,35	95,08	98,95

Source: Manufacturing Census, 1976, Department of Statistics.

production in large-scale, highly mechanized factories and 'industrial mines', basic production is carried out by a massified black proletariat neither differentiated by traditional skills nor having experienced the benefits of reform. These are the conditions for a rapid advance in class consciousness as the political resistance to apartheid gains momentum.[9]

While the transition to monopoly capitalism created the material conditions favouring industrial unionism, this did not mean that they emerged automatically without a struggle. In the first place growing capital intensity led to a rise in unemployment, creating a large reserve army of labour. This contradictory effect of the transition to monopoly capitalism weakened the ability of workers to organize, particularly where they were easily replaceable because of limited 'skill'. In the Eveready strike of 1978, for example, the managing director said:

It would only take a day to train workers to replace strikers and many applicants were at the gates looking for jobs.[10]

In the second place, the exclusion of blacks from the Industrial Council allowed management to take advantage of the government's alternative to trade unions, the liaison committee system, to pre-empt the organization of black metal workers, in particular the Metal and Allied Workers Union (MAWU),[11] formed in 1973. Thirdly, racial divisions within the workplace, reinforced by craft privilege, meant that the Confederation of Metal and Building Unions (CMBU) failed

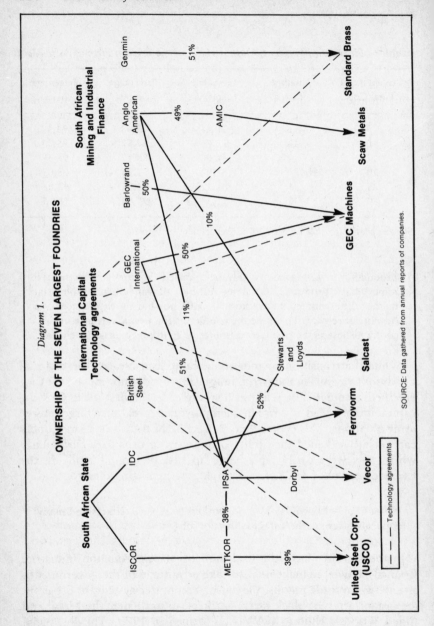

Diagram 1.

OWNERSHIP OF THE SEVEN LARGEST FOUNDRIES

SOURCE: Data gathered from annual reports of companies.

--- Technology agreements

Note: The ownership of the seven largest foundries was concentrated in the South African state through ISCOR and the IDC, international capital and local mining and industrial finance (Diagram 1).

to give concrete support to the emerging metal unions.

For a moment in 1976-77 it looked as though the pattern of non-transition to permanent organization would repeat itself; but the consolidation of monopoly capitalism had given black semi-skilled workers a strategic location in the labour process, and effective shop floor tactics were able to exploit this lever in spite of the obstacles to workplace organization enumerated in this chapter.

Phase One: Recruitment

The formal establishment of MAWU in Pietermaritzburg in April 1973 was a direct result of the wave of mass strikes of 100 000 African and Indian workers that took place in the Durban-Pinetown area in January and February 1973. In their pioneering study of those strikes, the Institute for Industrial Education (IIE) concluded that

> The strikes were a series of spontaneous actions by workers which spread by imitation, and the spread was 'multiplied' by the fact that three quite independent factors happened to coincide. The first factor was the initial strike at Coronation Brick. The second factor was the existence in Durban, strategically placed in each of the major industrial areas, of a number of factories belonging to one organization characterized by particularly low wages and bad labour relations — the Frame group. The third factor was the rising transport costs and the rumoured train boycott. What precisely sparked off the strike is not clear — however, once the strikes did occur, the sight of large crowds of workers out on strike encouraged workers in neighbouring factories, and the strike spread geographically road by road.[12]

However, the sociologically problematic nature of a purely 'spontaneous' strike is evident to the authors of the study. In an attempt to avoid 'spontanism', they draw three analytical distinctions: agitators, i.e., those unconnected with the work situation; activists, i.e., individuals who initiate action in the work situation; and influences, i.e., people whose public activities have an effect on the level of consciousness of workers. They acknowledged, furthermore, that 'the spread of spontaneous action of this kind will almost certainly depend upon and be influenced by pre-existing informal communication networks such as friendship groups, "home boy" groups, groups of people who "habitually commute together" and so on.'[13]

Unfortunately, however, the authors fail to explore further these central insights into spontaneous mass action and the reader is left with the actual dynamics of conflict in particular factories unexplained and unexplored. In part this omission is the result of the authors' political objective in writing the book, i.e., to explode the dominant managerial and state ideology that the strike was the result of 'agitators'. This, of course, the book does very effectively in Chapter 3, albeit in a defensive way.[14]

While the dynamics of actual conflict remain unexplored, it is possible to identify certain influences and networks of communication that began before the strike in 1972 and came together after the strike to form trade unions. Three seem to be central — the General Workers' Factory Benefit Fund (GWFBF), the Wages Commission, and the regrouping of trade union activists who were the survivors of earlier struggles. The Benefit Fund was formally established on 9 September 1972 to provide social security for workers employed in Durban and Pietermaritzburg, largely in the clothing and furniture industries.[15] Initial support came from the Garment Workers' Union of Natal and the Furniture Union. A second influence was the establishment in May 1972 of the university-based Wages Commission. The Wages Commission brought together white students who were increasingly critical of the dominant liberal opposition because they believed it was ineffective and focussed on race rather than class exploitation. Inevitably they were drawn to a working class in and around Durban that was increasingly aware of the need for trade unions. A third, less well-known influence, was the regrouping of trade union activists of the period of mass struggle of the 1950s and early 1960s in an attempt to revive the South African Congress of Trade Unions (SACTU) in 1972.[16]

Initial recruitment into the Benefit Fund was rapid and largely random. The mass strikes of January and February 1973 had led to a surge of working class militancy in Durban and Pietermaritzburg, and by the end of that year the Fund had ten thousand members.[17] It soon became clear that the Fund had signed on sufficient members in certain industries to establish industrial unions. Furthermore, members in certain factories were now eager to be organized into trade unions. The existence of considerable numbers of members in metal factories made it logical to establish a metal union. In April 1973 MAWU was formally established in Pietermaritzburg with Alpheus Mthethwa, an employee of the Fund, as the first secretary.

August 1973 SEIFSA circulated a model constitution for a 'Bantu' liaison committee to its members, which outlined the liaison committee's objective of providing 'a means whereby management may explain its policy to the workers'. Section 3b defined the limits of the committee's functions:

> The committe shall not, by resolution or otherwise, reverse or amend any instruction given by management, nor can it interfere with any disciplinary action undertaken by management.

Liaison committees were, it is clear, designed to pre-empt trade unions. While employers are advised in this memo to

> meet any approaches from persons allegedly representing the Bantu workers, employers should not accept stop orders from black unions or allow these organizers into 'the work precincts for recruitment purposes'. In the event of an illegal strike employers should not, under any circumstances, attempt to negotiate until work has been resumed.

Employers were advised to

> notify the nearest South African police station 'if at any time it appears that law and order are in danger'.[26]

Management's attempts to reassert control through liaison committees and MAWU's rejection of this form of worker representation emerges as the central issue in the first three years of the union's history. Numerous conferences were held by employer organizations to educate management on the need to improve communication with their black work force by introducing liaison and work committees.[27] To improve communication between black and white, management would invite experts on 'Bantu culture' to address their white personnel. The assumption underlying these presentations was that the most significant fact about African workers was not that they were workers but that they belonged to a different *culture* which had to be sympathetically understood. The lecturers tended to operate from a sympathetic, and at times a liberal, point of view but they gave a misleading picture of Africans as having only recently been exposed to western culture. In a set of lectures given at a large foundry, the first talk on 'characteristics of Bantu people' conveyed the misleading impression 'that the Bantu never knocks on a door. There were no doors'. It goes on to suggest that 'male-female relations amongst the younger people are an aggressive, morally lax association, characterized by uninhibited primitivism and sexual lecherousness.' The course ends with advice on 'fifty things to do with Bantu workers' which begins with the revealing remark, 'Treat him as a human being, he is one.' It then goes on to conclude, 'Use a spot of humour. The Bantu are easily triggered off into laughter.'[28]

This stress on the problem of communication ignored the dimensions of power involved in industrial relations. It rested on the assumption of an essential community of interest between an employer and a worker — the belief that the employer had the best interests of the worker at heart and that any conflict between the two arises from a misunderstanding, which can be cleared up by improved communication. As Hyman points out, this is based upon the assumption that 'industrial peace is the norm and conflict pathological. From this perspective disputes must be attributed to ignorance or to misapprehension; with knowledge of the facts workers would have no desire to strike. While some strikes may result from misunderstanding, it would be naive to assume that disputes typically arise in this way.'[29] Alan Fox identifies this frame of reference by management as 'unitary': it assumes a common focus of loyalty and one source of authority in the workplace.[30] The workplace is seen as one of harmony and trust where, if conflict does arise, it is attributed to faulty communication or agitators. But one cannot agitate successfully without widespread grievances. This does not mean that in certain situations militant representatives do not perform a significant role in articulating conflict. For conflict to take on a collective character it is usually necessary for some, initially at least, to take the lead in giving organizational form to workers' discontent. But to attribute conflict to agitators is to point to the instrument, not the cause.

From this perspective the trade union is seen essentially as an intrusion into a private contractual relationship. The essence of this intrusion, as seen by employers, is that the union systematically promotes distrust. It introduces distrust into employer/employee relations by encouraging its members to take 'a false conflict view' of the work situation. But to charge that the union introduces distrust implies that there was trust before.

In all four of the disputes dealt with, management had attempted to pre-empt the self-organization of workers by establishing a liaison committee modelled on the SEIFSA constitution.[31] In Defy and Conac Engineering, workers were not sufficiently organized to challenge the liaison committee and tried to get shop stewards elected to it. In Leyland and Heinemann they organized the whole shop floor, including coloureds in the case of Heinemann, into the union, and were able to pose the union as an alternative form of representation to the liaison committee.

The Leyland Struggle

In order to strengthen their bargaining position in Leyland, MAWU was forced to expand its offices to Johannesburg in 1975 as that company was established nationwide. The stoppage of work by 177 African employees at Leyland in March 1974 raised the question of recognition of MAWU. Large numbers of workers from Leyland had joined the GWFBF before MAWU was formed and they elected a committee in July to represent them. However, management had established a liaison committee earlier that year and rejected MAWU's request for recognition, arguing that 'the procedure for committee communication between employer and employee as laid down in the Bantu Labour Relations Act will be implemented and used effectively to develop a close liaison between management and the employers'. When workers decided to stop work until management conceded their demands, the secretary of MAWU phoned the plant manager with the intention of mediating a quick settlement of the dispute. The secretary received a blunt answer, to the effect that management was capable of handling its own affairs without the intervention of a 'third party'. Management consulted with the Department of Labour who advised that all workers be fired for striking illegally. When the secretary phoned Leyland's Johannesburg head office, he was informed that if the Durban workers were such 'hotheads' serious consideration would be given to closing down the Mobeni plant and transferring the Natal operations to Blackheath in the Cape. However, head office did agree to negotiate with worker representatives if they returned to work.

Meanwhile management had hired twenty new workers so that when the strikers returned to work some were discharged because, according to management, a three-day week in Britain had necessitated the retrenchment of sixty-five workers. The union rejected this move as victimization, as those workers who stayed on were forced to work overtime. They argued that management had 'carefully weeded out the strongest unionists to the best of their ability'. The dismissed men now faced unemployment with the added hardship that they would be endorsed out of the Durban area if they did not find work in thirty days. Furthermore, the Unemployment Insurance Fund (UIF) takes an inordinately long time to process claims and the actual payments are very small.

For MAWU the dispute at Leyland had far-reaching implications. In the first place it led to the beginning of the reformulation of the strategy mentioned earlier. 'Initially', the union wrote, 'we had been largely office based, but as a result of the ruptures at Leyland it was found necessary to become factory based in our structure and method of organization.' This implied intensive training of the shop stewards in order to improve their effective functioning. This was formulated more systematically in the MAWU report of August 1975:

> Previously, organization had been based on a mass drive for member-ship without a thorough assessment of the direction of the union or the consequence of such a drive. The heightened militancy of the Durban workers, following the strikes, made the mass organizational drive appear successful, but the subsequent lessening of militancy on the part of the workers and the need to train suitable qualified personnel to deal with the problems of the union had necessitated a reassessment of strategy. Broadly speaking, this reassessment had resulted in two major changes in strategy — a) decentralization, and b) concentration of resources on a few carefully selected factories.[32]

A move in the direction of consolidation had already been taken in January 1974 when the Trade Union Advisory Co-ordinating Council (TUACC) was established as a coordinating body of the new unions, in the MAWU Offices in Pietermaritzburg. TUACC was formed, it was reported at a council meeting in June 1974, because it was found that 'in our present socio-economic and political climate the growth and *survival* of the union necessitated our acting collectively'.[33] Acting collectively also involved defining an area of independence from the KwaZulu government. This was a difficult and delicate task as a dispute had broken out between the Chief Minister, Gatsha Buthelezi, and a rival minister, Barney Dladla, and it had been suggested that the unions were giving support to Dladla. Consequently the first three objectives of the TUACC constitution referred to its role in advising and informing the KwaZulu government on matters pertaining to labour. A second implication of the Leyland dispute was the need to establish a nationwide union to negotiate with a company such as Leyland that had plants in Johannesburg, Cape Town and Durban. With this in mind, the secretary of the union went to Johannesburg in

November 1974 to explore the possibility of establishing a branch on the Rand. One of the bodies with which contact was established was the Industrial Aid Society (IAS), formed in December 1973 as a complaint service and advice body for workers. It was mainly an outgrowth of student interest in the labour movement and its initial committee consisted mainly of academics, students and black workers who had contact with the academic community, either because they worked on the university campus, or because they had worked with the Student Wages Commission. At the request of MAWU in Natal, and after considerable internal controversy about the nature and structure of worker organization, a Transvaal branch of MAWU was formed in 1975 based on some of the IAS membership in metal industries. The IAS acted as a service body to the MAWU branch, supporting it with finances, education, transport and administration.[34]

On the secretary's first visit to Johannesburg, he met Gavin Anderson, who had left university to work full-time in the IAS.[35] Anderson became the first acting secretary of MAWU in Johannesburg and S. Kubeka (who had recently lost his job in a victimization case in Imextra) became the first union organizer. It was during this trip, when Alpheus Mthethwa began recruiting at Leyland in the Transvaal, with the help of Anderson and Kubeka, that they were accosted by members of the Security Police. The security men told the secretary that he should accompany them to their offices in Germiston. He was told that there were a number of charges that could be laid against him, and that no problem was anticipated by them in justifying his arrest. They said that he could be charged with being in the Witwatersrand area for more than 72 hours without a permit; or with distributing pamphlets in the area of Germiston, which is an offence in terms of the by-laws of the municipality. The Security Police also confiscated from the workers the pamphlets which the secretary had already distributed. The secretary was detained for fourteen hours and only released when his whereabouts were established by friends who telephoned the Security Police and asked for his release. At the same time, a colleague working in Johannesburg, who had been assisting the secretary in organizing Leyland, was detained and interrogated at the same place. MAWU believed that the Leyland management had invited the Security Police action in order to pre-empt union organization and smear the union:

It is obvious here that the SB (Security Branch) were called in at the request of the Leyland management in an attempt to block the organization of workers at the Elandsfontein plant into the Metal and Allied Workers' Union. The activity of the SB in detaining the secretary and in confiscating pamphlets from workers was clearly designed to intimidate workers.[36]

The Leyland dispute is significant for a further reason. It was the first occasion on which MAWU used overseas pressure in an attempt to gain recognition. International pressure on South Africa to improve the conditions of black workers had led in 1973 to the House of Commons investigation into the wages and conditions of Africans employed by British firms in South Africa. Lord Stokes, managing director of Leyland, had given evidence before this commission, telling them:

> From conversations I have had out there I gather there are problems in negotiating with Africans because they prefer to discuss vertically as there seem to be various families or groups of families that they like to negotiate with rather than, even if we tried to organize it, with a cross section; it would not work very well because they have allegiance to various tribes.[37]

Arising out of these investigations, the British government set up a series of guidelines for British employers which pointed out *inter alia* that 'there is nothing to prevent a company from recognizing and negotiating with a trade union representing African workers'.[38] At the end of 1974 the British embassy appointed a labour attaché, Bill Vose, to monitor these changes; he established contact with MAWU. In October 1975 the British embassy invited the secretary overseas to visit British unions. Although the secretary was unable to obtain a passport to travel overseas, this British interest encouraged MAWU to see international pressure as a weapon in their struggle for recognition.

As a tactic this was to prove controversial, both with regard to the state and inside the unions. The government amended the General Laws Amendment Act in 1974 to 'prohibit the furnishing of information on a company's activities at the request of anybody from outside South Africa, except with the permission of a Minister.'[39] Inside the unions the tactic of overseas pressure was raised in the February 1976 TUACC meeting and the secretary of MAWU was asked to evaluate its success. Mr Mthethwa stated that there had been a change in management's attitude and that management had cooperated in the election of a shop steward group during working hours. There were problems though, in that although management was being pushed closer to recognizing the union, they were using many tricks to avoid the union gaining more strength in the factory.

The secretary of TUACC replied

that there was a danger of using outside foreign pressure to win union recognition and this may encourage workers to rely on this outside pressure rather than relying on the unity of the factory.[40]

The Heinemann Struggle

The most dramatic challenge to the liaison committee — and the only dispute that led to a prosecution — was at Heinemann in March 1976, when MAWU members consistently boycotted the liaison committee introduced by management. This led to a baton charge of the workers by the police, with large numbers being badly beaten. The secretary and organizer were charged with inciting a strike and obstructing the police in their duty under the Bantu Labour Relations Act, the Industrial Conciliation Act, the Riotous Assembly Act and the Police Act. They were eventually found guilty on one charge of inciting employees not to accept re-employment. Four of the workers were arrested on Elandsfontein station and charged under the Riotous Assembly Act, the Bantu Labour Relations Act, and the Industrial Conciliation Act. These workers were twice refused bail and it was only after an appeal to the Supreme Court that bail was permitted to them. They were found not guilty and discharged. The union eventually succeeded in winning a R20 000 assault case against the Minister of Justice.   [R40,000 for costs etc. - Anderson interview DOC.]

A worker at Heinemann gave this account of a meeting called by the managing director and representatives of SEIFSA when they attempted to persuade workers to accept the liaison committee (December 1976):

Management asked us what was wrong with the old liaison committee. We answered that nothing came of complaints that were offered to it. Also it was felt that it was not established properly. People were given a list of names and asked to vote. Management said they knew others that were working well and offered to allow us to visit these factories. He said workers could keep their union membership but it had no legal standing. He told us that he was not saying that we should leave our union but it was their own decision if they wanted to continue to pay twenty cents a week. The union was a third party and couldn't get into the factory to negotiate.

The fundamental rejection of these two bodies by workers is best illustrated at the subsequent trial of the two organizers:

Prosecutor: Why did the workers boycott the election?

Accused: Because they felt the liaison committee was not what they wanted.

Prosecutor: Were there any discussions between you and the workers prior to the elections?

Accused: Not between us and all the workers of the factory. The union and shop stewards meeting every week, certainly there were discussions on the liaison committee during February.

Prosecutor: Between yourself and the shop stewards. Were you present?

Accused: I was present at the discussion.

Prosecutor: Was accused No. 2 present?

Accused: I think he was.

Prosecutor: Was his advice to shop stewards that they must see that these elections are boycotted?

Accused: No, in fact the shop stewards took all the decisions themselves. The function of the union official at meetings like this is to take minutes of the meeting and to carry out mandates from these main meetings.

Prosecutor: Without any advice at all?

Accused: They take part in discussions but at these meetings it is not a question of persuading anyone that the liaison committee was a bad thing. It was a question of people knowing that the liaison committee was a bad thing and deciding what to do about it.[41]

Before the final confrontation management made an attempt to persuade workers to accept the liaison committee. According to union sources a systematic offensive against the union now began:

Shop stewards were moved out of their departments and isolated from other workers. Some foremen attempted to prevent workers speaking to each other in the factory. There was also an attempt to introduce discrimination along racial lines within the work force. A group of four coloured workers were called to the office and told that the management preferred them to the African workers. The coloured workers were urged not to ally with African workers but to join a registered union which by law they were permitted to do. Rumours also spread through the factory that the African workers were going to attack the coloured workers.[42]

Although the accused were found guilty on one count, the magistrate conceded that widespread rejection of the liaison committee by the workers existed when he said, 'it has not been proved that the accused engineered the beginning of the strike, and that being so it appears to me that events would have taken much the same course even if the accused had played no role'.

Management's chief weapon in facilitating this pre-emptive tactic was the fear of dismissal — strengthened by the fear of unemployment in a recessionary climate (1976-1978), and of endorsement out of the urban area if you were a contract worker. Having limited skill (eighty-six per cent were unskilled or lower semi-skilled), MAWU members were easily interchangeable. A dismissed worker in the dispute in Heinemann attributes his dismissal to his membership in MAWU:

> I believe that I was fired because I was active in recruiting people to the union. About a week before I was fired the foreman of my section came to me at my machine and said he didn't want to see me making groups with other workers to tell them about the union. He said I talked too much about the union. The union, he said, didn't work in that factory. If he saw me talking again he was going to fire me. He said I stopped people from working. But I only talked to people at tea time or lunch time. On Thursday at 4.45 p.m. the foreman called me from my machine and we were called to the training office where we were told that the firm was going down and so they were reducing staff.

The Defy Struggle

The dispute at Defy illustrates the way in which the pre-emptive tactic was facilitated by the fear of dismissal. A dispute broke out in May 1975 in the assembly department of Defy Industries in Jacobs when management attempted to increase the intensity of work by altering the bonus system in its favour. Established as the first mass production foundry in 1936 (then Durban Falkirk), Defy was forced in 1974 to increase productivity in order to maintain profit levels. 'In order to minimize the effects of inflation and the high cost of holding excessive stocks', the 1974 annual report noted, 'stock levels will be reduced and maximum efficiency and higher productivity will be achieved in manufacturing.'[43] The board expected a difficult market in 1975 because of lower spending on durables and the competitive effect of the introduction of television. Similarly the 1975 annual report noted that 'profit increases are going to be difficult to achieve because of the down-swing in building'.[44] The interim result for August confirmed the board's pessimism, recording that the extent of the drop in profits was greater than anticipated.[45]

As part of management's attempt to increase productivity a new assembly line was installed in 1974. However, the introduction of new technology, such as air-operated screwdrivers, had increased assembly workers' bonuses to 'unrealistic levels', creating 'an imbalance' with wages in the rest of the factory. To correct this 'imbalance' an agreement was reached in September. In April 1975 management again attempted to alter the bonus system by refusing to include defects in calculating the bonus. Matters came to a head on Friday 16 May when assembly workers received only approximately half the bonus they would have received under the old system. Two representatives were immediately mandated to talk to the foreman. He suggested that as it was late they should raise the matter on Monday 19 May. When approached by representatives on Monday, the foreman lost his temper, instructing the representatives to resume production within two minutes or take off their overalls and leave the premises. Refusing to negotiate, the foreman then ordered the workers to leave unless they were prepared to accept, unconditionally and indefinitely, the existing bonus system.

A quarter of the workers involved in the dispute were Indians who belonged to the registered Engineering and Industrial Workers' Union (EIWU) which had begun to recruit members in 1975. Half of the African workers in the department were members of MAWU which was not recognized by management, although Alpheus Mthethwa had made approaches to management on behalf of the union. Both Indian and African workers had gone on strike in February 1973 and it is this action that may have provided the impetus for union recruitment. By May 1975, 153 of the 578 African workers had joined MAWU (40 by November, 103 by 1974 and 10 in 1975). Management had responded to these shop floor pressures by establishing a liaison committee and appointing a black personnel officer to 'improve relations between management and workers'. Management had proposed a liaison committee in August 1974, inviting six nominations from the factory (two from the foundry and one each from the enamelling, fettling/sand blasting, maintenance, and despatch sections). The chairman and secretary were appointed by the company and an *induna* acted as interpreter. The constitution of the liaison committee was identical to the model constitution circulated by SEIFSA in August 1973, and an analysis of the minutes confirms the intentions of its designers to limit that body's function to communicating management policy to black employees. The chairman of the committee quoted Clause 2b (which specified that the committee could not reverse a managerial decision) when a worker representative on the committee requested that, if an employee was to be dismissed, the matter should be referred to the committee.

Against this background it is not surprising that management responded to the May dispute by demanding unconditional acceptance of its decision. The assembly department workers reacted to this lock-out by turning first to the registered EIWU — who simply referred them to the Department of Labour — and then to SABS who accepted management's definition of the dispute as a strike. The next day they returned to the factory to find that management had counter-attacked with two tests for them. One was a speed sorting test involving nuts and bolts, the other an IQ test involving shapes. After these tests had been completed, all but nineteen of the workers (eleven Indians and eight Africans) were re-employed. The bonus system was scrapped and the basic wage was raised, but this only meant that workers were left with the equivalent of the old basic, plus the low bonus rate which had occasioned the dispute; the effective overall wage had dropped considerably. Management could see the whole operation, in terms of ends, as a successful exercise in trimming for productivity and efficiency. The workers had lost the dispute.

Although there was continuing evidence of workers being dissatisfied with the liaison committee, attempts to establish a significant trade union presence at Defy failed. A shop steward committee started to meet in the union offices from September 1975, but never established sufficient support in the factory to be able to challenge the liaison committee. In February 1976, however, the secretary felt they had sufficient membership to approach management. He argued that since the company was eighty-four percent British-owned 'it is in Britain where it can be expected of management to seriously consider the question of union recognition. [Further], we may consult with the British unions to put pressure on the company for recognition of MAWU.'[46] Although a decision was taken at this meeting to approach management, it was clear from the discussion that union support was tenuous. In fact one of the shop stewards said he did not wish to continue to collect signatories for a petition calling for recognition 'because of the hardship he had met trying to get people to sign'.[47]

Consequently when the managing director was reported in the *Daily News* as saying that the liaison committee was functioning well, the chairman of the new shop stewards' committee pointed out that 'it was not surprising that he could say that because the workers have not as yet taken action to register their dissatisfaction with the liaison committee'.[48] He suggested the union should supervise a petition demanding an election at Defy in which workers would be asked to choose between the union and the liaison committee. This was to be the last meeting of the shop stewards' committee — no members had been recruited since May 1975 and those that had joined had stopped paying subscriptions by mid-1976.

The major reason for the union failing to win support lay in the fear of dismissal or retrenchment. A number of the active members had not been reinstated after the May dispute and this had become common knowledge among workers. A man who joined Defy in 1976 and became a union organizer later, described attitudes to the union as follows:

> I was told by the old workers that if any worker had tried to get workers to join the union he would be dismissed. I was still new and although I had been a member of NUTW in South African Fabrics, I was scared. No new members joined in 1976. They belonged to the union but they did not want it to be known that they were members. They didn't even want other workers to know. Two of the members of the shop stewards' committee were also on the liaison committee — they kept contact with the workers secretly. They would talk to workers in the toilets about the union. When someone came in who they did not trust they would keep quiet or pretend they were discussing something else. I was warned by a shop steward not to speak too loud about the union. He warned me to watch out because there were spies. He told me I would be dismissed if I kept talking about the union. If I was interested, he said, I must come to the union offices and not discuss this inside the factory. When the members of the liaison committee came back to the workers, they would tell members of the liaison committee that they were sell-outs. Then I

would tell them that it was only the union that can help us, but the workers would say to me that I must forget about the union if I want to go on working at Defy. Few joined from the compounds because they had no permit to stay in the township. They felt they would lose their jobs if they joined the union.[49]

Accompanying this tactic of fear was the tactic of smear. The characterization of the union as 'illegal' or 'corrupt' was a common tactic of managerial resistance during this period. One respondent interviewed in the Union Membership Survey of MAWU members in 1975 said, when asked why more workers did not join the union, 'they fear employers who always give the impression that unions are dangerous and adventurous bodies and threaten to dismiss anyone who joined the union'. Union members recalled in December 1976 that at the meeting called by Heinemann in March 1976,

> management said the union is a business, especially MAWU. Here in Transvaal it was fighting for membership with the Engineering and Allied Workers' Union (EAWU) and the more membership they got the better jobs they got. They even said these people are crooks, coming to do business out of us.

By the end of 1976 the technique of pre-empting the union had proved highly successful in repulsing attempts by MAWU to organize black metal workers. Large numbers of members had virtually ceased to pay their subscriptions. Two-thirds of the Union Membership Survey sample had lapsed, i.e., they were twenty-eight weeks in arrears. In February 1977 the Transvaal MAWU reported to TUACC that only about R30 per week was being collected in subscriptions.[50] In November 1976 the union was hit by a further blow when four of the union organizers were banned for five years under the Suppression of Communism Act. Natal MAWU reported that they had retrenched their organizers during that year and with the banning of the two remaining organizers in November 1976, the union had no full-time organizers left.[51]

Yet while the union had lost all these disputes, they were not victories for either the state or management. In 1977, in an attempt to salvage the liaison committees, the Bantu Labour Relations Regulation Amendment Act was amended (again!) to provide for 'negotiation over wages'. MAWU, in a detailed memorandum, argued that from their experience over the preceding four years, the 'committees are basically undemocratic, open to all types of pressures from management, and unable to negotiate meaningfully on most issues'.[52] Experience had shown, they said, that committees functioned as inadequate and ineffective safety valves: 'They have been perceived as such by workers in the factories who uniformly distrust the workers who are members of these committees.' More especially, they argued, in some factories the *indunas* and 'boss-boys' were automatically appointed to the committee; there was no report-back and the proceedings of meetings were not discussed with workers — meetings were often held irregularly and no time was given to canvass opinion. In spite of their inadequacies, the memo suggests, 'in almost every firm which MAWU has approached management, management has either tried immediately to create a liaison committee or, when one already exists, has insisted that the committee works effectively, and so it is unnecessary for them to talk to the union'.

Amongst more far-sighted members of management, there was a growing realization that liaison committees had failed to win the support of black workers. Barlow Rand, Heinemann's parent company, implied this when they released this statement after the 1976 dispute:

> We feel obliged to negotiate within the framework created by law and cannot opt out of industrial agreements which apply to the whole industry. This does not imply that we are happy with the existing industrial relations legislation. We believe it needs drastic revision.[53]

The changed nature of production, in particular the strategic location of black metal workers in production, had given them a leverage on the shop floor that could no longer be ignored. Management was increasingly dependent on these workers to increase production. The precipitating incident that led to the dispute in Defy had been management's desire to increase output by reducing the bonus. At Conac Engineering, management attempted to increase output through compulsory overtime. It was in the context of these changing forms of exploitation that disputes took place during this period.

However, while these factory struggles, in particular the Heinemann struggle, were clearly a necessary condition for a change in state and management policy, they were not a sufficient condition. It was the outbreak of the urban unrest in 1976 that was to provide the final impetus for a realization of the need to make more drastic changes. Although organized labour remained aloof from the unrest, fearing that they would be suppressed if they became involved in a 'political strike' it had become clear to management and the state that support within the black population needed to be widened.[54] The initiative by Mr H Oppenheimer and Mr A Rupert in November 1976 in establishing the Urban Foundation with the clear objective of creating a black middle class illustrates this strategy. Its director, Justice Steyn, described the Urban Foundation's objectives in these terms:

> Urban distortions and exploitation played a significant role in the tragic events of 1976. The elimination of these distortions, or at least their amelioration, must lie close to the heart of every thinking South African. I cannot see any thinking businessman declining to participate in South Africa's future through the Urban Foundation. His dividend would be the emergence of a black middle class and a greater stability in our urban society.[55]

The establishment of the Wiehahn Commission in 1977 to investigate labour relations is a further example of a recognition of the need to widen support within the black population.

Yet it would be misleading to exaggerate the importance of trade unions *per se* in explaining the change in state strategy. The Wiehahn Commission was also to see in the unions' weakness an opportunity for controlling the pace of union development. African unions, it said, are not subject to 'protective and stabilizing elements in this system or discipline and control.' In fact they were seen to enjoy greater freedom than registered unions insofar as they participated in party politics and could use their funds for any purposes they saw fit.[56] It would be better, the commission concluded, to permit African unions to register at an early stage.[57]

More pressingly, the state feared that the resurgence of popular-democratic struggle in 1976 would lead to the re-establishment of links between organized labour and the popular struggle similar to those in the 1950s and early 1960s. Although such continuity was present in certain individual members, as we demonstrated earlier, MAWU had been concerned to 'establish an independent worker position'.[58] Sophisticated strategists for capital and the state had come to realize that a certain form of trade union recognition could in fact facilitate a separation of 'economic' and 'political' struggle, and thus hope to weaken the role that organized workers could play in the national popular struggle. Thus state repression (banning the more political leaders) was not inconsistent with reform attempts to control the unions from above through statutory recognition. The success of this politically repressive campaign against the unions raised the potential for the other side of the restructuring process to succeed — reform. This restructuring must be seen as a contradictory process, involving repression and reform simultaneously.

In this chapter it has been shown how a major obstacle to the struggle for recognition by black metal workers was the attempt by management, through its association SEIFSA, to pre-empt the union through liaison committees. This tactic of managerial resistance was facilitated by the threat of dismissal (the tactic of fear) and allegations of union corruption and incompetence (the tactic of smear). When state recognition limited these tactics, the unions were able to win space in their attempt to move beyond the struggle for recognition. In the improved climate after 1977, they were able to move beyond the second phase to the phase of negotiating an agreement.

This was seen in the case of MAWU, which doubled its membership on the East Rand in 1981 and is now firmly in the third phase.[59] Uneven as it was, shop floor struggle against management's system of control in the period 1973 to 1976 laid the basis for a strategy that reflected and emphasized the shift in the balance of power in the factory. The union as an institution among black metal workers had become a permanent feature of the industry; on this there could be no turning back.

Notes

1   These are phases, not stages, as they do not operate in simple chronological form. The process of union development is uneven and in periods of recession, for example, gains made in a tight market situation may be lost and the union will find itself moving from phase three back to phase two, or even phase one.

2   A. Flanders, 'What are trade unions for?' in W.E. McCarthy, ed., *Trade Unions* (Penguin Books, Harmondsworth, 1972), p.23.

3   For further information on these unions, see E. Webster, ed., *Essays in Southern African Labour History*, (Ravan Press, Johannesburg, 1978).

4   Monopoly refers here to a situation in which producers have significant discretionary market power. The term covers what economists call monopoly (single seller markets) and oligopoly (few seller markets). For a

description of the nature of monopoly capitalism in South Africa, see Report of the Commission of Inquiry into the Regulation of Monopolistic Conditions Act, 1955, March 1977, RP 64/1977.

5   G. Bloch, 'The development of manufacturing industry in South Africa, 1939-1969', M.A. thesis, University of Cape Town, 1980, p.212.

6   *Ibid.*, p.213.

7   Quoted in *ibid.*, p.214.

8   R. Edwards, *Contested Terrain: The Transformation of the Workplace in the Twentieth Century* (Basic Books, New York, 1979), p.128.

9   D. Hemson, 'Trade unions and the struggle for liberation', *Capital and Class*, VI (1976), p.37.

10   *The Star*, Johannesburg, 30.10.1979.

11   I focus on the Metal and Allied Workers' Union (MAWU) because it has the largest proportion of black foundry workers. However, not all examples in this chapter are taken from foundries. For an analysis of the tactics of managerial resistance to the other major black metal union, the Engineering and Allied Workers Union (EAWU) during this period, see L. Douwes Dekker, 'The development of industrial relations by companies in South Africa, 1973-1977', M.A. thesis, University of the Witwatersrand, 1981, pp.206-19.

12   Institute for Industrial Education, *The 1973 Durban Strikes* (Ravan Press, Johannesburg, 1974), pp.99-100.

13   *Ibid.*, pp.91-92.

14   Maree develops this argument in a review of the book, 'Seeing strikes in perspective', in *South African Labour Bulletin* (*SALB*), II, 9 (February, 1976).

15   'Report of the General Workers' Factory Benefit Fund', *SALB* I, 3 (July, 1976), p.52.

16   'When Albert Dhlomo [a SACTU activist] came off Robben Island in 1970 after serving a prison sentence for being an ANC member, he had the idea that we [fellow activists] should revive the unions. We started off in 1972 by issuing out pamphlets to workers in certain factories. Workers responded spontaneously by calling to the office to join in the afternoons. They were former SACTU union members who brought in new members to join. I think it could be argued that there was some continuity from the past.' (Author's interview with B. Nxasana, May 1981.) Nxasana was a shop steward in the African Textile Workers' Union (a SACTU affiliate) until he was imprisoned for one year and then banned for two years from 1967 to 1969.

17   'Report . . . GWFBF', p.52.

18   E.P. Thompson describes the relationship between the benefit societies and early English unions in these terms: 'In the very secretiveness of the Friendly Society, and its opaqueness under upper-class structuring, we

have authentic evidence of the growth of independent working class culture and institutions. This was the sub-culture out of which the less stable trade unions grew, and in which trade union officers were trained. Union rules, in many cases, were more elaborate versions of the same code of conduct as the Sick Club.' E.P. Thompson, *The Making of the English Working Class* (Penguin Books, Harmondsworth, 1963), pp.460-61.

19   D.L. Davies, 'Report on the GWFBF', personal collection.

20   For a report on the incident see 'Report . . . GWFBF', p.52. See Thompson for a discussion of how the Combination Acts of 1799 and 1800 forced the trade unions into an illegal world.

21   The MAWU secretary spoke to the Trade Union Advisory Co-ordinated Council (TUACC). TUACC Council Minutes, August 1975, personal collection.

22   Sixteen percent were difficult to classify and were labelled 'other'.

23   The idea of focusing on management's defences against unionization is drawn from Donald Roy's account of resistance to the organization of textile workers in the American South. 'Fear stuff, sweet stuff, and evil stuff: management's defences against unionization in the South', in Theo Nichols, ed., *Capital and Labour, A Marxist Primer* (Fontana Paperbacks, Glencoe, 1980).

24   The liaison committee is a joint management-worker committee, with equal representation for both groups. In addition, the employer is empowered to appoint the chairman (Section 7/1(c)). The committee may 'make such recommendations concerning conditions of employment as the committee may at any time deem expedient' (Section 7/2). In the first draft of the bill, published on 4 April 1973, the emphasis was placed on works committees, where all members are elected, rather than liaison committees. In the final version, at the instigation of the employers' associations, this was reversed, leaving the South African Institute of Race Relations (SAIRR) to comment that 'there has been a decided shift of emphasis in the employers' favour between the earlier and later bills.'

25   Letter from the Department of Labour to all employers' organizations, 11 February 1975, personal collection. The IIE was to conclude a survey of employers undertaken a month after these strikes by suggesting that 'employers seem to believe that they will be able to re-establish their customary total control of the work force by means of a few relatively minor concessions' (*The Durban Strikes*, p.83). These conclusions are confirmed by a study undertaken among employers in the Durban area in 1972 where executives interviewed tended to opt for works committees as the most appropriate form of organization for black workers (sixty-eight percent). Twelve percent were prepared to support the idea of registered African trade unions, two percent the possibility of Africans in mixed unions, and four percent merely suggested some form of

organization would be advantageous. The respondents' perceived disadvantages of African unions emerged in the following order of importance: they cause unnecessary trouble; they are vulnerable to outside infiltration and agitation; they make management responsible for the malpractices of other firms; they are a waste of time; they develop patterns of leadership which are authoritarian/dictatorial; they are the first step to communism; they have leaders who speak for themselves, not for the workers; running the unions is beyond the ability of Africans. The authors concluded that 'the general impression emerging from these results is that the basic orientation of representatives of management as regards African labour relations is defensive and, in various ways, antipathetic to the idea of organized and clearly defined negotiation as between two factions with interests which are opposed in many respects'. L. Schlemmer and M. Boulanger, 'Race and employment patterns among larger employers in Durban in a brief case study of employment policy relation to social change', in *Change, Reform and Economic Growth in South Africa*, eds. L. Schlemmer and E. Webster (Ravan Press, Johannesburg, 1978), p.187.

26 SEIFSA, Memo on Bantu Labour Relations Regulations Act, August 1973, personal collection.

27 In 1973, for example, the first African-directed consultancy to improve communication with black workers, African Manpower Services, under Wells Z. Ntuli, was set up.

28 Lectures prepared by R. Silberbauer, delivered to management at Salcast. For a critical discussion of this 'popular mythology', see D. Webster, 'A review of some "popular" anthropological approaches to the understanding of black workers', *SALB*, III, 1 (July 1976), pp.53-65.

29 R. Hyman, *Strikes* (Fontana and William Collins, London, 1972), p.60.

30 A. Fox, 'Management's frame of reference', in A. Flanders, ed., *Collective Bargaining* (Penguin, Harmondsworth, 1969), pp.391-92.

31 My account of the dispute at Defy is drawn from M. Kirkwood, 'The Defy dispute: questions of solidarity', *SALB* II, 1 (May/June, 1975), pp.55-61; from the records of MAWU in its Jacobs office; and from the author's personal interview with Vusi Shizi, organizer at Jacobs, August 1981. My account of the dispute at Conac Engineering is drawn from an account of it by *SALB*'s Durban editors, 'Conac Engineering and the Department of Labour', *SALB*, II, 9/10 (May/June, 1976); and the author's personal interview at the time with Brian Cutler, the Pietermaritzburg organizer at Conac Engineering, October 1981. Leyland is covered in two articles in *SALB*: J. Copelyn, 'And what of Leyland?' *SALB*, I, 3 (June, 1974), pp.12-16; and A. Mthethwa and Pindele Mfeti, 'Report on the Leyland Motor Corporation and the Metal and Allied Workers Union', *SALB*, II, 5 (1975), pp.36-47. The Heinemann strike is

covered in the article by MAWU, 'Workers under the baton: an examination of the labour dispute at Heinemann Electric Company', *SALB*, III, 7 (June/July, 1977), pp.49-59; from Anderson and Kubeka vs. the State, Case SH(1) 371/76, regional court, Germiston, June-August, 1976 (housed in the Historical and Literary Papers, University of Witwatersrand Library); from the author's interview with Anderson and Kubeka, September 1981; and from an account of a meeting between management and workers, as reconstructed by Mandla Masengu, Elizabeth Mayisela and Emily Ndlovu (December 1976). All references to these disputes are drawn from the above sources.

32 E. Webster, 'A profile of unregistered union members in Durban', *SALB*, IV, 8 (January/February, 1979), pp.53-56.

33 TUACC Council Meeting, 16 June 1974, personal records.

34 This account of the IAS is drawn from their minutes beginning March 1974, MAWU file, 1077 (University of the Witwatersrand Library archives).

35 Author's interview with Gavin Anderson, Johannesburg, September 1981; and with Alpheus Mthethwa, August 1981.

36 Mthethwa and Mfeti, 'Report on the Leyland Motor Corporation', p.43.

37 M. Legassick, 'The record of British firms in South Africa in the context of the political economy', *SALB*, II, 1 (May/June, 1975), p.75.

38 *Ibid.*, p.75.

39 See editorial comment, 'Prohibition on furnishing of information', *SALB*, II, 1 (May/June 1975), p.5, for a discussion of this amendment.

40 TUACC Minutes, February 1976, personal collection.

41 G. Anderson and S. Kubeka vs. the State, p.432.

42 MAWU, 'Workers under the baton', p.53.

43 Defy Industries, *Annual Report, 1974*, quoted in M. Kirkwood, 'The Defy dispute', p.56.

44 *Financial Mail* (Johannesburg), 21.3.1975.

45 *Financial Mail* (Johannesburg), 15.8.1975.

46 Minutes of Shop Stewards' Meeting. 10.2.1976.

47 *Ibid.*

48 Minutes of Shop Stewards' Meeting, 2.3.1976.

49 Author's interview with Vusi Shizi.

50 MAWU Transvaal report to TUACC, February 1977, TUACC minutes.

51 *Ibid.*

52 The quotation refers to the committee system. MAWU memo on the BLRRA Act 1977, p.4, MAWU records, personal collection.

53 MAWU, 'Workers under the baton', p.58.

54 For an evaluation of the lack of direct involvement of organized labour in the stayaways that followed the Soweto uprising, see E. Webster, 'Stayaways and the black working class: evaluating a strategy', *Labour,*

Capital and Society, XIV, 1 (April, 1981), pp.10-38.

55 *Financial Mail* (Johannesburg), 11.3.1977.

56 South African Labour and Development Research Unit (SALDRU), 'The Wiehahn Commission: a summary', para.3:35:5, *SALB*, V, 2 (August, 1979), p.21.

57 *Ibid.*, para.3:35:15.

58 MAWU's tactical caution arose out of direct experience with state harassment when such links were established by some unions in 1972. That period was recalled in an interview with Nxasana: 'We set up an office in Durban in 1972 and workers started coming in. We took joining fees. Then the Special Branch arrived and took me to their offices and told me we couldn't do this and must disband. So we contacted the Wages Commission and they took over for our members and established a Benefit Fund. This was the start of the unions.' (Interview, B. Nxasana, August 1981). Tactical caution was to develop into a critique of the nature of SACTU's alliance with the ANC (African National Congress). Lambert expresses this position most clearly in a review of Feit's study of SACTU: 'Because of SACTU's subordinate position, decisions to launch national strike campaigns were taken with little reference to the level of preparedness and maturity of working class organization. It was the dominance of the ANC and SACP (South African Communist Party) in the alliance that finally led to the smashing of SACTU, at the very point that it was both developing a mass base and an experienced leadership.' Rob Lambert, 'Political unionism in South Africa', *SALB*, VI, 2/3 (1980), p.104.

59 E. Webster, 'MAWU and the Industrial Council — a comment', *SALB*, VIII, 5 (April, 1983), pp.14-18.

CHAPTER 7

Opening the Closed Unions: Restructuring the Racial Division of Labour

It was suggested in Part 1 that craft unionism depends upon the capacity of the union to restrict entry into the job. In Chapter 3 it was shown how, under the pressure of technical change, the craft skill of the moulder was diluted and the union was forced to open its membership to non-craftsmen. Further undermining of their privileged position forced the moulders to redefine themselves in racial terms by introducing *de facto* job reservation in the 1968 Industrial Council agreement. However, faced by a systematic onslaught from employers to open up 'skilled jobs' to Africans, and being unable to provide them with union members, the unions were forced to allow non-union (i.e. black) workers to take the new positions. Yet opening union jobs to non-union members could only make the registered unions even less representative of a semi-skilled work force which threatened to lower the standards of the skilled men. As had happened sixty years earlier in the United Kingdom, the opening of the 'closed unions' became an imperative for survival. 'Since the general conditions of effective closed unionism are an occupational stability on the part of the workers it organizes and a system of restricting entry to their jobs', observes Turner, 'the most obvious cause of such a transformation in a closed union's character is a technical change which undermines the permanence or blurs the identity of its members' occupation.'[1] He concludes that 'whether the union will in fact then modify itself depends largely on the pace of the technical revolution with which it is confronted'.[2]

Yet the victory of the imperatives of technical change is not guaranteed, at least not in the short term. It has been shown that privileged workers were able to retain their 'standard' through transforming the closed shop into *de facto* job reservation. Two unions, the Y & S and to a lesser extent the AEU, have continued this racial strategy, refusing to open their unions to blacks. This chapter is concerned with three of the craft-diluted engineering unions which, faced by a crisis in craft control, and taking advantage of the change in state strategy, opened up their membership to Africans. The lever employers used to persuade the craft unions to open was the threat of a skill shortage. However this threat concealed an attempt to increase the productivity of labour. All three unions, in opening their ranks, have attempted to retain control by the established unions — either through parallel unions, as in the case of the South African Electrical Workers' Association (SAEWA), or by restructuring one union into separate racial branches, as has happened in SABS and the IMS. But whereas SABS attempted to transform itself into an industrial union, the IMS showed little interest in expansion, concerned simply to retain its restricted entry and content to survive as a small union. Whether SABS is likely to achieve its expansionary objectives or the IMS its restrictive objectives will be assessed in Part III. Significantly, the IMS is able to contemplate restricted survival because it is able to limit entry into the job through a double closed shop.

The mechanism employers have used to pressurize the unions to open up restricted jobs is to challenge their capacity to find union members to fill the vacant positions. Unions responded to this challenge by giving employers exemptions in the Industrial Council to employ non-union labour. By 1970 the number of exemptions had increased so rapidly that a SEIFSA circular informed its members that a special committee of the National Industrial Council had been set up to issue exemption certificates. Members were circulated with a *pro forma* application to speed up this process.[3] The perennial prediction of skill shortages had become such a pillar of conventional wisdom by 1970 that it was exceedingly difficult for unions to question it.[4]

This chapter traces the manner in which employers were able to take advantage of the widespread acceptance of a skill shortage to undercut the white craft unions. Not surprisingly, predictions of skill shortage were usually linked to calls to take advantage of black labour and remove job reservation. In 1964, the Bureau of Economic Research at the University of Stellenbosch cautiously suggested that 'if, in certain sectors of the skilled labour market, the required white manpower supply has been exhausted, and sufficient numbers cannot be recruited by means of immigration, present needs dictate that recruits be sought in other sectors of the population'.[5] In its second report the 1961 Educational Panel convened by the University of the Witwatersrand concluded that 'practically all economically active whites are now engaged in skilled work, so that if the proportion of the total population which is engaged in such work is to rise (as it must do), all the new recruits to the skilled ranks needed to bring about this must be non-whites'.[6]

Faced by this ideological onslaught, the craft unions were forced to retreat from *de facto* job reservation to opening up jobs, and eventually the unions themselves, to black workers. Precisely because employers' arguments were seen as a pretext to take advantage of cheaper black labour, the craft unions remained sceptical of management's motives in opening up these jobs, questioning the nature of the skill shortage. Nicholson, secretary of SAEWA, expressed it bluntly in these terms:

> The apprentices are there for the taking. Employers have been shirking their obligations to train skilled labour. They want to use the shortage of artisans to force the trade unions into accepting the fragmentation of skill — cheap labour that can be exploited.[7]

The nature of this 'skill shortage' in the foundry must now be examined.

The precise nature of the so-called skill shortage and the 'crisis of control' facing the craft union is revealed most clearly through an analysis of the occupation of moulding. According to the *Manpower Survey* foundries were never really faced with a serious shortage of moulders, certainly not production moulders and core-makers. Between 1969 and 1979 a maximum 1% shortage of production moulders was recorded, and a 7.5% shortage of journeymen.

Table 7. Estimated Skill Shortages Among Moulders (1969-1979)

Date	Artisan & Apprentices	Production Moulders & Core Makers
1969	1.3%	0%
1971	7.5%	1%
1973	6.2%	0.5%
1975	3.6%	0.001%
1977	3.7%	0%
1979	0%	0.003%

Source: *Manpower Survey*, Nos. 8, 9, 10, 11, 12, 13.

1. *A foundry floor in the early years.*

2. *A Krugersdorp foundry in the first decade of the century.*

3. The 'architect of the
   foundry process':
   the skilled pattern
   maker.

4. A production moulder releases sand from the moulding machines.

5. A 'cast boy'.

6. *Modern casting: molten metal being poured into moulds.*

7. *A furnace.*

8. *As the molten metal is poured, spillage from the mould occurs.*

9. *A bare-handed attempt is made to dab up the spillage.*

10. *The shake-out: the casting is being thrown into the barrow at far right. Red-hot castings remain on the grid.*

11. *Fettling.*

12. *The core is placed into the mould by the core maker.*

In large part this non-shortage of production moulders and core makers lay in the fact that the occupation had, by 1979, ceased to be a 'white' job.

Table 8. Racial Proportion in the Occupation of Production Moulding and Core Making (1979)

Whites	Coloureds	Blacks
539 (20%)	974 (36%)	1 202 (44%)

Source: *Manpower Survey*, No. 13.

The crux here is the manner in which this 'blacking' of the moulding trade concealed a process of cheapening labour.

Moulding was preserved by the union as a predominantly 'white' job in the Transvaal until the 1970s. 'Up until two years ago in the Transvaal', said the IMS secretary Crompton in 1972, 'there wasn't a coloured production moulder in the industry. Today he virtually out-numbers the whites and the white cannot get a job in the industry, because the employers are running this industry cheaper now than they have ever done in their lives. They are running it on basic rates, not on premium rates, as occurred before these people came in.'[8] In October 1972 it was reported in the press that the Transvaal Malleable Foundry (TMF) had taken on ten coloured production moulders and had retrenched ten white production moulders.[9]

The IMS then called upon the Department of Labour to intervene and asked for a meeting of the Industrial Council. The secretary claimed that the society had not been able to place a white production moulder in any Transvaal foundry for eighteen months. He maintained that the foundries would take on only coloured moulders because they could pay them the minimum rate of R1.05 an hour while the going rate for whites was R1.30 an hour. He warned that 'if this sort of thing carries on there will be the greatest upheaval this country has ever known'. It was later reported that the Minister of Labour had ordered the foundry to reinstate the ten white workers.[10] However, this resistance by the IMS to encroachment on white jobs, and the doubtful legitimacy of the Department of Labour's intervention, was only transitory: by 1981 all these jobs in the TMF were occupied by coloureds.

It was the introduction of non-union Africans into moulding jobs that was to bring out most clearly the crisis of craft control. Speaking at the TUCSA conference of African trade unions in 1972 Crompton said:

> The realities of the position are such that already in this industry 70 per-cent of persons employed are people who are not able to belong to a trade union. People are living on less than 27 cents an hour: the remaining percentage comprises of Indians, coloureds and whites, and they are getting comparatively high wages. But make no mistake about it, we are becoming more unrepresentative of the workers in the industry every year, and to close our eyes to the fact that the African cannot, and will not be permitted to belong to our unions, is something we cannot tolerate. We also cannot open the flood gates to this unorganized horde, it will bring our standards right back to ninety or one hundred years ago.

Crompton's solution was that all moulders should be organized into one non-racial union and he opposed the earlier attempt by TUCSA to establish a parallel union in the engineering industry for Africans.[11] This position was reiterated in 1975 by his successor, Barnard, at the second meeting of the newly-formed South African Coordinating Council of the International Metalworkers Federation (IMFSACC).

> The IMS is not against the establishment of black unions under the con-trol of a registered union, or the establishment of black unions as such, they are against the establishment of a black Iron Moulders' Society.[12]

It has been argued that the labour process in foundries had been radically restructured to a point where only limited numbers of crafts-men were required. This is best illustrated through Autocast, established in a border area seventeen kilometres from Bophuthatswana in 1976. In a letter applying for exemption from the Industrial Council on 31 March 1978, Autocast made it clear that it had established the foundry in a border area in order to employ black labour at cheaper rates than were enforced in the industrial areas of South Africa. It began its request by citing the government's white paper on the report of the inter-departmental commission on the decentralization of industries:

> Industrial Councils are expected to cooperate in giving effect to govern-ment policy by granting, where necessary, exemptions from their

Industrial Agreement so as to enable industrialists to employ lower wage rates in the border areas.

However, Autocast's argument for an exemption rested not so much on the higher cost of white labour as on the fact that the labour process had been restructured to a point where skilled labour was no longer required:

> we have highly automated equipment which does not warrant the employment of skilled labour. It would therefore be a waste of manpower to employ skilled whites to perform the jobs concerned.[13]

Autocast was established to provide a local grey iron casting centre to service South Africa's motor industry after the introduction of a local content programme in the early sixties. Autocast is an equal partnership between Messina and Birmid Qualcast, the largest independent foundry group in Europe.[14] It has, as a consequence, automated modern equipment set up by Birmid technical staff. Whites, Autocast assured the National Industrial Council, would be retained simply to supervise all the operatives; production was a push button operation requiring minimal skill.[15] The core setter 'places cores into a core carrier in pre-determined order for transfer into a mould automatically . . . cores are not laid manually into the mould . . . only into a core carrier'. Moulding is done by automatic moulding machines imported from Europe (Disimatic from Denmark and Hansberg from Italy) averaging between 120 and 280 boxes per hour. In addition, according to the company handout, they 'enable castings to be made with high quality surfaces and to a closer tolerance than by most other casting methods'.[16] The task of the moulder is simply to attend an automatic moulding machine under supervision — 'he does not undertake any moulding operations'. Core production is automated and core transfer is by means of conveyor. The task of the core maker is simply 'to attend the automatic core making machine and offload the cores on to a conveyor belt. No core making operations are done manually by the attendant.' Similarly the core assembler 'places a small purpose-made auxiliary core in a predetermined position into an incomplete core assembly'. And the core dipper takes 'the core off the conveyor belt, dipping it into a blacking solution and placing it on to a drying rock'.

After visiting the foundry and discussing it in the NEC, the IMS refused under any circumstances to allow this work to be graded lower than D, or to be done by blacks (Autocast had proposed grades between E and I).[17] On 20 April 1978, the National Industrial Council, in reply to Autocast's request for an exemption, reminded it that all castings produced for the motor industry were covered by the engineering industrial council agreement, and opposed the application for exemption. Autocast then appealed to the Minister and was given an exemption. Opposition from the IMS and the NIC continued but Autocast had achieved their objective which was, in their own words, 'simply that we want natives on the job'.[18]

Further evidence of the questionable nature of the skill shortage argument is revealed when one examines apprenticeship training. Woodward has shown how in the United Kingdom the conflicting objectives of production and learning are reconciled by placing the apprentice in a low skill occupation as the artisan's mate, where he serves as an alternative to the unskilled labourer who would normally occupy this position. This is possible in the U.K., he says, because apprentices' wages are lower than those of the average skilled or semi-skilled worker.[19] Of course in South Africa the existence of cheap labour in the unskilled and semi-skilled categories undercuts this practice. The average wage rate for lower skilled operatives and labourers was 0.91 cents in 1979; except for in the first year, apprenticeship rates were all significantly higher — fifth year R2.19, fourth year R1.50, third year R1.25, second year R1.00 and first year R0.75.[20] In addition, the employer is required to provide the additional cost of allowances for education and block-release for apprentices. Meth concludes his examination of the economics of training in the private sector by suggesting that, in spite of levies and grants to individual employers,

> It is difficult for a firm to recoup training expenses and provide adequate training. The basic reason for this is the existence of the cheap black labour force which discourages firms from using apprentices as inexpensive artisan's mates, as is the custom in the United Kingdom. Apprentices' wages cannot be driven down low enough to make them competitive with the lower paid blacks.[21]

As a consequence of the uneconomic nature of apprenticeship training, employers did not encourage apprenticeship: yet they argued that a skill shortage existed. How do we explain this apparent paradox? In the opinion of the IMS it arose out of the fact that employers were engaged in psychological warfare against craft workers:

In the foundry industry, the employers granted 100 certificates of apprenticeship in the last ten years. Such a small increase in the intake of apprentices is difficult to understand at a time of expansion in the foundry industry. We believe that the argument of a shortage of skilled labour is the kind of psychological warfare waged by the employers against all workers to frighten them and make them work harder if they want their jobs.[22]

'Psychological warfare' was to reach a climax in 1979 when the employers, in anticipation of Wiehahn, proposed for the first time to the National Apprenticeship Board that apprenticeship training be opened to blacks.

The IMS was quick to object to what it perceived as race discrimination. The secretary pointed out that whites are required to undergo military training for at least two years, although they do get eight months off:

Now when the black comes in, they are not doing military training, therefore they have got an advantage over the white man. All apprentices should be treated on the same level and we cannot say they must take blacks because we are losing whites . . . Blacks must also go into the army. If we do not adhere to these lines then it will mean that our white boys go to the army and when they come back all the jobs will be taken by the blacks.[23]

Sceptical of employers' motives in opening up artisan work, and afraid of undercutting by cheaper (black) labour, the IMS was once again redefining the boundaries between craft and non-craft workers along racial lines. Their scepticism was confirmed later that year when, during Industrial Council negotiations, employers proposed a further downgrading of the artisan jobs to allow grade AA (non-journeymen) moulders to make any size of mould. In support of this demand, and in direct contrast with their public statements on the skill shortage, the employers argued forcefully that the advances in foundry technology, in particular the CO_2 process, had removed the skill from moulding jobs. Challenging the IMS representatives, Boustred, chairman of the employer caucus in the NIC, said the employers 'would like the union representatives to tell them where the skill was acquired by the rate A1 man'. 'They were at a loss', he said, 'to know why a skilled man was needed in rate A1.' The contested nature of the concept of skill is revealed clearly in these negotiations as union members on one hand tried to define the nature of the job as skilled, in spite of technological change, and the employers on the other hand demanded that the skill be demonstrated. As negotiations unfolded it became clear to the IMS representatives that they could no longer defend their position on the grounds of skill alone; their best line of defence was to accept 'deskilling' and demand a rate for the job. The employers took advantage of this breach of craft ideology in the negotiations, then proposed a compromise. Grade A1 moulders would be allowed to make boxes over 1.5 metres, while grade AA men could make boxes between 1 and 1.5 metres.

It is clear that there was no real shortage of 'craft' skills in the foundry. The unions were faced by a radically transformed labour process in which job dilution and fragmentation were taking place. Growing numbers of blacks occupied jobs previously held by white (i.e., union) members. This process of dilution took a number of different forms. The first and most obvious mechanism for dilution was the employment of non-union labour on grades of work that had been designated as union labour in 1968, i.e., grades A to D. In 1979 grade D work was opened to Africans in terms of a supplementary agreement to the main agreement.[24] It was estimated that this opened up ten thousand jobs to Africans.[25] In 1973 grade C work was opened — an estimated 8 000 jobs.[26] Support from the union was gained by a guarantee that white workers who were displaced by blacks would automatically be promoted to a job at a higher rate, and that in the event of a recession the employer would be forced to give preference to union labour.[27]

However, resistance to African advancement was to surface in 1976 when grade B and grade AB work was released from the closed shop.[28] Unions demanded racial segregation on the shop floor where blacks and whites were performing grade C and D jobs, insisting that they be 'employed in separately demarcated areas, or sections, or annexes or departments, or identifiable work places'.[29] In particular, SABS was to object to the introduction of 850 Africans in grade AB welding jobs arising out of the establishment of Sasol Two.[30] This was one of the reasons why SABS withdrew from TUCSA in 1976. According to Bouwer, the union's general secretary at the time,

> our policy differs from TUCSA's. We have thousands of coloured and Asian members whose jobs we have to protect. We can't do this at the same time as putting Africans in these unions as proposed by TUCSA.

We can't allow African workers to move into their jobs.'[31]

This strategy of dilution was to culminate in 1978 when the supplementary agreements were scrapped and all classes of work from A1 to D were opened to union members. The unions countered what they saw as an attempt to lower wage costs by demanding increases of up to 42 percent on union rates of pay in grades A to D. Nicholson, general secretary of the CMBU (previously named the MUJE), described the reasons behind the unions' demand in these terms:

> SEIFSA's public attitude is based on moral considerations, but employers have never been bothered with morals before. The charge we level at them is that they want unlimited access to cheap labour. Our demand for higher minimum wages is a test of the employers' sincerity with regard to the so-called code of ethics. If they try to keep wages low, the scrapping of job reservation will merely mean an attempt to exploit cheap labour.

The union advanced two reasons why it did not believe the rate-for-the-job was adequate protection: the first was that the going rate was well above the statutory rate; the second was that wages would be set too low for whites to accept:

> If they are sincere, they will concede these minimum rates without any argument at all as they are in fact less than the existing going rate in the higher categories. In our experience, once blacks go into top jobs, they stay. And there are enough blacks to occupy all jobs. If a job market is completely open there will be an access problem, especially for coloureds and Indians. There must be some form of protection for minority groups. Before we are even prepared to consider SEIFSA's proposals, they will have to come up with some other form of protection.[32]

SEIFSA did not concede the minimum wage demands, and wages in engineering remained low in these grades. Instead, Section 35 was offered as a form of protection. Section 35 simply consolidated the principles of the previous supplementary agreements, extending them into the main agreement providing for preference in re-employment to retrenched workers (clause 3). In addition, the 'orderly promotion' clauses provided for the promotion of blacks into higher grades, provided no whites were willing to accept training for this job and those involved had been consulted (clause 5c). 'Employers', announced Drummond, secretary of SEIFSA, 'who brought in outsiders [i.e., blacks] to "leap-frog" over existing workers [i.e., whites] would be in trouble.' Ben Nicholson said that the unions would attempt to build these principles into other agreements in which they were involved. The new agreement meant that they were getting rid of racial protection while giving union members confidence that the changes would not cost them their jobs. This job security for union members led to the agreement being welcomed by Borman, general secretary of the Y & S.[33]

In reality the protection Section 35 offered union members was largely illusory: in the first place, legal opinion held, its vagueness made it void:

> Section 35 is void by reason of its vagueness and is therefore unenforceable as presently worded. It seems that the employer has got the better of the bargain. The employees' protection under Section 35 is illusory.[34]

Harris, an official in the IMS, shared these opinions when he asked the secretary at a committee meeting whether a man who was retrenched would be taken back on the same pay:

> What is to stop an employer laying off say twelve men because there are no jobs — then at a very high rate — and afterwards the firm decides to take the men back at the basic minimum rate of R2.08 an hour?[35]

The implication of the use of cheaper non-union (black) labour in these trades was made clear by Van der Watt, secretary of SABS:

> Since the introduction of Section 35, skilled black workers have been employed in increasing numbers in the plants where SABS have traditionally organized. This not only weakens the union's strength in terms of membership, it also weakens its control over the supply of labour to the 'skill' trades.

Van der Watt held that an active system of 'reverse discrimination' was taking place, as white and coloured workers were being squeezed out of the more skilled jobs. The black worker is preferred, he said, for four reasons:

1) he can be employed at the same job at the minimum rate of pay;

2) under the black In-Service Training Act of 1976[36] the employers prefer to train blacks because of the tax concession which re-imburses the employer for all training costs — including equipment, salaries and materials. This was particularly advantageous where the need for rapid training of various specific jobs was concerned. Previously, the employer would have had to train an apprentice for three to four years, at a considerable cost, in order for that task to be done. A cheaper black worker with three months intensive (effectively cost free) training could perform a specific coded-welding task, that an experienced white apprentice would merely encounter as an aspect of his three year training;

3) an additional incentive for the employer to train and employ the black skilled worker is the likelihood that he is not organized into a union. He therefore has no organizational base from which to bargain for better working conditions, higher wages and benefits;

4) finally, the provision in Section 35 that excludes blacks from doing grade A work, i.e., artisan work, has had the effect of increasing job fragmentation. Blacks could be trained up to artisan level, and be put through the artisan trade test at Babeligi. Although this certificate cannot be used in the urban areas to qualify for the rate A job, the black artisan is employed at the rate immediately below rate A — A1 — and put to work in the artisan job of moulding and core making by creating a special rate, A1, in the 1978 foundry division of the agreement.[37]

The most important consequence of the 1978 agreement did not lie in Section 35, which it has been suggested was a consolidation of previous agreements; its significance lay in accelerating the rate of job fragmentation, i.e., the down-grading of the less skilled aspects of the job. In the foundry section of the 1968 agreement the 'rubbing off of hard and core fins, including patching and inspection', was classified as grade B work. In the 1978 agreement this aspect of grade B work had been down-graded to grade D. Similarly, in the 1974 agreement the 'making of exothermic sleeves and/or feeding pads' and the 'making of runner cups' were classified as grade D work. In the 1975 agreement this aspect of grade D work had been down-graded to DDD. The degree of down-grading of the 'making of runner cups' is illustrated by the fact that in the 1949-51 agreement the job was classified as journeyman's work. The most common form of job fragmentation involved the complete detachment of white workers from direct production and their transformation into supervisors. For example, supervising spin casting masks (grade AA), or supervising smelting (grade B), supervising dye casting (grade C) or supervising annealing heat treating (grade B). Supervision is defined in the agreement as 'being performed in the vicinity of a rate A, AA or AB employee or chargehand or person specifically so appointed to exercise supervision, so that the person who has to exercise the supervision is able to sight the operation in question'. The important change here is in the social relations of production where increasing numbers of whites are allocated into directly supervisory functions.[38]

However, in spite of the limited significance of Section 35 *per se*, 1978 was a turning point in the history of the engineering unions. It was the year when the craft unions actively returned to their strategy of trying to absorb Africans into the registered trade union structures. In Chapter 5 the establishment of TUCSA's first parallel union for Africans in the engineering industry was described. The way in which they were encouraged to work through the registered unions in the Industrial Council was also discussed. In the next chapter the IMF's attempts to revive this strategy in 1972 will be examined. The significance of 1978 is that this attempt to incorporate black workers is in harmony with, rather than in opposition to, the new state strategy on labour. Significantly Professor Wiehahn, the chairman of the inquiry into labour legislation appointed the year before, opened the 1978 conference of SAEWA. Giving a clear indication that the commission's work would result in far reaching change in labour relations, he urged trade unions to face up to the new climate.

> I want to emphasize that trade unions without the desire or means of change will run the serious risk of losing their existence.

Referring to the conference's forthcoming debate on black membership, he said:

> May you find the strength in your conviction that your decisions will be in your organization's and our country's interests.

The TUCSA's general secretary, Mr A Grobbelaar (a member of the Wiehahn Commission) told the meeting that tremendous changes were coming very soon.

Trade unions will have to take certain steps or go out of existence. If they do not equip themselves for a changed situation that will face all trade unions then they will not survive.

At this conference delegates unanimously adopted a resolution instructing their National Executive Council to initiate procedures to organize a trade union for black electrical workers.[39]

Having been centrally involved in introducing the abolition of the job colour bar in the Industrial Council Agreement through Section 35, SAEWA was to be the first craft union in the 1970s to organize a black trade union. Formed later that year, the black Electrical and Allied Workers' Union formed the third section of an 'umbrella system' under which the white union and the coloured EATUSA have a separate existence but a common general secretary.[40] In proposing this change, the general secretary, Ben Nicholson, stated that if the law were amended to allow for racially mixed unions, then the membership of the three unions would decide whether they should continue under the umbrella system or whether they should form one combined union for all electrical workers.[41] He explained that the effect of the umbrella system was to ensure that the three trade unions would operate with a common policy towards common goals, by allowing each union control over its internal affairs. Referring to the other major resolution of the 1978 Congress — that workers irrespective of race or colour would be eligible for training as electricians — Nicholson stated that

compelling reasons of an economic and political nature have made it imperative for us to reject the colour bar. But, most important, the elimination of the colour bar will give us better job protection. By allowing workers of all races to become artisans we are countering the employer's pressure for more semi-skilled workers — for the fragmentation of our trade and the cheapening of labour. High standards of training for workers of all races, equal pay, equal fringe benefits and equal privileges — these are the principles which underlie our resolution, and these are the principles we intend to fight for with the trade union strength of electrical workers of all races.[42]

Similarly SABS was to recognize the need for unionization of Africans as large numbers of African workers had entered skilled job categories. Explaining the necessity for unionization Van der Watt said in 1979:

Black job advancement is inevitable — we simply haven't got enough whites and coloureds to do all the skilled jobs. The only way we can guarantee the survival of our members, is to organize these African workers who are moving into the higher skilled jobs. It is in our interest to organize skilled African workers. The recognition of black trade union rights would stop the super-exploitation of black workers and put an end to the process of undercutting white and coloured workers by cheaper and unorganized black workers.[43]

In 1980 SABS began recruiting African members into a separate branch for Africans. In contrast to SAEWA, who had expelled their coloured members creating a separate union after the 1956 Act, SABS had retained the coloured membership but had established separate branches. As a consequence of retaining coloured members SABS had a larger proportion of non-journeymen members (50 percent) than the all-white SAEWA (90 percent) and were forced to confront earlier the advancement of Africans into jobs previously confined to union members.[44] As early as 1973 the executive of SABS had discussed the need for unionization of the African workers in their plants and had met with MAWU to discuss this issue. It was agreed by SABS at this meeting that it would not attempt to 'poach unskilled members from the unregistered unions'.[45] They considered, partly after the incident at Metal Box described in the next chapter, that conflict with MAWU and EAWU should be avoided. SABS, explained Van der Watt, began organizing the skilled workers from the top downwards and the unregistered unions began organizing from the bottom upwards. Both unions, he said, were now beginning to organize in the same grades.[46]

The problem came to a head in the period between 1976 and 1978 when further grades were opened up to Africans. Van der Watt said:

> There had been an increase of skilled blacks into the plants where SABS previously had 100 percent membership. In some plants the membership had dropped to being only 70 percent of the total workers in these grades.[47]

Clearly it was now in the interest of SABS to have these workers unionized, preferably in their own union. MAWU, in turn, was not keen to lose the potential membership of the black skilled worker and particularly not the semi-skilled worker. But MAWU drew its membership predominantly from the ranks of the unskilled and lower semi-skilled, and with a subscription of 80 cents per month could hardly offer the benefits that SABS offered its members for R4 a month.[48] With these problems in mind SABS approached MAWU with three possible alternatives:[49] that SABS should organize skilled African workers; that the unregistered unions should organize skilled African workers; that SABS should provide funds and facilities to employ an organizer of the unregistered union's choice who would then organize the skilled African workers into the unregistered unions.

The outcome of these negotiations was inconclusive in that SABS applied for an exemption to recruit skilled black workers, concentrating on grade D and above. However, while MAWU only applied for registration of semi-skilled and unskilled workers, it would be wrong to conclude, as Nicol does, that they had an agreement with SABS not to recruit skilled workers.[50] Sharp distinctions between what counts as skilled or semi-skilled work are, it has been suggested, difficult to establish. However, as SABS has been forced to transform itself from a craft into an industrial union, it has increasingly come into contact with MAWU, an industrial union attempting to unionize all workers in a particular establishment. The contradictions raised by attempting to transform a racially-based craft union into a non-racial union will be dealt with in Chapter 10. What is already clear is that once mechanization had removed the skill from many jobs held by members of SABS they could not maintain control over their traditional job categories without organizing African workers. Yet even SABS, which had opened its membership with more enthusiasm than any of the other craft engineering unions, made the decision on the understanding that it would lose coloured and white members. Van der Watt said at the beginning of 1980:

> there is not a shadow of doubt in my mind, and my executive know and are aware of this too, that if the Minister grants us the exemption, there will be a sharp decline of our white, even our coloured and Asian members for the first three years or more. But there is also no doubt in my mind that in fifteen years time I shall still have a union, and a stronger one — how big will the present Y & S be in fifteen years time? If indeed they still have a union.[51]

This assessment will be evaluated in Chapter 10.

Thus the strategy of 'opening' the 'closed' unions to blacks was part of a strategy of protecting entry into the trade. With the advancement of non-union blacks into artisan work the threat to craft control could now only be overcome by opening the union to blacks. 'What happens', said Nel of the IMS, 'if the blacks come into the trade and they cannot join the union?' 'It would be best', said the secretary, 'to let blacks into the trade and after 1 October 1979 you can ask for exemption for blacks to belong to the Iron Moulders Society.'[52] On 29 October the IMS sent a letter to the Minister of Manpower applying for exemption to enrol Africans.[53] It was, the IMS proudly notes in its minutes, the first registered union to open to blacks.[54] The executive made it clear that the move was part of its strategy to restrict entry into the moulding trade. This objective could now best be achieved by bringing blacks into the IMS, rather than allowing them to be organized by a rival black union. 'It was generally felt that we must have the blacks with us where we can keep an eye on them, otherwise if they have their own union they can cut our feet from under.'[55]

The engineering craft unions were about to embark on changes undertaken earlier in the century in Britain and the USA. They were able, Greenberg suggests, to 'maintain a more effective monopoly over their skills over a longer period of time than unions in non-racial settings'. His conclusion that the Webbs' confidence in the 'incessant revolutionizing of industrial processes' may be misplaced in a racial order would seem to be correct.[56]

Unlike SABS who opened their union in an expansionary mood with a clear intention of transforming themselves into an industrial union, the IMS opened their union defensively and without any intention of expanding beyond the traditional moulding trade. How do we account for the different responses of SABS and the IMS? By 1979 mass production in large scale mechanized foundries had become dominant in South Africa, rendering the craft skill in the mass production foundries redundant. In the 1979 Industrial Council negotiations over job fragmentation a member of the NEC of the IMS stated the effect of these changes in clear terms:

> The problem was that the whole industry today was all on CO_2; at the foundry where he worked they were making every job with CO_2. The bigger foundries wanted to get rid of the moulder because they could put any size mould in a loose board . . . and they did not need a skilled man.[57]

However, because of the uneven transformation of the labour process, the craft of the moulder was still required for jobbing work, mostly in the smaller foundries. So long as jobbing work existed, employers assured the union, the skills of the moulder were required.

> There would never be enough moulders to handle jobbing work; there were always the jobs which companies could not afford to mount; they could not afford the money for the one-offs . . . sheer economics drive them into jobbing.[58]

Open or industrial unions, it has been suggested, are forced to rely on the strength of numbers and are therefore expansionist by nature. Over half of the total affiliation of the British TUC belongs to six unions only, out of some 180 affiliates in all.[59] Accompanying the rise of these large unions is the apparent comfortable survival, despite the general trend to merger and amalgamation among unions, of a number of relatively small organizations like that of the pattern makers. These smaller, stable unions, Turner suggests, are predominantly closed.

> They are restrictionist, not merely in the sense that they base themselves on a capacity to control the supply of labour to particular occupations and maintain an exclusive trend to employment within these occupations, but also in the sense that they have little intrinsic interest in increasing their numerical strength. Indeed, their interest lies rather in the opposite direction, of limiting the intake of labour to the jobs that they control and thereby restricting also the membership of the union itself. Thus the shape of British trade unions in general might be described as one in which open or expansionary unions have spread around islands of stable closed unionism.[60]

A fully restricted union, such as the IMS, is likely to make only those changes that are necessary to retain its restricted entry to moulding jobs. This, it believes, is possible with only limited constitutional change by simply opening the union to blacks. So long as jobbing exists in foundries the demand for the skill of the moulders will continue and their restricted entry into the trade can be maintained through the double closed shop.[61]

Faced by an incapacity to provide sufficient union members to fill union protected jobs, the three engineering craft unions discussed in this chapter opened their membership to Africans. As a result of these changes black metal workers were now confronted by two rival forms of worker organization in the foundry. In the next chapter we will examine some of the ways in which the emerging unions were to challenge the dominant position of the craft unions in the metal industry during the 1970s.

Notes

1   H.A. Turner, 'The morphology of trade unionism', in ed. W.E.J. McCarthy, *Trade Unions, Selected Writings* (Penguin, Harmondsworth, 1972), p.108.

2   *Ibid.*, p.108.

3   Letter from SEIFSA to members. Special exemption to deal with labour shortages, 15.10.1970. Records of MAWU housed in the Historical and Literary Papers Collection, University of the Witwatersrand Library, Accession No. AH 1077.

4   For a summary of the conflicting evidence on the skill shortage debate, see Chapter 6 of E. Webster, 'The labour process and forms of workplace organization in South African foundries', Ph.D. thesis, University of the Witwatersrand, 1983.

5   Bureau of Economic Research, University of Stellenbosch, 'A survey of contemporary economic conditions and prospects for 1961' (Stellenbosch, 1963), p.31.

6   *Education and the South African Economy*, Second Report of the 1961 Education Panel (Witwatersrand University Press, Johannesburg, 1966), p.25.

7   *Rand Daily Mail*, Johannesburg, 22.1.1980.

8   TUCSA, *Africans in Trade Unions?* (TUCSA, September 1972), p.31.

9   South African Institute of Race Relations, *Survey of Race Relations 1972* (Johannesburg, 1972), p.257.

10   *Ibid.*, p.258.

11   TUCSA, *Africans in Trade Unions?*, p.32.

12   IMS Records, NEC, 17.4.1975.

13   Autocast to National Industrial Council, 31.3.1978.

14   Interview with Du Plessis, Personnel Manager, Autocast, March 1980.

15   Autocast to NIC.

16   Autocast, *Quality in Quantity* (company publication).

17   IMS Records, NEC, 17.4.1978.

18   *Ibid.*, 27.6.1978.

19   W. Woodward, 'The economic evaluation of apprentice training', *Industrial Relations Journal*, VI, 1 (Spring 1975), p.34.

20   R1319, Gazette No. 6083, 23 June 1978.

21   C. Meth, 'Trade unions, skill shortages and private enterprise', *SALB*, V, 3 (October 1979), p.86.

22   F. de Clerq, 'The organized labour movement and state registration: unity

or fragmentation?' *SALB*, V, 6 and 7 (March 1980), p.34.
23 IMS records, NEC, 22.9.1979.
24 No. 3721, 1.12.1972.
25 South African Institute of Race Relations, *Survey of Race Relations 1972*, p.250.
26 *Ibid*, 1973, p.229.
27 In terms of Section 5(1)(a) and 5(4).
28 No. 5273, 3.9.1976, Supplementary Agreement.
29 *Ibid*, Clause 3.
30 IMS Records, NEC, 27.1.1977.
31 South African Institute of Race Relations, *Survey of Race Relations 1976*, p.316.
32 Riaan de Villiers, 'Clash looms on colour bar', *Rand Daily Mail*, Johannesburg, 2.5.1978.
33 South African Institute of Race Relations, *Survey of Race Relations 1978*, p.181.
34 Advocate Bassey, legal opinion on Section 35 for MAWU, 1978.
35 IMS Records, NEC, 25.5.1978.
36 This Act removed industrial training from the Department of Bantu Education and created a separate council to coordinate industrial training for Africans either through government training schemes, or else through generous government support for employer initiated schemes.
37 Interview with Van der Watt, conducted by M. Cullinan, 'Deskilling, technical and industrial training, and white craft unions', Industrial Sociology Honours, University of the Witwatersrand, February 1980.
38 These examples of job fragmentation are the result of an analysis of the foundry section of the Industrial Council agreement in 1944, 1949, 1950, 1951, 1952, 1955, 1956, 1960, 1968, 1970, 1974, and 1978.
39 All speeches at the SAEWA 1978 Conference are taken from *South African Journal of Labour Relations*, II, 4 (December 1978), pp.46-47.
40 *Ibid.*, p.47.
41 In November 1980 the three parallel electrical unions decided to set up a Federation of Electrical Trade Unions of South Africa. The unions retain separate organizations but are governed by a national council on which they have equal representation. The council meets every quarter. 'The possibility', Nicholson said, 'now exists for establishing one union, but the problem is we lose our three seats on the Industrial Council if we do.' Interview, August 1981.
42 *South African Journal of Labour Relations*, II, 4, p.47.
43 F. de Clerq, 'The organized labour movement', p.35.
44 See survey among union officials, E. Webster, 'The labour process', Appendix B, A2 and A4.
45 Interview with Van der Watt conducted by M. Cullinan, p.95.
46 *Ibid.*, p.95.

47   *Ibid.*, p.96.
48   See Chapter 9 for a detailed discussion of the skill level of MAWU members.
49   Interview with Van der Watt conducted by M. Cullinan, p.97.
50   Nicol wrote in 1980 that '[MAWU] had agreed not to oppose the formation of a new parallel union by [SABS] on condition that it only recruits black workers in skilled jobs'. M. Nicol, 'Legislation, registration, emasculation', *SALB*, V, 7 (March 1980), p.51. This oversimplifies the issue. MAWU was not in a position to oppose the extension of registration by SABS into skilled African grades as it had few members in those grades. Neither had MAWU agreed not to recruit in those grades. Increasingly the two unions are competing for similar members.
51   Interview with Van der Watt conducted by M. Cullinan, p.110.
52   IMS Records, NEC, 22.9.1979.
53   *Ibid.*, 24.11.1979.
54   *Ibid.*, 4.10.1980.
55   *Ibid.*, 19.1.1980.
56   S. Greenberg, *Race and State in Capitalist Development* (Ravan Press, Johannesburg, 1980), p.280.
57   IMS Records, NEC, 4.7.1979.
58   *Ibid.*
59   H.A. Turner, 'The morphology of trade unionism', p.98.
60   *Ibid.*, p.99.
61   Automation seems to have advanced furthest amongst welders in the engineering industry. They are members of SABS. The first industrial robots have now been introduced into the engineering industry on the Reef. Three were said to be in operation in welding by February 1982. The robots weld at up to three times the speed of the skilled man and require only one or two skilled welders to programme and supervise them. 'Three robot welders on the Reef', *The Star*, Johannesburg, 16.2.1982. In November 1979 *FWP Journal* organized a tour of overseas foundries and the editor reported on his return that 'robots are growing in popularity because they can replace workers in hazardous, unhealthy environments; reduce man-hours per ton and achieve higher quality castings with lower scrap rates. Industrial robots can be used to cope with the rising cost and general shortage of labour, lack of capacity, and to comply with various government regulations.' *FWP Journal*, November 1979, XIX, 11, p.62.

CHAPTER 8

The International Factor: The IMF in South Africa, 1974 — 1980

The role of international trade unionism in the development of black worker organizations in South Africa is a subject that has received little attention.[1] While this chapter does not attempt to evaluate all the activities of the International Metalworkers' Federation (IMF) in South Africa, it does provide a starting point for such an analysis by examining the regional activities of the metal workers' international — the IMF's South African Coordinating Council (IMF SACC).

The council was established in 1974 to coordinate the activities of all metal unions in South Africa. This chapter traces how the comfortable imperial relationship between the IMF and its local craft affiliates (the established unions) was challenged by the emerging unions in the 1970s. The council was to provide a lever and a platform for the beleaguered emerging unions, enabling them to establish a common position on certain key issues. As a result the council reflected the major struggles between the established and emerging unions between 1974 and 1982.

The IMF and South Africa

The International Trade Secretariats (ITSs) emerged in the late nineteenth century when craft workers in particular trades established international networks. In contrast to the First International (1864 — 1876), the ITSs were purely trade union bodies.[2] Whereas the First International covered issues ranging from the political rights of workers to the representation of their workplace interests, workplace issues were of central concern to the ITSs. This distinction was clear-cut by the time of the Second International (1889 — 1914), when political interest in socialism was represented through the political parties affiliated to that body.

The IMF was founded in Zürich in 1893. By 1981 it claimed more than 14 million blue and white collar worker members in 140 unions in more than 70 countries. Employed in machine shops, foundries, shipyards, steel mills, and automative, electrical, electronic and aerospace plants, these metal workers belong to the largest of the 14 ITSs.[3] Membership of the IMF is distributed as follows:

Europe	—	6 million
North America	—	3,5 million
Asia	—	2,3 million
Latin America & West Indies	—	1 million
South Pacific	—	260 000
Near East	—	100 000
Africa	—	200 000

As in other ITSs, its members are overwhelmingly from Europe, North America and Japan.

The rise of the multinational corporation in the post Second World War period led the IMF to recognize the need 'to oppose the united front of capital with the united strength of trade unions' everywhere these companies invested.[4] In 1966 World Company Councils (WCCs) were established linking together workers from all over the world in companies such as Ford, General Motors, Chrysler and Volkswagen.[5] In 1971 the 22nd Congress of the IMF concluded that multinational corporations 'play a divide-and-rule game calculated to pit each national group of workers against the others in this policy of buying human labour and raw materials in the cheapest markets'. Concern was expressed by some delegates from developed countries that jobs would be 'exported' to 'cheap labour' countries. South Africa was mentioned at this congress as an example of the way in which multi-national companies 'make full use of discriminatory domestic racism to maximize profits'.

This direct interest in black workers in South Africa by the IMF Congress was to place both the IMF Secretariat and its South African affiliates, the established unions, in a dilemma. The established unions, such as the South African Boilermakers Society (SABS), the South African Electrical Workers Association (SAEWA) and the Amalgamated Engineering Union (AEU), formed a privileged labour

aristocracy of skilled, mainly white workers who constitute a powerful caucus, the Confederation of Metal and Building Unions (CMBU).
These unions have over the years acted largely in the interest of their
predominantly white members, often at the expense of less skilled,
non-unionized, but numerically dominant black workers. In 1972 the
IMF sent a delegation to South Africa to examine this situation more
closely. In essence their report endorsed the CMBU perspective that
the founding of independent black unions was not practical. The best
possibility of building unions, they argued, was 'step by step through
the protective umbrella of a registered union', i.e., the parallel union
approach.[6] In making this recommendation, the delegation was ignoring the claims of the only existing emerging metal union at that time,
Jane Hlongwane's Engineering and Allied Workers Union (EAWU).

The IMF's uncritical acceptance of the view of black workers
presented by its CMBU affiliates was challenged by the outbreak of
mass strikes among black workers in Durban in 1973. In April of that
year a further independent black metal union, the Metal and Allied
Workers Union (MAWU), was established in Natal. At the 23rd
Congress of the IMF in 1974 it was recommended that 'all IMF
affiliates in South Africa should cooperate in organizing the unorganized workers in the metal industry'. EAWU, and an emerging
black motor union, the National Union of Motor Assembly and
Rubber Workers of South Africa (NUMARWOSA), attended this
congress, at the end of which it was decided to launch a regional committee of the IMF in South Africa — a decision consistent with the
general tendency inside the IMF to regionalize its structures. 'The S.A.
delegates', Hlongwane wrote later, 'found they did not know each
other and were not helping each other. After this event, with the
assistance of the general secretary of the IMF, the inaugural meeting of
the IMF SACC was held in Port Elizabeth in September 1974.'[7] In
addition to the CMBU members its founder members included the
four emerging unions, MAWU, EAWU, NUMARWOSA and its
African associate, the UAW.

Thonnessen, assistant general secretary of the IMF, began the
meeting by pointing out that few workers were organized in South
Africa:

> As a start, I suggest that trade union pressure should be applied to multi-
> national companies operating in South Africa to grant model wages,
> working conditions, trade union rights, etc. IMF affiliates in countries

with parent companies with subsidiaries in South Africa can and will put pressure on these companies to obtain full information about the treatment of black workers and to upgrade their conditions.

In order to exert this pressure the IMF would require 'regular information reports on the problems facing the black, coloured and white members in South Africa to be able to give positive assistance'.[8] The IMF was prepared to break the economic boycott of South Africa called for by anti-apartheid forces if, as a *quid pro quo*, local multi-national corporations with the cooperation of the CMBU would encourage trade union recognition.[9] Difficulties in implementing this strategy soon emerged. At the August 1975 meeting of the IMF the chairman reported a request from the Toyota World Company Council regarding Nissan-Toyota in South Africa. After noting the amendment to the General Laws Amendment Act which prohibited the furnishing of information to overseas companies, 'it was agreed that the consequence of contravening the Act is of such a serious nature that the IMF affiliates in South Africa should be advised of the provisions of this amendment and that the S.A. Coordinating Council should completely refrain from submitting any information such as that prohibited by the said Act'.[10]

Struggles Inside the Council

The council was to reflect four major struggles between the emerging and established unions between 1974 and 1980: the attempt by established unions to form parallel unions; the lack of support from the established unions in the struggle for recognition by MAWU; the attempt to establish democratic representation on the Industrial Council; and the role of the CMBU in the Eveready strike.

The first issue to emerge in the council was parallel unionism. On the basis of the support given to this strategy in the 1972 IMF report, Tom Murray, secretary of the SABS, had informed the inaugural meeting of the council that an important management 'had invited the SABS to organize African workers into a multi-racial union'. When it was pointed out by an established union that African unions often used 'union membership' as a party political platform, Murray made it clear that 'for over seventy years or more the trade union movement as a whole has never ever tolerated party politics'. Murray suggested instead that the emerging unions 'approach the registered unions when they have any problems that require the attention of the Industrial Council, and thus use the offices of the registered union as a means of rectifying their problems'. This line was supported by the other registered unions. The AEU felt 'it would be in the interests of these unions to seek the advice of the secretariat of the various registered unions before lodging complaints or endeavouring to put forward demands for an agreement'. The IMS declared that although it was opposed to a parallel union it was 'not against the establishment of black unions under the control of a registered union'.[11]

At the second meeting of the IMF SACC in March 1975 SABS declared that it was going to set up a parallel union at Metal Box under its guidance. Murray stressed that SABS had become involved 'at the express invitation of Metal Box, because they wanted a union with national representativity to take control of their employees'. He then said that management had suggested that a referendum be conducted in Metal Box 'to ascertain whether the employees are desirous of becoming unionized'. He appealed to all unions in Natal to encourage their members to vote in favour of SABS. Failure on their part to cooperate in this respect would result in Metal Box being unorganized for ever.[12] Alpheus Mthwetha, secretary of MAWU, objected to Murray's proposal, believing it to be unfair as an African union, MAWU, already existed in Natal. They should, he said, consult with the other African unions involved, including the South African Tinworkers' Union (SATWU), a founder member of SACTU. Murray dismissed SATWU as a union 'that in a matter of thirty years had only managed to organize 200 members'.

The referendum held in June came as a shock to SABS when workers overwhelmingly rejected a proposal to join it by 1 139 votes to 31.[13] Both MAWU and SATWU had called on members among Metal Box staff to vote against the proposal. MAWU rejected the proposal because it saw it as an attempt to preempt its own more democratic, non-racial approach in favour of a management-initiated, company-style union in collaboration with an established union that had shown no previous interest in organizing African workers.[14] By challenging SATWU, SABS had revealed an ignorance of the history of the struggle for recognition at Metal Box by a union whose history is deeply rooted in the Indian working class in Durban. In a letter to Metal Box after the rejection of SABS, SATWU said that 'the union had catered for its members (500 coloureds and Indians) for 38 years, and they see no reason to change now to something which they would have little say in'.[15] Again, they wrote to Metal Box, 'we have every reason to believe that the new body your company is contemplating to enforce on workers is going to be segregated in character with its entire office bearers and executive members consisting only of whites'.[16] Founded after the Durban Falkirk strike of 1937, SATWU had been an active member of SACTU. State harassment and managerial resistance in the early 1960s had restricted its active presence at Metal Box. Nevertheless its support among the workers was obvious from this referendum.

The first CMBU union to set up a parallel union was SAEWA when it established the Electrical and Allied Workers Union (EAWU) in 1978 in anticipation of the Wiehahn Commission recommendations.[17] Archie Poole of the coloured Engineering Industrial Workers' Union (EIWU) followed when he established the National Union of Engineering Industrial and Allied Workers (NUEIAW) as a parallel union for African workers in early 1979.[18] Faced by what they saw as 'unfair competition' the emergent unions turned to the council to arbitrate. A disputes committee was set up by the IMF SACC, its secretary recorded, 'because the existing unions have been denied facilities or recognition by management, whereas the parallel unions were formed at the request of management and enjoy facilities from management'.[19] In November 1979 this committee met to discuss an attack by Poole at the TUCSA conference on the emerging unions for being 'ineffectual'. In addition the committee was asked to arbitrate in a dispute between MAWU and EIWU over the organization of African workers at Non-Ferrous Metals in Durban.[20]

While the council had provided the emerging unions with a platform from which to attack the parallel unions, equal hostility was soon being expressed by workers themselves outside the council. After initial rapid recruitment boosted by management assistance, these unions faced a lack of credibility in the eyes of African workers as 'white controlled unions'. They were rapidly outpaced by the more militant emerging unions.[21]

The lack of concrete support on the council for the emerging metal unions was revealed in March 1976 when MAWU appealed to the council after Heinemann management had refused to recognize it, thus engineering a confrontation with the union. Instead of offering the union support, the council criticized it for its 'unethical approach to management' and set up a sub-committee of the council to visit

Heinemann, excluding MAWU from this delegation.[22] While the head office of the IMF in Geneva sent R1 000 to support the striking workers, the limits of international support were demonstrated when Rebhan, the general secretary of the IMF, tried to win support for black workers in the Heinemann plants in North America. He said 'none of the IMF affiliates has a collective bargaining agreement with any of the thirteen plants of Heinemann in the United States or Canada'.[23] The conclusion he drew from the Heinemann incident was that black metal workers should organize their recognition strategies around those companies that were well organized in Europe and America. He said, 'this is another important lesson which we have to keep in mind if we start to fight about the recognition of a black union by a multi-national corporation. The selection of a target should be made in the light of trade union strength in the mother country.'[24]

Scepticism about the IMF in South Africa, and its reasons for establishing the local council, existed inside MAWU from the outset.[25] But the union could gain little, it believed, by staying out of the council. 'If they stayed out of the Coordinating Council the established unions would gain financially and morally.'[26] Thus during the first three years of the council's existence (1974 — 1977) MAWU concentrated on testing the limits of the council's commitment to its shopfloor struggle. The Metal Box and Heinemann contests had demonstrated these limits. In October 1976 MAWU took this tactic one step further when it challenged the representativity of Africans drawn from liaison committees sitting as observers on the Industrial Council. MAWU suggested instead that only African representatives endorsed by representative unions should be allowed to take advantage of this concession. At the October meeting of the council they proposed that:

> at an industry level registered unions which are members of industrial councils will try to ensure that only representatives of African workers who have been endorsed by unregistered unions in the Coordinating Council would be admitted to, and given standing at, meetings of the Industrial Council.

MAWU's scepticism seemed confirmed when, after lengthy discussions, the established unions concluded that the proposal was 'too wide and far reaching for it to be acceptable in its present form'.[27]

The state's offensive against MAWU, unleashed in November 1976 with the banning of all four of its full-time organizers, revealed the intentions of some of the members of the council more clearly. After refusing to support MAWU's request that African observers on the Industrial Council have the support of the emerging metal unions, Nicholson promised at the January 1977 meeting that EAWU would be present at the Industrial Council negotiations that year in the capacity of an observer. No MAWU representatives were present at this meeting, having been told that the meeting was to be held the following day.[28] Nicholson made it clear that he believed MAWU was controlled by 'white agitators' and showed a clear preference for what he believed was the more moderate EAWU.[29] Jane Hlongwane, secretary of EAWU, had continued to receive support from the IMF SACC even after she was suspended by her executive in 1977 for allegedly autocratic methods. In fact the four emerging metal unions (UAW, NUMARWOSA, EAWU and MAWU) were to accuse the IMF secretary, Thonnessen, of 'interfering in the internal affairs of EAWU' and encouraging the establishment of a splinter union, the Steel, Engineering and Allied Workers Union (SEAWU).[30]

The first indication of a challenge to the established unions' control over the council emerged in January 1977 when Freddie Sauls, secretary of NUMARWOSA, raised the issue of the statement released by the Trade Union Council of South Africa (TUCSA) after the bannings of trade unionists in the previous year. NUMARWOSA had already become disillusioned with TUCSA, resigning in December 1976 when it was all but driven out of the Congress after sponsoring a motion that TUCSA affiliates should deregister and admit African workers. It had begun sounding out the idea of an alternative federation of like-minded registered and unregistered unions and a date had been set for March 1977 to discuss the feasibility of this idea.[31] Sauls queried what the activities were that were allegedly 'outside the ambit of trade unions', as TUCSA's general secretary, Grobbelaar, had said in his statement. At the March 1977 meeting of the council, MAWU successfully proposed that the council reject the minister's reasons for banning the trade unionists and condemn TUCSA.[32] The first effective challenge to CMBU control over the council now began to emerge.

The growing polarization within the council came to a head in November 1978 over the response of the CMBU members to the Eveready strike in Port Elizabeth. A strike had taken place when 320 coloured workers were dismissed after management had refused to negotiate with their union, NUMARWOSA.[33] At a special meeting of the council called in November NUMARWOSA opposed the resolution that a delegation should meet the Minister of Labour to discuss the role played by the Department of Labour in the dispute. NUMARWOSA opposed this decision as it was satisfied with the role that the Department had played. When the delegation, consisting of the CMBU members, met the minister and departmental officials, they were informed about the proceedings of the Conciliation Board meeting and given other information. As a result of the meeting, the CMBU delegates decided to launch an investigation into the strike and circumstances leading to it. CMBU representatives in Port Elizabeth met the local Department of Labour officials and together with a representative of Yster en Staal, which had members in Eveready, met the company management and spoke to the workers. Matters came to a head when the CMBU representatives reported back on their findings at a council meeting held on 29 November. There was an immediate clash with Sauls and he walked out, accompanied by representatives of all the emerging unions in the council.

According to various press reports, NUMARWOSA and the other unions involved in the walk-out accused established unions of siding with the government and management against NUMARWOSA. Delegates involved in the walk-out took the view that a member union had been undermined by the investigation without being consulted. Sauls said the delegation had acted outside its mandate, which was only to discuss the role of the Department of Labour. He said the walk-out was the culmination of the long-standing failure of some 'white unions' on the council to cooperate. 'They don't treat us as equals. They don't consult us and seem to care more about talking to management and the government than us.' The walk-out was seen by both sides as critical to the future of the council. Bower, general secretary of the SABS, wrote an urgent letter to the IMF headquarters in Geneva, claiming that NUMARWOSA was acting irresponsibly and appealing to the body to send a mediator to South Africa to resolve the dispute. At the beginning of 1979 Thonnessen came to South Africa and, after a week of negotiations, convened a council meeting on 20 January at which the rift was healed. A conciliatory statement suggested that lack of cooperation might have led to misunderstandings: attempts would be made to remedy this, and affiliates reaffirmed their determination to work in accordance with, and in the spirit of, the council's constitution. A full-time secretary would be appointed to improve the council's services to its affiliates.[34].

Collapse of the Council

However, in spite of these statements of good intent, the Eveready dispute reinforced the conviction of the black metal unions on the council that they should continue to meet as a regular caucus. In March 1979 they drew up a set of criteria for participation in the council identifying 'genuine shop-floor cooperation as the most important area'. They were concerned that existing divisions and prejudices should be overcome at the workplace if there was to be 'cooperation to the ultimate benefit of all'. Solidarity action over recognition and opposition to the presence of liaison committee members on the Industrial Council were also mentioned. The document concluded by suggesting that it was no longer acceptable for craft unions to 'use race as a means of protecting craft privilege'.[35] These five black metal unions were to come together with other independent unions in April 1979 to form the non-racial Federation of South African Trade Unions (FOSATU).[36]

With Ike van der Watt as chairman of the council and Bernie Fanaroff, an organizer in MAWU, as secretary, the CMBU members were no longer in complete control of the coordinating council. Two camps had emerged in the metal industry, representing two different styles of unionism. One, the CMBU group, emerging from a history of craft and race privilege, was attempting late in the day to open up to blacks, either through parallel unions or through opening membership to blacks in separate branches; the other, the emerging black unions, was struggling in the face of race discrimination to win basic trade union rights. After the establishment of parallel unions from 1978 onwards to take advantage of the change in the Industrial Conciliation Act, the relationship between the two camps was inevitably competitive. The unsuccessful attempt to get the council to act as arbitrator was the last straw. In April 1980 a fragile unity finally crumbled and the FOSATU metal unions withdrew from the council.

At the international level the conflict culminated two years later when, in June 1982 at the meeting of the IMF Central Committee in Rome, the FOSATU metal unions made allegations concerning the activities of certain IMF affiliates in South Africa. Written statements were filed about the activities of the Radio, Television, Electronic and Allied Workers Union, EIWU, SAEWA and the AEU. It was alleged that these unions practised racism, showed an attitude of paternalism rather than of cooperation, and in some cases actively undermined fellow IMF delegates.[37]

Five substantial charges were made against the CMBU members. Firstly, it was stated that, during disputes at Heinemann in 1976, Eveready in 1978 and Dorbyl in 1981, the unions concerned had undermined strikers and in some cases collaborated with management and the Department of Labour to force a settlement against the wishes of the unions involved in the disputes. Secondly, it was claimed that the unions had ignored requests to caucus about wage demands before wage negotiations in which they had been involved. Thirdly, they were accused of objecting to MAWU's registration application on racial grounds, contrary to internationally accepted principles and those of the IMF. Fourthly, it was charged that the four unions had submitted a memorandum to the Wiehahn Commission asking that blacks should be required to do military service on the border before they were given apprenticeship training. The fifth charge was that they had practised segregation either by working only amongst white workers, or by having parallel unions for workers of different races, which were dominated by the white unions. After considerable debate SAEWA and the AEU were expelled, while the other two unions were given a year 'to get rid of apartheid' in their organizations.

As the expulsion of these two leading CMBU members clearly showed, the impact of the international factor on South African industrial relations had been considerable. 'It is the first time', *FOSATU Worker News* noted, 'that a major international body has taken action against South African unions for practising apartheid.'[38] Initially dominant, the established unions had lost their hold over the council in the face of the growing challenge from the black unions. For these emerging unions the council provided both a platform and an opportunity to develop a common set of organizational principles. In the case of MAWU and the black motor unions — the UAW, NUMARWOSA and the Western Province Motor Assemblies Workers' Union (WPMAWU) — the council helped to cement an alliance that led to these unions playing an important part in the establishment of FOSATU.

What challenged the position of the established unions inside the council was not the intervention of the IMF but the self-organization of black metal workers in South Africa itself. Ultimately, the IMF had no power to direct events inside the IMF SACC. In a situation where the IMF accepted that it had to work within the status quo, the established unions continued to dominate the council. This confirms

Neuhaus's conclusion that 'the ITSs have very little power in their own right. Theirs is a proxy power: in implementing their decisions, especially in international actions, they depend on the voluntary backing of their affiliates, who jealously guard their autonomy.'[39] However once the balance of power began to shift and the lines were redrawn, the IMF acted decisively. Once charges were filed alleging racist practices in certain established unions, these unions were investigated and the racists expelled from the IMF. The effect that these expulsions will have on the CMBU and the IMF SACC, revived formally in 1983, remains to be seen.

Notes

1   For an analysis of international trade unionism see G.K. Busch of *The Economist* Intelligence Unit, *Political Currents in the International Labour Movement, Volume 1, Europe and North America*. For an argument that these international activities constitute a form of trade union imperialism, see D. Thompson and R. Larson, *Where Were You Brother?* (War on Want, 1978). For the Cold War nature of these activities in South Africa, in particular the attempt to set up alternatives to SACTU, see K. Luckhardt and B. Wall, 'Organize or Starve: The History of SACTU' (London, 1980), especially Chapter 11.

2   See W. Olle and W. Scholler, 'World market competition and restrictions upon international trade union policies', *Capital and Class*, No.2, pp.56-75.

3   R. Neuhaus, *International Trade Secretariats* (Fredrich Ebert Stiftung, 1981), p.71.

4   IMF 22nd Annual Congress, 26-30 October 1971. Personal collection.

5   Olle and Scholler, 'World market competition', p.65.

6   Report of the IMF delegation on their visit to South Africa, 11-27 March 1972, p.35. Personal collection.

7   J. Hlongwane, 'The emergence of African unions in Johannesburg with reference to the engineering industry', in J.A. Grey Coetzee, *Industrial Relations in South Africa* (Cape Town, 1976), p.207.

8   IMF SACC Minutes, 14.10.1974.

9   A gathering of international labour representatives called for a boycott of South Africa in 1973 in Geneva: 'International trade union conference against apartheid', in Luckhardt and Wall, *Organize or Starve*, p.101. Similar conferences have, of course, been called since then, but this was the most representative.

10 IMF SACC Minutes, 19.8.1975. In fact, provisions of this Act have never been used.
11 *Ibid.*, 14.10.1974.
12 *Ibid.*, 20.3.1975.
13 *Ibid.*, 19.8.1975.
14 Interview with Alpheus Mthwetha, 31.8.1981.
15 Letter from SATWU to managing director, Metal Box, 18.7.1975, FOSATU archives, Central Court, Durban.
16 *Ibid.*, 21.2.1975.
17 J.D. Farrell, 'Focus on labour in South Africa', *South African Journal of Labour Relations*, II, 4 (December 1978), pp.46-47.
18 'Shop floor battle looms', *Financial Mail*, 27.07.1979.
19 Minutes of the Disputes Committee of the IMF SACC, 25.10.1979.
20 *Ibid.*, 20.11.1979.
21 For a discussion of the ineffectiveness of the metal parallel unions see Chapter 10.
22 IMF SACC minutes, 12.3.1976.
23 IMF SACC, Rebhan to Bouwer, 4.5.1976.
24 *Ibid.*
25 See report on the discussion between MAWU (Natal) and the IAS in June 1975, IAS records.
26 Interview with Alpheus Mthwetha.
27 IMF SACC minutes, October 1976.
28 The MAWU was clearly under the impression that this was a deliberate exclusion. A letter from its secretary, June-Rose Nala, to the secretary of the IMF SACC on 20 March 1977 makes this clear:
    'The executive committee of MAWU is extremely disappointed that it was not possible to attend the council meeting in January 1977 due to the failure of the secretary to inform the union of the sudden change of date. They are particularly concerned that this prevented MAWU from raising and participating in discussion on the TUCSA action on bannings. How could proper discussion take place without those most affected being present?'
    Correspondence, IMF SACC.
29 'MAWU is controlled by white agitators and the black secretary [Nala] is simply a figurehead who couldn't move without the whites', interview with Ben Nicholson, SAEWA, August 1981.
30 'EAWU and the activities of the IMF in this matter', IMF SACC.
31 P. Bonner, 'Focus on FOSATU', *South African Labour Bulletin (SALB)*, V, 1 (May 1979), p.11.
32 IMF SACC minutes, March 1977.
33 This account of the strike is drawn from R. de Villiers, 'Eveready strike', *SALB*, V, 1 (May 1979), pp.25-26.

34   *Ibid.*, p.34.
35   Joint statement on the IMF SACC issued by EAWU, MAWU, NUMAR-
     WOSA, UAW and WP MAWU (which joined the council in 1978).
36   Bonner, 'Focus on FOSATU'.
37   'IMF expels two SA Trade Unions', *FOSATU Worker News*, July 1982.
38   *Ibid.*
39   Neuhaus, *International Trade Secretariats*, p.149.

PART 3

The Experiment Begins: The Search for a New Form of Control in the Workplace

Part II suggested that the contradictions generated by capitalist development, in particular the transition to monopoly capitalism, created a crisis of control in work relations. This crisis operated on two levels. On one level capital's need to increase the productivity of labour was limited by the success of the diluted craft unions in maintaining a monopoly over certain jobs. The increasing dilution of these jobs, previously held by whites, made the opening of the 'closed' unions a necessity for the protection of jobs. The withdrawal of state support for the racial exclusion of blacks from the Industrial Council system provided the opportunity for the IMS to open its membership to blacks.

The more significant crisis of control over work relations in the foundry arose from the racially despotic nature of management's control over black labour. As reliance on the white supervisor and his *induna* gave way to more sophisticated control through management-initiated liaison committees, growing resistance was encountered from organized black metal workers. Responding to the presence of a growing number of semi-skilled black workers in the industry, black unions emerged in the early 1970s. Yet management's strategy of preempting the union through the liaison committee, facilitated by the tactics of 'fear and smear', inhibited the transition of black metal workers from phase two (the struggle for recognition) to phase three (negotiating and maintaining an agreement). It was, ultimately, the popular struggle in the townships in 1976 that widened the nature of the crisis, forcing capital and the state to search for new forms of social control in the workplace.

The conclusion drawn from Part II of this study is that although capitalist development intensified race discrimination, the transformation of the labour process in South Africa led in the long run to the opening of closed unions and to the independent organization of black semi-skilled workers in industrial unions. But while this transformation of the labour process created new opportunities for workplace organization among semi-skilled workers, it would be misleading to explain these developments solely in terms of the labour process. This conclusion confirms the assertion made at the beginning of this study of the need to widen analysis of the labour process to take into account determinants that go beyond the workplace.

This emerges most clearly in Part III of this study when we turn to an examination of the Wiehahn/Riekert experiment which attempted to incorporate and redivide black workers. The experiment began in 1977 when the government set up a commission of inquiry to investigate labour law (the Wiehahn Commission) and a commission to examine the use of manpower (the Riekert Commission).[1] The Wiehahn Commission heard evidence from most of the parties involved in the engineering industry, although the unregistered unions expressed reservations about appearing before the commission because of the absence on that body of any representative from their unions.[2] Nevertheless their two central demands — the rejection of the committee system and the right of workers to join the organization of their choice — were forcefully put by the largest of the unregistered groupings.[3] When these commissions eventually reported two years later, they recommended the deracialization of the established industrial relations system by incorporating black workers into the Industrial Council system (the Wiehahn solution).[4] The other side of the incorporative strategy involved the redivision of African workers between those with permanent residence rights in the urban areas and those without (the Riekert solution).[5] In both cases the contradictions generated by the specific racial nature of South African capitalism led to worker resistance cutting across the incorporative strategy of the state and capital.[6] This resistance in the metal industry was facilitated, a month before the Wiehahn report was released, by the establishment of FOSATU on a nation-wide basis to coordinate and direct the responses of black workers.[7]

The incorporative strategy, and resistance to it, were to be sharply influenced by the widening economic crisis that hit the foundry industry in particular and the metal industry in general in 1982. The onset of recession was to lead, as we show in Chapter 11, to dramatic retrenchment of predominantly unskilled migrant workers. In extreme cases, as in B & S, plants have been closed down.[8] Increasing numbers of foundry managers have been persuaded to take advantage of capital subsidies and lower wage costs to relocate foundry production in border areas such as Brits (Autocast) or 'homeland' sites such as Isithebe in KwaZulu (Apex) and Dimbaza in the Ciskei (Dimbaza Foundries). This is usually accompanied by a desire to enter the international foundry market. Announcing that the giant multinational Lonhro company had bought a 51 percent interest in the Dimbaza Foundry, its production manager, Neville Rosser, observed that

> the foundry industry appears to be on the decline in developed countries, mainly due to the resources of minerals and labour that are available in developing countries. Obviously, having Lonhro as a partner, being relatively close to large mineral and labour pools, and having an under-utilized harbour on our doorstep places us in a strong position to break into the struggling foundry market overseas in a big way.[9]

This restructuring of the labour process in the face of economic crisis has threatened the delicate industrial relations system that was beginning to emerge on the shop floor. On one hand, the recession has strengthened management's position in negotiation, leading to a resurgence of the 'free market' ideology and a reassertion of 'managerial prerogatives'.[10] On the other hand, unions have demanded, and sometimes won, retrenchment procedures at plant level which have reduced the numbers of workers retrenched. The retrenchment of union members has highlighted the lack of adequate social security for black workers. The contradictory nature of the Wiehahn/Riekert strategy is now clear: attempts at deracialization in the workplace, unless they are accompanied by deracialization in the society at large, will lead to a widening, and not a narrowing of demands in the workplace. This contradiction is sharpened in periods of economic crisis. The effect of this differential incorporation of workers into the capitalist system is illustrated, in the conclusion, through a description of the home and work lives of the five foundry workers introduced in Chapter 1.

Notes

1   For the terms and composition of the Wiehahn Commission see P. Bonner
     and E. Webster, 'Background to the Wiehahn Commission', *South
     African Labour Bulletin (SALB)*, V, 2, pp.1-2; for the Riekert Commis-
     sion see L. Ensor and C. Cooper, 'Summary of the recommendations of
     the Riekert Commission', *SALB*, V, 4, pp.7-9.
2   'The government has also ignored the wishes and concerns of the
     unregistered trade unions by refusing to appoint to the commission
     anyone with any experience of the political problems of the members of
     these unions. It is not sufficient that an African has been appointed to the
     commission. What is required is someone with practical experience of the
     unregistered unions.' Press statement released by the unregistered unions
     after giving evidence to the Wiehahn Commission (for details of unions,
     see footnote 5).
3   Memorandum submitted to the Wiehahn Commission by the Council of
     Industrial Workers of the Witwatersrand (comprising the Transvaal
     MAWU), the Trade Union Advisory Coordinating Council (comprising
     inter alia Natal MAWU), the National Union of Motor Assembly and
     Rubber Workers of South Africa, and the United Automobile, Rubber
     and Allied Workers. They submitted joint evidence and represented in
     total 75 000 workers, the largest grouping of unregistered unions. They
     were to form FOSATU in April 1979.
4   For a detailed summary of the Wiehahn Commission see, 'The Wiehahn
     Commission: a summary', *SALB*, V, 2, pp.13-52. For a detailed critique
     see, 'Critique of the Wiehahn Commission and the 1979 amendments to
     the Industrial Conciliation Act', *SALB*, V, 2, pp.53-79. The commission
     and the White Paper are treated together as the basic framework for 'the
     solution' was laid by the commission.
5   For a detailed summary of the Riekert Report, see 'Summary of the
     Riekert Report', *SALB*, V, 4, pp.7-36; for a discussion of the report, see
     articles by Maree, Claasens, Duncan, Nattrass, De Villiers, Le Roux, all
     in *SALB*, V, 4.
6   Initially capital went along with the Industrial Council incorporative
     strategy but protested against the exclusion of migrant workers from
     unions. However, in the face of the 'challenge from below', capital was,
     as discussed in Chapter 11, prepared to enter into plant agreements out-
     side the NIC.
7   P. Bonner, 'Focus on FOSATU', *SALB*, V, 1.
8   J. Keenan, 'The B and S Closure: rationalization or reprisals?', *SALB*, X, 1.
9   Rosser, in *Induna* (King William's Town, December 1984), p.8.
10   'Barlow Rand and FOSATU', *Financial Mail*, 23.12.1983.

CHAPTER 9

Workers Divided: Labour Market Segmentation in the Foundry

A recent paper applied labour market theory to South Africa, formulating a model of racial dualism. Cassim postulates

> a white sector and a black sector which are the results of an historical process of segmentation of the labour market, in which the distribution of individual jobs and incomes has become dominated by the superficial characteristic of race.[1]

The racial dualism of the South African labour market is illustrated, he argues, by an examination of the occupational distribution of different race groups.

Table 9. The Occupational Distribution of Different Racial Groups

Occupational Category	Percentage of Race Group			
	African	Asian	Coloured	White
Professional and Technical	23.0	3.5	10.0	63.5
Managerial and Executive	2.0	2.0	1.0	95.0
Clerical	14.7	7.5	8.3	69.4
Sales	24.4	8.8	10.6	56.0
Production Workers	69.8	4.0	12.1	14.0
Unskilled	85.1	1.2	12.5	0.5

Source: Department of Labour Manpower Survey, 1979. Data in the above table excludes agricultural and domestic workers. Reproduced in F. Cassim, 'Labour Market segmentation in South Africa', African Studies Institute seminar paper, University of the Witwatersrand, 29 March 1982.

Such an examination indicates that the higher rungs of the labour market are dominated by whites, whereas Africans form the bulk of the lower end of the job queue.[2] However, a close examination of Table 9 reveals an intermediate category of coloured and Asian workers (for example, under the occupational category of unskilled the table records 85.1 percent Africans, 13.7 percent coloureds and Asians, and 0.5 percent whites). This threefold segmentation of the South African labour market is confirmed if we follow Cassim's advice and undertake a detailed microstudy of a particular labour market, namely, South African foundries.[3] Following Edwards, this chapter will distinguish between three labour markets — the secondary market, the subordinate primary market, and the independent primary market.[4] These segments are defined, he says, not by any fundamentally decisive characteristic but by a cluster of characteristics. To illustrate these characteristics, this chapter will refer to the biographies of men who work in the foundries, introduced in Chapter 1.

The Secondary Market

The secondary market consists in the first instance of jobs that require limited skill. These tasks are essentially repetitive, involving mostly manual effort from light duties to heavy physical tasks. They require only from one to a few days' induction. Here is a typical example:

> My job involves loading and finishing castings on a wheelbarrow and pushing the wheelbarrow to the grinding areas. On Saturdays I clean the knock-out area.[5]

The majority of the jobs could be classified as semi-skilled in that they require the acquisition of elementary skills. However, there is very little scope for initiative and decisions are characterized by the use of simple check lists.

What marks these jobs as secondary is the casual nature of the employment. The work almost never requires previous training and many of the tasks do not require any formal education at all. Fifty percent of the shop stewards had no formal schooling. They are simply hired, usually by the 'boss boy', on a trial basis and training is done on the job. One furnaceman said:

You are just put there at the fire, even though it is dangerous, and you do what the others do. Some people will take two weeks to get used to the job. Some people never adapt to the fear of the fire in the foundries. They get dismissed.

Given this situation, Claasen concludes, management's policy of not training workers but pushing them straight into these jobs makes more sense:

The jobs are so unskilled that productivity is much less a function of training than of being able to cream off the best workers. The selection process is achieved by the high ratio of dismissals. The slow and cheeky are quickly weeded out. Given the high rate of dismissals, to train people before dismissing them is a waste of money.[6]

A crucial feature, then, of the secondary labour market is that it offers virtually no job security. Yet, in spite of this the average tenure for secondary workers in foundries is very high. Thirty-four percent of the sample had worked for the same firm for over fifteen years, and 54 percent for over ten years (see Table 10).

Table 10. *Length of Service of Shop Stewards in a Sample of Foundries*

Number of Years	Percentage in the Same Firm	Percentage in the Same Job
0 – 2	0	16
2 – 4	12	46
5 – 9	34	12
10 – 15	20	22
15 – 30	30	4
30 +	4	0

Source: Data drawn from Shop Steward Survey

These figures, drawn from a sample of shop stewards, were compared with all black workers in the largest foundry in the sample. A detailed investigation of the 2 220 black workers revealed that 57 percent had worked for over ten years at the same firm and qualified for Section 10/1(b) rights. (Of the 2 220 black workers in March 1982, 1 100 had worked for over ten years. Two hundred were born in the area, and the balance of 920 were on contract.) Why do secondary workers have high tenure? These findings reinforce the view that it is the lack of job security and the ever present possibility of an immediate replacement by others from the 'reserve army' that marks a secondary job. This is underlined where the majority of workers only have the right to employment and residence in the urban areas, provided that they are in the employ of that firm. Fifty-four percent of our sample were contract workers, and another thirty-eight percent had acquired residence rights by continuous employment with one employer for over ten years (Section 10/1(b)). The power management has over the secondary worker and the dependence it creates on the part of workers is vividly illustrated by Sipho.

> Our employers don't treat us like human beings, but animals, because they know that as soon as they expel you you would lose a place of residence, because you would not be able to pay for the hostel fees without the money which they provide. And the pass office is going to be indifferent and will instruct you to go back where you come from. That is very painful.

Thus if some secondary workers respond to this insecurity by changing jobs frequently, others assess their chances differently and remain with one firm.[7] All secondary workers, however, mentioned a lack of job protection and the immediate possibility of replacement.

Wages in the secondary labour market in the foundries, including overtime, are on average below the household subsistence level (HSL).[8] Wages associated with secondary work range from one sixth to one third of the wages for independent primary jobs.[9]

This research seems to bear out the conclusion that the secondary market is indeed a distinct market, characterized by different market outcomes and different market conditions. Secondary jobs are dead-end employment in the sense that additional experience does not mean higher earnings. They are also dead-end jobs in the sense that the promotion ladder is confined to advancement within the secondary labour market.[10] As Edwards concludes:

> It contains low-pay jobs of casual labour, jobs that provide little employment security or stability. These are dead-end jobs offering little opportunity for advancement, and requiring few skills . . . . Since employers have little investment in matching workers and their jobs, they feel free to replace or dismiss workers as their labour needs change.[11]

The Subordinate Primary Market

In contrast to secondary jobs, primary jobs offer some job security, relatively stable employment, and higher wages — all primary jobs share the characteristic of offering well-defined occupations. 'The biggest group of subordinate primary jobs', says Edwards, 'are the jobs of the traditional industrial working class — production jobs in the unionized mass production industries; plant jobs in auto-assembly, steel making, machine manufacturing, etc.'[12] In the foundry the jobs of the unionized production moulders and core makers, held largely by coloureds, come closest to Edwards's concept of the subordinate primary job.

These jobs are distinguished from the casual labour jobs of the secondary market most fundamentally by the presence of a union, the IMS. Chapter 5 of this study indicated how the dilution of the craft nature of moulding was to reduce the significance of the apprenticeship system and place the closed shop at the centre of the IMS's defensive strategy.[13] Through this mechanism moulders were able to restrict entry into the job, control the supply of labour, and thus maintain the privileged income of the moulder. Here is a clear example of a worker-enforced segmentation of the labour market which lends support to Rubery's argument that labour market theorists have neglected the role of worker organization.[14] As a result of the union's closed shop the jobs of production moulder and core maker are better paid than the jobs in secondary employment, with a ratio of two, sometimes three to one.[15] In addition to the joint union-management medical aid fund and provident and life fund, the union also has its own funeral benefit, sickness and accident fund, and unemployment benefit fund.

On the other side, however, subordinate primary jobs are distinguished from independent primary jobs in that their work tasks are repetitive, routinized and subject to machine pacing. In Part I of this study the emergence of mechanized moulding was discussed, first in Durban Falkirk and then more extensively after the Second World War. The skills required are learned rather quickly, within a few days or weeks, and they are often acquired on the job. They offer the worker little opportunity for control over the job and were, from their inception, a threat to craft control. The nature of this threat to the craft worker was given a racial form when management introduced coloured workers as production moulders in the 1930s. Historically then, coloured workers were seen as part of an attempt to breach craft control and were brought reluctantly into the union to protect the white members. As the IMS argued in 1959 when applying for an exemption for coloured workers to belong to a separate branch of the IMS:

> Unless coloured production moulders were organized, they were likely to be a danger to the living and working conditions of our members built up by the society over a period of forty years'.[16]

Both constitutionally and in practice, control of the IMS remains firmly in the hands of the white National Executive Committee based in Johannesburg.[17].

In spite of the fact that some coloured workers have become craft workers (43 out of a total of 2 003 members of the society in December 1980), all coloured workers in the IMS share a common subordinate primary status because they do not exercise the same degree of control over the most important distinguishing characteristic of their market status — their union. The subordinate primary market, then, contains the jobs of the predominantly coloured production moulders and core makers.

Independent Primary Market

Jobs in the independent primary market differ from subordinate primary jobs in that they typically require skills obtained in advanced or specialized schooling; they often demand education; they are likely to have occupational or professional standards of performance; and they are likely to require independent initiative or self pacing.[18] Of the three groups of jobs that dominate the independent primary market — technical/supervisory, craft and professional — craft workers (grade A) will be considered here.

The central characteristic of the independent primary market — the possession of general and self-paced, rather than specific and machine-paced skills — is best illustrated by the artisans in the foundry — the pattern makers and the journeymen moulders. The pattern makers are the architects of the production process as they conceive of the pattern, i.e., the outside shape of the mould to be cast. The designing of patterns is a crucial aspect of the trade as the pattern maker has to ensure that the moulder will be able to make the mould into the shape in which the metal will be cast. The craft moulder is distinguished from the production moulder by the fact that he does not operate a machine: his skill lies in the tools of his trade.[19]

If occupational distribution in the foundries can be defined in terms of three racially segmented labour markets, what forces account for this division? 'Labour markets are segmented', Edwards says, 'because they express an historical segmentation of the labour process; especially, a distinct system of control inside the firm underlies each of the three market segments.'[20] Edwards distinguishes between three different systems of control inside the firm. The essence of the first, simple control, is the arbitrary power of foremen and supervisors to direct work, to monitor performance, and to discipline or reward workers — such a system can permit little job security.[21] The secondary labour market is the market expression of workplaces organized according to simple control.[22] The second form of control, technical control, emerges only when the entire production process of a plant or large segments of it are based on a technology that paces and directs the labour process.[23] The subordinate primary market contains these workplaces under the 'mixed system' of technical control and unions.[24] The third form of control, bureaucratic control, is the institutionalization of hierarchical power. 'Rule of law — the firm's law — replaces rule by the supervisor's command.'[25] The independent primary labour market reflects a bureaucratically controlled labour process.[26] Thus, for Edwards, the fundamental basis for division into three segments is to be found in the workplace, not in the labour market.[27]

Diagram 2. How Labour Markets Correspond to Systems of Control

Market	System of Control		
	Simple	*Technical*	*Bureaucratic*
Independent Primary (White)			Pattern Makers Journeymen Moulders
Subordinate Primary (Coloured)		Production Moulder Core Maker	
Secondary (Black)	'Cast-boy' Grinding Knock-out		

In essence, Edwards is turning labour market theory on its head; it is not lack of schooling or experience that explains secondary market, i.e., low black income; instead, blacks have secondary market jobs *because* of a system of control in the labour process. Such an analysis was already present in our account of the characteristics of the labour market; in fact, it forms a central expectation in the formulation of this study. Diagram 2 relates the evidence in this chapter to the Edwards hypothesis.

The Interconnection Between Control Inside and Outside the Foundry

While it is clear from the evidence in this chapter that the distinct form of control exercised on the job is crucial in shaping the labour market, this distinctiveness cannot be explained only by the type of control exercised over the job inside the firm. There is a vital interconnection between the form of control *inside* the firm and the form of control exercised over black workers *outside* the firm. The vast majority of secondary market jobs are occupied by migrant workers (most of them on contract) who, through influx control, constitute the most controlled and vulnerable section of the work force.[28] As a consequence, control over black workers inside the firm is facilitated by, and takes place within, the wider political context of white power and black powerlessness. It is the intervention of this racial state, primarily through influx control, which binds the black workers to dangerous and dirty secondary market jobs, and whites (and to a lesser extent coloureds), through the Industrial Council system, to more privileged primary market jobs.

The majority of secondary market jobs are occupied by men who are separated from their families in the rural areas (88 percent of the shop stewards had their families living either in KwaZulu or the Transkei). The men live in single sex hostels (either company or Administration Board owned), or as lodgers in the township or in servants' quarters in the white suburbs. In other words, their lives are defined by the geographical and institutional separation of the processes of maintenance (the day-to-day sustenance of the productive worker) from those of renewal (the rearing of children).[29] However, in spite of this separation they remain insolubly interdependent as reflected in the oscillating movement of migrants between work and home. On one hand, removal processes are dependent on income left over from maintenance, which is remitted home by the productive workers. On the other hand, productive workers require continued support from their families engaged in renewal at home, because they have no permanent legal or political status at their place of work.[30]

Although most of those who had families in the rural areas had some livestock and access to some land, 90 percent said they did not have enough land to survive on and their families were dependent on them for wages earned in the city. They indicated that their lands were not large enough for cultivation and that they would have to sell their livestock for an income. As one man put it:

> I do have access to land but the area is so dry that my family cannot feed themselves. They are dependent on the money I earn as a worker.

Even those few (three) who had larger numbers of livestock stressed the fact that their cattle were dying and that their families could no longer survive without their wages.

The precise nature of the legislation that controls the movement of black labour from countryside to town is crucial to any understanding of how control outside the foundry facilitates control of black workers inside the foundry. When rural African work-seekers reach the age of fifteen they must register and be classified under a particular category of work at the local labour bureau.[31] The work-seeker may not leave that area to take up employment elsewhere unless his contract for employment has been attested locally.[32] No contract may be attested for more than one year.[33] Permission to take up employment in the urban area can be refused by the municipal labour officer if adequate accommodation is not available.[34] Once the contract has been terminated the employee must return to his labour bureau, report to the local labour officer, and wait to be recruited again.[35] No black may remain in an urban area for more than 72 hours unless he/she qualifies for urban residence.[36]

In practice the labour bureau is increasingly being bypassed in the recruitment process in favour of either the 'one stop service' (an open requisition), or by 'shooting straight' (specific requisition).[37] The first system involves the Administration Board directly in recruiting and contracting labour in the rural area.[38] The second system, 'shooting straight', involves the workseeker making his way independently to the city, bypassing the rural control, finding employment, and then having his contract approved.[39] Those who manage to find legal employment by 'shooting straight' return with a specific requisition and the contract is then attested in the rural area. Foundry recruitment follows a similar pattern. (See Table 11).

Although an equal number of employers recruit through requisitioning the Administration Board ('one-stop service') as those who rely on worker self-recruitment ('shooting straight'), the latter practice is clearly against the Riekert Commission's recommendations accepted in the White Paper. These recommendations favoured employers giving preference to local (Section 10/1(a) or (b)) labour and were strongly opposed to employers recruiting labour illegally in the urban area, i.e., employing those who were 'shooting straight'.[40] Since 1980 the East Rand Administration Board has encouraged employers on the East Rand to accept these recommendations.[41]

Table 11. *Methods of Recruitment Among a Sample of Foundry Employers*

	Number	Percentage
Requisition Administration Board	17	47
Self-recruitment, often by word of mouth or homeboy networks	17	47
Employers themselves recruit in the rural areas	2	6

Source: Foundry Management Survey.

However, the Riekert Commission also found that workers with Section 10/1(a) or (b) rights would rather remain unemployed than accept work not to their liking, especially manual work.[42] It pointed out that, apart from mining, the sector for which most contract labour was 'imported' was the manufacturing industry where manual labour was unpopular with urban Africans.[43] These observations were confirmed by the Foundry Management Survey in which nineteen (53 percent) employers indicated a clear preference for 'homeland labour' rather than local labour.[44] Most of the employers felt that local labour was not prepared to work in the foundry as the work was too exacting:

Locals don't want to work in the foundry.

Locals say it's too heavy.

Homeland labour is still quite happy to work with a pick and shovel.

Town labourers are not too keen on manual labour.

Employers also felt that homeland labour was more compliant and 'reliable':

Homeland labour is very reliable and has a very low turnover.

Homeland labour works harder and they are more obedient and conscientious.

Locals do not want to do this kind of work.

Local labour is drunk, rebellious and if they have a disagreement with you they pull out a knife and stab you, especially the young ones.

Others stressed the 'loyalty' of the rural worker because they are subject to influx control.

They aren't so free to change and are consequently more loyal and they stick with the job.

One employer mentioned that it was easier to prevail on homeland labour to work overtime as they often lived in the company's hostel.[45]

Increasingly the East Rand Administration Board has been forced to give employers an exemption to requisition for foundry labour in the 'homelands'. The growing pool of unemployed labour in the rural areas is the single most important factor facilitating control over secondary market jobs. Claasens found in 1978 that in seventeen of the KwaZulu districts she visited, no evidence could be found of recruitment for manufacturing.[46] She concluded that in certain districts of KwaZulu a process of marginalization is occurring — a process whereby a growing number of unemployed join the ranks of those who will never be absorbed into wage labour. In Mahlabatini, for example, the number of requisitions of labour from employers outside the district has steadily declined: in 1974 twenty-three requisitions, 1975 eighteen, 1976 sixteen, 1977 six, 1978 seven. Two further studies report a similar process of withdrawal of recruitment from the remote rural areas. The Labour Research Committee (LRC) conclude that:

in general, workers in the bantustans may only get what are known as contract worker jobs, the jobs that city people refuse. However, the people in the most remote areas do not even have access to the full range of contract worker jobs as do those in the less remote areas. They are on the bottom of the scrap heap of the industrial reserve army.[47]

Greenberg and Giliomee conclude that:

While previously TEBA relied upon labour agents to seek out labour in the remote rural areas, the ready supply of labour in recent years has made such a network superfluous . . . but the demise of the agents, a Transvaal official observed, is 'one of the penalties of the oversupply of labour'.[48]

As Sipho remarked:

We get lower jobs than township people. In those plants where workers are gently treated we are not needed. We are only needed in those places where there is rough work.[49]

The Contradictory Nature of Migrant Labour

Control over the black labour force outside the foundry, in particular the system of migrant labour regulated through influx control, facilitates control over black workers inside the foundry. Yet, while clearly the existence of migrant labour has an important function in cheapening, controlling and dividing the work force in the foundry, to emphasize how functional migrant labour is for capital is to underplay its contradictory nature. The functions of migrant labour for foundry employers must first be summarized.

In the first place migrant labour performs an economic function. Migrant labour provides employers with access to a large 'reserve of labour' from the 'homelands'. These unemployed workers, through active competition on the labour market, exercise a continuous downward pressure on wages, disciplining those in wage labour. Migrants end up doing the least desirable jobs on the labour market — those jobs the employer would have to improve if there was a free choice of jobs. Migrant labour also irons out the upswings and downswings in the economy, providing access to labour that can be drawn on and expelled at little cost to employers. Above all a system of migrant labour lowers the cost of reproduction of labour power. In other words it cheapens labour power. However, this last point raises the question: cheaper for whom?[50]

Migrant labour cheapens the cost of foundry labour for the individual employer because he need only pay the cost of maintenance — the costs of renewal are displaced to the reserve economy. It is sometimes suggested that high labour turnover accompanies migrant labour, and is costly for employers because migrant labourers are less likely to acquire skills in their work.[51] However, as indicated in Table 11, long service in the foundry is common among contract workers. Through the 'call-in card' system management can minimize the cost and inconvenience of having to renew the contract annually. The cost to the state of renewing labour is also cheapened — functions normally performed by the state, such as provision of welfare facilities, education, social security and housing — are transferred to the reserve economy and the provision of urban amenities is limited to those required by single productive workers only.

Burawoy, however, points out that the question of whether migrant labour is cheap for a particular employer involves an examination not only of the direct costs experienced by that individual employer, but also of secondary costs such as taxation appropriated by the state.[52] Savage, for example, concluded that it cost R112.8 million, at a conservative estimate, to implement influx control over a single year (1974).[53] He arrived at this figure by costing arrests and summonses, patrolling and policing; prosecuting; loss of production; costs of imprisonment; issuing and updating documents, and operating labour contracts, labour bureaux, aid centres and transit camps. The additional cost of subsidized transport must, with the increasing price in petrol, be a major item in secondary costs. H. Houghton calculated in 1964 that if one assumed that the average contract was for eighteen months, migrants would travel an extra 370 million man miles each year, in addition to the normal daily journey to work.[54] By posing the question 'Cheaper for whom?' Burawoy may have simplified the problem, but the question still needs to answered.

In the second place migrant labour facilitates management's control over black workers. Contract workers are only legally entitled to live in an urban area so long as they are in the employ of a particular employer. Hundreds of blacks are sent to jail every day by commissioners' courts for being in urban areas longer than 72 hours without permission and for failing to produce their reference books on demand. In a study of pass offences Monama and Dugard found that typical pass offenders appear in court without legal representation and are tried, convicted and sentenced in less than three minutes.[55] If contract workers go on strike they can be dismissed and then endorsed out of the urban area. Other migrant workers are readily available as strike breakers in such a situation. Recently in one foundry, the union organizer said, union members were on strike and most of them were dismissed.

> That company had already started recruiting migrant workers before the workers were dismissed . . . that suggests management is always looking for migrants to replace those on strike, because they realize it is difficult for the local people to take the jobs of the striker and instead they go to the homelands because the people in the homelands are not well informed about trade union activities.[56]

Furthermore, a 'troublesome worker' or a worker dismissed for striking may find that he has been blacklisted. Troublesome workers may find that their contracts are not renewed at the end of the year. 'Take the question of call-in cards', one personnel manager said. 'The managing director has instructed me to draw up a black list of all union members and they intend not to renew their contracts.'[57] The dismissed worker may find another job, but when he goes to reregister his new contract his previous employers may refuse to transfer the contract.[58]

Less dramatically, contract workers are often controlled in their jobs through employer accommodation. Josias, for example, was suspicious of his employer's motive for building a company compound. He wanted an assurance that the compounds would not be used to control workers — if contract workers lost their jobs, he said, they would lose their accommodation and be ineligible for registration until accommodation was found elsewhere.[59] In addition, of course, contract workers have an incentive to stay on in the job hoping to qualify for permanent status.

Finally, migrant labour functions to divide workers. There are social and cultural differences between the migrants and urban people. Peskin and Spiegel conclude their analysis of hostels on the Witwatersrand by suggesting that

> migrants tend to be perceived by township residents as being culturally and geographically separate from the townships. There are various

derogatory terms coined by township residents such as *amaoveralls* (the overall wearers) that accentuate their aloofness from the hostel dwellers and illustrate the general attitude of disdain.[60]

More significantly, these cultural and social divisions coincide with the division of labour in the foundry. Respondents interviewed perceived this connection:

We contract people are different; we do the rough work while the location people do the easy work.

Or:

We from the homelands are much poorer — the others despise us. The local people don't like work and they can choose the jobs they like. As for us, if an *induna* fires us we are grabbed and arrested.[61]

Some have suggested that migrant labour divides the working class into two strata, giving the indigenous working class a consciousness of themselves as a 'labour aristocracy'.[62]

While it is clear from this summary that migrant labour performs an important function for capital, a functionalist explanation underplays important contradictory effects of migrant labour. In the first place, herding together large numbers of contract workers into hostels facilitates communication between them, making trade union organization easier. The MAWU Transvaal secretary, also a resident of the Vosloorus Hostel, explained that

it is easy to get hold of everyone in a hostel. It is an advantage when you organize. They are close to each other, living in the same conditions. It brings together a lot of different factories, some times ten representatives in one room. And they preach unions to each other all the time.[63]

Another union organizer stressed the advantages of organizing inside the compound, once access has been gained:

We started organizing in the foundry in May 1980 and we used to meet guys outside the compound and explain to them about the union. We did this for three days and then the security guards dismissed us off the property. After that we went into the compound secretly and signed up people. Through this method I got about ten members and security could not touch us. I would visit them in their rooms and we managed to get about six hundred members this way. Then I wrote to the personnel manager and asked for access to be granted to the compound. Once access was granted in February 1981, membership increased very rapidly. It was easy to organize as all the workers were in one place.[64]

In the second place the presence in large hostels (such as Vosloorus with 15 000 men) of large numbers of workers with a shared set of grievances generates two processes which Sitas regards as irreversible — a process of public class knowledge, and a process of defensive combination. Class knowledge is defined by Sitas as the public knowledge built from the experience of manual workers in such hostels as Vosloorus. The first and most immediate grievance that workers expressed was the fact that the hostel was dirty because it was not adequately serviced, in particular the toilets.[65] However, the grievance that workers felt most deeply about was the 'black-jacks' (municipal police) and their associated system of spies, the *impimpi* as they are called. The black-jacks are the front line of state control over migrant workers, constantly searching for illegal hostel residents and those who have not paid hostel rents. The main bitterness towards them arises from the fact that they wake residents in the middle of the night, banging on the metal doors. They talked at length on these grievances and how they intended to overcome them.[66]

But underlying all the hostel dwellers' grievances was a shared sense of having been deprived of a stable social life. Such grievances were usually expressed less directly — complaints about the lack of privacy (sixteen to a room); about the fact that they had to cook their own food after a long day at work; about stealing; about excessive drinking over the weekends; and about violent assaults.

This process of 'public class knowledge' is linked to the process of defensive combination. Migrants are already combined, Sitas says, the moment they enter the hostel or the factory. People from the same region or clansmen will immediately organize their lives on group lines.[67] Most of the respondents to the shop steward survey said they had been recruited through their fellow workers or the hostel. Few mentioned the union organizer. Workers usually joined the union in groups. In the case of Rely Precision, the first group of workers joined in July 1979 and by May 1980, 55 of the 60 workers had joined — a few groups every month. They came from three different districts in KwaZulu, lived in Vosloorus Hostel, and consequently shared a common set of grievances.[68]

However, it is at the workplace that these men become aware of their common interests. 'The first thing that makes people aware of their unity', said Sipho, 'is that they learn it in the factories.'[69] Contrary to conventional wisdom and the conclusions of the Wiehahn Commission, migrant workers were not less but more responsive to trade unions than local workers in the foundry.[70] Claasens concluded that this was so because of their bad wages, bad conditions and vulnerability.[71] Migrants are more militant, one shop steward said, because they are in jobs where conditions are worse. He argued that because migrants have such a small chance of getting other jobs, they concentrate on trying to improve the conditions in the factories where they must work.

> It is very difficult to change the factories because of the contract. All you can do is join the union to improve your situation.[72]

This was contrasted to the situation of permanent people. A common argument is that permanent people are in a good position in the firm:

> They are not so poor, they are satisfied with conditions. They don't have to be committed to struggling because they can always change jobs if they don't like their conditions.[73]

In an interview the organizer summed up his view of the function of migrant labour and how to challenge it:

> Influx control says that one cannot live in an area because of the colour of your skin . . . . As I mentioned earlier there can be no change without the contribution of the working class. It is not going to be an easy thing for the authorities to change their mind or for the regime to change from what it is at this point in time and scrap influx control . . . except if workers can be the ones that can be pushing them by means of negotiation and possibly there can be mass action planned by workers to protest against the whole system . . . . Influx control was due to the introduction of capitalism and capitalism is the one that has been in favour of influx control in order to control the labour force that is floating into the towns. That is why they have got things like influx control — to control how many people must be in the cities and how many people must be left out. So that when the people that are employed in the cities turn against their employers, and the employers

know very well that there are many people in the reserves so that they can replace the people that are against them.[74]

The union's awareness of the way in which migrant labour acts to control, divide and cheapen the work force is clear, as is the union's belief in the importance of worker organization in resisting the state's strategy (the Riekert solution) aimed at redividing workers.

In this chapter the racial division of labour in the foundry has been conceptualized in terms of three racially segmented labour markets — the independent primary labour market (Bob and Len), the subordinate primary market (Morris), and the secondary labour market (Sipho and Josias). These segmented labour markets, Edwards suggests, arise because of an historical segmentation of the labour process.

But while the labour process is crucial in shaping these labour markets, there is a vital interconnection between the form of control inside the foundry and the form of control exercised over black workers outside the foundry. The vast majority of secondary market jobs are occupied by migrant workers who, through influx control, constitute the most controlled and vulnerable section of the work force. However, explanations that focus on the function of migrant labour underplay important contradictions generated by migrant labour that make these workers a militant force in the foundries on the East Rand. Facilitated by changes in the labour process that have encouraged the emergence of industrial unionism, these unions have begun to challenge the state's strategy of redividing workers. This has focussed workers' attention on the need to challenge influx control if they are to change their labour market status from the secondary to the primary labour market.

Notes

1   F. Cassim, 'Labour market segmentation in South Africa', seminar paper (29.3.1982), African Studies Institute, University of the Witwatersrand, p.11.
2   *Ibid.*, p.13.
3   A total of 8 065 employees were employed in the 36 foundries interviewed in the foundry survey.
4   R. Edwards, *Contested Terrain: The Transformation of the Workplace in the Twentieth Century* (Basic Books, New York, 1979), Chapter 9.

5   Survey of foundry management.
6   A. Claasens, 'Riekert and Wiehahn: union and migrants', Industrial Sociology Honours dissertation, University of the Witwatersrand, 1980.
7   P. Stewart, 'Pushing the frontiers of control: a shop floor struggle', *Africa Perspective*, No.19.
8   On my calculations the average worker received R13.15 per week less than the Household Subsistence Level for the area. See Memo to the Secretary, Light Castings Shop Steward Committee, 22.2.1982.
9   See Table 11 of 1980 IMF survey on wages and social conditions in the foundry, compiled by B. Fanaroff and E. Webster.
10 Claasens, 'Riekert and Wiehahn', p.92.
11 Edwards, *Contested Terrain*, p.170.
12 *Ibid.*, p.171.
13 See Section 23 of the Industrial Council Agreement for the closed shop clause.
14 See J. Rubery, 'Structured labour markets, worker organization and low pay', *Cambridge Journal of Economics*, II, 8 (March 1978), pp.17-36 for an extended critique along these lines of dual labour market theory. Edwards illustrates the conventional neglect of worker organization: 'With a few noteworthy exceptions . . . the notion of worker-enforced segmentation does not seem plausible.' (pp.164-165).
15 1980 IMF Survey.
16 See Chapter 5.
17 Rule 31(3), Union Constitution.
18 Edwards, *Contested Terrain*, p.174.
19 See Chapter 2.
20 Edwards, *Contested Terrain*, p.170.
21 *Ibid.*, p.183.
22 *Ibid.*, p.178.
23 *Ibid.*, p.113.
24 *Ibid.*, p.178.
25 *ibid.*, p.21.
26 *Ibid.*, p.178.
27 *Ibid.*, p.178.
28 Estimates of the proportion of migrants in basic metal give a figure of 80-90 percent. See Sitas, 'Drought in the city', paper delivered at the University of the Witwatersrand History Workshop, 1980, p.33, and M. Lipton, *Optima* II/III, 29, p.91.
29 See M. Burawoy, 'Migrant Labour in South Africa and the United States', in T. Nichols, *Capital and Labour: A Marxist Primer* (Fontana, Glasgow, 1980), pp.138-139.
30 *Ibid.*, p.139.
31 Section 6(1) and 7, Regulations for Labour Bureaux at Bantu Authorities,

Government Notice No.R.74, *Gazette Extraordinary*, No.2029, 29.3.1968.

32 *Ibid.*, Section 21.

33 *Ibid.*, Section 13(1).

34 Section 27(a) of the Black Urban Areas Consolidation Act No.25 of 1945.

35 *Ibid.*, Section 6(2).

36 An exemption to be in an urban area is given if a black person qualifies for urban residence by birth (Section 10/1(a)) or continuous employment for not less than ten years or for not less than fifteen years (Section 10/1(b)) or as a wife or dependant of someone who qualifies under (a) or (b).

37 See S. Greenberg and H. Giliomee, 'Labour bureaucracies and the African rural areas: a field research report' (Urban-Rural Workshop Report 82/8, Institute of Future Research, University of Stellenbosch, 1982) for a discussion of this distinction.

38 'The East Rand and North Central (Pretoria) administration boards send their requisitions for labour directly to the Northern Transvaal (admin.) board which proceeds to recruit and contract for labour, with only formal reference to the homeland officials . . . . How the introduction of the administration board into the homeland serves to further control is best described by an administration board official: "The ideal is that his documentation should be ready when he leaves his homeland. That is why we are trying to get this one-stop system to work. This is a form of influx control. That is the ideal — before a person leaves the homeland, he must have a job and accommodation."' *Ibid.*, p.5.

39 *Ibid.*, p.20.

40 For a summary of Riekert, see *South African Labour Bulletin* (*SALB*), V, 4, p.22 in particular.

41 For ERAB see interview in Claasens, 'Riekert and Wiehahn', p.39; and foundry survey. For a discussion of the application of the urban black labour preference policy on the Witwatersrand, see Black Sash Report February 1981 — January 1982, Johannesburg.

42 *SALB.*, V, 1, p.13.

43 *Ibid.*, p.27.

44 Seven (19 percent) said they preferred locals because of administrative difficulties. Ten (28 percent) said it made no difference.

45 Similar conclusions were reached by a survey among eighty migrant workers on the East Rand conducted by the Economic Research Committee at the University of the Witwatersrand in 1979-80. See p.44 of the unpublished report for a summary of migrant worker attitudes. See also Morris and Kaplan, 'Labour Policy in ISCOR', *SALB*, II, 6 (January 1976); for employers' reasons for preferring 'homeland' labour, see *ibid.*, p.26.

46 *SALB.*, V, 4, p.57.
47 *SALB.*, VI, 7, p.64.
48 Greenberg and Giliomee, 'Labour Bureaucracies', pp.13-14.
49 Stewart, 'Pushing the Frontiers', p.81.
50 Burawoy, 'Migrant Labour', pp.140-143. For a discussion of the reasons for the ultra-cheapness of black labour, see F. Johnstone, *Class, Race and Gold* (Routledge and Kegan Paul, London, 1976), pp.34-45.
51 F. Wilson, *Migrant Labour* (Ravan Press, Johannesburg, 1972), pp.174-175.
52 Burawoy, 'Migrant Labour', p.142.
53 *African Affairs*, LXXVI, 304 (July 1977).
54 Wilson, *Migrant Labour*, p.177.
55 *Rand Daily Mail*, Johannesburg, 6.3.1979.
56 B. Goldblatt, Interview with shop steward, Industrial Sociology II research project, University of the Witwatersrand, October 1981.
57 Interview with personnel manager of East Rand foundry, November 1981.
58 For further evidence of this practice, see *SALB*, VI, 7, p.81.
59 Goldblatt, Interview, p.24.
60 E. Webster, 'Stay-aways and the black working class: evaluating a strategy', *Labour, Capital and Society*, XIV, 1 (August 1981), pp.10-38.
61 Claasens, 'Riekert and Wiehahn', p.53.
62 See, for example, Castles and Kosack, 'The function of migrant labour in Western European capitalism', *New Left Review*, 73 (May/June 1973), pp.3-18. They use the concept of labour aristocracy.
63 Interview with Transvaal regional secretary of MAWU, November 1981.
64 Interview with Wadeville organizer of MAWU, November 1981.
65 Stewart, 'Pushing the frontiers', pp.71-72.
66 *Ibid.*, pp.55-59.
67 Sitas, 'Drought in the city', p.50.
68 Analysis of union records, June 1980.
69 Stewart, 'Pushing the frontiers', p.60.
70 For the Wiehahn conclusions on migrant labour, see paras 3.58.1; 3.58.2; 3.58.7.
71 Claasens, 'Riekert and Wiehahn', p.45.
72 *Ibid.*, p.48.
73 *Ibid.*, pp.41-48 for a discussion of this issue.
74 Goldblatt, Interview, pp.20-21.

CHAPTER 10

Reform from Above: First Steps in the Deracialization of the Industrial Council System

It has been shown — in Chapter 7 — that the engineering craft unions opened their membership to blacks, a development that will now be considered further. Meanwhile, how have the other trade unions which are party to the National Industrial Council (NIC) responded to the tentative attempts at deracializing the industrial relations system in the period of the Wiehahn Commission and after?

The first response from a union within the NIC — Yster en Staal — expressed a keen sense of betrayal. 'To my mind', said Wessels Borman, general secretary of the Y & S:

> the report boils down to nothing less than a plea for total labour integration which in turn will eventuate into social integration of all races . . . if the report is accepted . . . it must be clearly understood that the fault should not be sought at the door of white workers and their unions — evidently notice was only taken of certain representation.[1]

Although the Y & S was supportive of the National Party in the early apartheid period, after the 1960s it placed less faith in the state as the guardian of its position. Some members of the Y & S had shifted their support from the National Party to the Herstigte Nasionale Party (HNP). When statutory job reservation failed, as in the engineering industry of the early 1960s, they were forced to accept the necessity of 'African advancement', and sought to control the pace of change by demanding that white workers were either retrained or promoted to supervisory positions. This phase culminated in the 1978 Agreement which, it was suggested in Chapter 7, increasingly relocated white workers to supervisory positions.[2] Thus Borman's opposition to the Wiehahn Commission's recommendations on job reservation were qualified by his statement that job reservation should only be abolished where effective protection for 'minority groups' had been established:

a process of demarcation which reached the absurd level of literally drawing lines between black and white workers on the shop floor in one case study of the application of Section 35 of the Agreement.[3]

The nub of the Y & S's opposition to Wiehahn was the Commission's recommendation that the state should recognize black unions. 'Blacks', Borman said, 'are not ready for trade unions. Liaison committees should be continued.'[4] Clearly black unions were seen as a political threat: 'since pressure for one man one vote will continue, a concession as far as trade union rights are concerned can only be seen as a step in this direction'.[5] Furthermore, he said, 'blacks don't want mixed unions. Unions will never be multi-racial. Whites don't want it and blacks don't want it. TUCSA tried and failed; unions should either be black or white.'[6] Yet even here there is a certain ambiguous acceptance of the inevitability of change, suggesting that in part their opposition was rhetorical. 'When we saw that black unions were inevitable we insisted that they must be registered. Now there is resistance to registration. Why is that? It makes us think we were right from the start.'[7] More pragmatically, one Y & S shop steward said that 'I don't object to blacks being setters provided they get paid the same as whites. Black unions will come. Some of them are already joining the Boilermakers' Society.'[8]

The Y & S, along with the Mineworkers' Union, were to oppose the pace of change envisaged in the recommendations of the commission at a meeting of the South African Confederation of Labour (SACL) on 11 May 1979. However, when they lost their motion by 13 votes to 11 (5 abstentions), the Y & S urged further consultation with the Minister of Labour and not direct action.[9] Even the much feared 'white backlash' from the shop floor did not materialize as anything more than mass meetings where racist statements about black workers were made.[10] In fact the SACL's membership had been steadily declining. In 1975 it had 25 affiliates with 206 511 members. By the end of 1980 it was down to 132 211 members with 15 affiliates. Besides the divisions within the confederation as to how to respond to Wiehahn, important affiliates such as the South African Technical Officials were expelled when they decided to open their membership to coloureds.[11]

The second response — that of the three engineering craft unions identified in Chapter 7 — involved opening membership to blacks, either by establishing parallel unions as SAEWA did, or by applying for permission to recruit blacks, which was the course chosen by the IMS and SABS. These unions opened their membership to blacks, it has been shown, in an attempt to control entry into the job.

Greenberg suggests that the reason for these differences in the responses of the Y & S ('exclusive industrial unions') and the engineering craft unions ('artisan unions') lies in their different capacity to control entry into jobs: artisan unions are not threatened by the organization of African workers because they control the job, whereas industrial unions depend on organization at their workplace and the protection of the state.[12] However, the homogenization of the labour process in the engineering industry has made craft skills increasingly less central to the 'artisan unions' position. (See Parts I and II of this book.) In particular, distinctions between the Y & S and the other engineering unions have been blurred. In the survey among union officials conducted in 1981, the Y & S had a forty percent proportion of journeymen; this was more than the IMS (thirty-three percent), the same as the AEU, but less than SABS at fifty percent, and SAEWA at ninety percent.[13]

Although the engineering craft unions differ in their strategies towards black unions — whether they should be racially separate branches or parallel unions — they all aim to incorporate African unions into the present NIC. Increasingly, in the face of the challenge from below, this incorporative strategy points to a restructuring of the NIC. However, over the forty years of its operation in the engineering industry, the NIC system has come to exemplify, for the trade unions party to it, the conditions for stability in the industry. From the trade union point of view it has functioned not in their interests only but also in the interest of the employer. Faced by the threat of statutory job reservation in the late 1950s the craft unions defended the Industrial Council system for reasons such as those put forward by the secretary of the IMS, Cliff Crompton:

> without industrial council agreements the wage bill would be an unknown factor;
>
> the employers cannot be undercut by a rival tenderer employing cheaper wage rates and lesser conditions than the conditions he extends to his own workers;
>
> there are less disputes and wildcat strikes within the workshops where labour is organized and the shop steward well knows that there is likely to be serious repercussions involving himself in particular should he not be sure of the grounds of his representation to the employer'.[14]

Deracializing: Three Problems

Suspect Motives

The attempt by the engineering craft unions to deracialize has faced three problems, the first of which is that their drive to unionize black workers is seen by the latter as an attempt at control in the interests of the existing white membership. This perception arises from the experience of black workers in the post-World War II period discussed in Chapter 5 and from the immediate past history of parallel unions. The IMF visit in 1972 provided a further impetus to the parallel union strategy. Announcing the decision of the CMBU to establish parallel unions in 1973, E H McCann stated that

> by setting up responsible African trade unions and maintaining effective communication with them, we believe we can protect the existing standards of the white, coloured and Indian workers as such trade unions will be the only way to prevent undercutting in both rates of pay and standards of work. Furthermore, we believe African trade unions are inevitable and that it is in the interests of industrial peace and economic progress that a start be made now to train responsible African trade unions.[15]

A few weeks later at the TUCSA conference a decision was made to recommend to affiliates the establishment of parallel unions.[16] However, industrial relations in the engineering industry had changed since the early 1960s — EAWU had survived the period of exclusion from TUCSA and had grown rapidly between 1972 and 1975. Furthermore, as discussed in Chapter 6, MAWU had also expanded and was an independent presence in the engineering industry. Because of this past history of attempted control, when the diluted craft unions amended their constitutions to include blacks or set up parallel unions in anticipation of Wiehahn they faced resistance from black workers.

In anticipation of the recommendations of the Wiehahn Commission, SAEWA had set up a black parallel union (the E&AWU) in 1978.[17] Encouraged by employers, the E&AWU began to recruit black members in the second half of 1979. In August, for example, the liaison committee minutes of GEC Machines recorded that the personnel department of GEC had arranged for representatives of SAEWA and the E&AWU to visit the company.[18] It was, the management said, a responsible union recognized by the company. At the next meeting of the liaison committee in September 1979 the committee was informed 'that over half the black employees had expressed an intention of joining the union and two of the liaison committee members had been nominated shop stewards'.[19] In October the committee was informed that membership dues of fifty cents per week were being deducted before the union was registered and that this was a breach of the agreement in the Industrial Council.[20] However, by March 1980 the initial 'rush' to join the E&AWU had 'dropped off considerably and at present very few applications are received by the personnel officer'.[21] By the middle of March the personnel officer reported that the shop stewards had 'stood down' because they had been 'intimidated'.[22]

What lay behind the failure of the E&AWU to maintain the momentum of its initial breakthrough? Black workers in GEC Machines began to question the motives of the union when the secretary of the 'parent union', SAEWA's Ben Nicholson, said that blacks should do military service on the border before they were apprenticed.[23] More particularly, its credibility as a union was questioned by workers because of its close links with management. An account by a worker in GEC Machines captures this perception:

> Workers were called individually to the black personnel officer. He told them about the union. He told workers the union is good when you lose your job because it gives you some money. He said the liaison committee will stay the same — that is, it is working well. He also said that the union cannot argue about the workers' wages. The workers must work hard to make production for the firm. Management alone will decide whether to give an increase — workers felt that this personnel officer was trying to force them to join the union. They report that he told them that they would lose their jobs if they did not fill in the form. He told them that management wants everyone to belong to the union.[24]

It would have been difficult for the craft engineering unions to conceal from black workers the pragmatism that lay behind their decision to open membership — a pragmatism clearly revealed in this interview with the National Organizer of the IMS:

> We are letting some blacks into the union. But we are doing this because we have to. We didn't ask for these blacks. The employer brought them into the foundry. But once they are in the foundry and they are doing the same job they must become members. That has been our policy. As I tell the managers, once they join the union they are no longer kaffirs,

they are an integral part of the union. That means that the employer is not going to be able to treat them like donkeys and make them work until they drop. They must be treated fairly. They can't be dismissed just for anything.[25]

By August 1981 the IMS had recruited 128 blacks, who had joined, according to the organizer, because of the closed shop.[26] In fact, a strike took place in 1982 over the requirement that African production moulders join the IMS because of the closed shop. While the IMS was initially insistent that these production moulders join the society, it was forced to retract when 280 workers stopped work over the right to belong to the union of their choice (MAWU). Although these moulders have now joined the IMS they retain their membership of MAWU: thus the response of black workers has in the end been equally pragmatic.[27]

Entrenched Racial Divisions

The second problem facing the engineering craft unions is that of deracializing a union when racial divisions remain deeply entrenched in the society at large. SABS has decided that the interests of blacks inside the union can best be served at present by separate racial branches for white, coloured and African workers with racial representation on a proportional basis for each group in the governing council and the executive committee.

The existence of separate branches is a means of ensuring that newcomers are given an opportunity of being represented at general council and executive committee levels and are not dominated by members with entrenched positions.[28]

They give three reasons for this policy: residential segregation makes it difficult to get representative attendance at any mixed branch meeting; factors outside the job situation such as transport affect each population group in different ways; and, finally, blacks at this stage lack experience of unions and their interests may be overridden if specific provision in the constitution is not made for them.[29] To date the IMF has accepted SABS's bona fides that this is an interim stage which will allow a strong black leadership to emerge.[30] However, a less generous critic might see in SABS's separate branch structure a paternalism that conceals a desire to maintain white control.[31]

The Bureaucratic Nature of the Established Unions

The third problem facing these unions is possibly the most difficult to resolve: the engineering craft unions have, over the years, found a comfortable niche in the industrial relations system and have come to rely on their access to management and the industrial councils rather than on organization on the shop floor. Although there may be individual shop stewards in a plant (quite often appointed by a foreman) only SABS maintains shop steward committees constituting an organized presence on the shop floor with paid time off to service membership needs. Union recognition is negotiated through the NIC rather than at plant level, and consequently these unions do not maintain specific grievance or dismissal procedures requiring shop floor mobilization. They do not see these as necessary: they feel that the Industrial Council provides an adequate forum for individual grievances and leave the Industrial Council's agents to fulfil many shop steward functions.

They have also largely abandoned the strike weapon. In fact the AEU complained that the police were not taking action against black workers during the wave of illegal strikes in 1981 in the East Rand engineering industry.[32] They are against any direct links with a political party or any community organization. Workers join their unions, officials feel, because of the benefits they offer. They have become in many senses benefit societies. Greenberg concludes his survey of artisan unions by suggesting that:

> these officers reflected an indifference born of security and job control that has allowed most artisan unions now and in the past to step back from the racial order. The artisan unions have used specific racial exclusions to powerful effect.[33]

The transformation of these craft unions into bureaucratized benefit societies is best illustrated by the IMS. At a meeting of the NEC in May 1977 to discuss the agenda of the next conference, it was suggested that the society's conference be held every three years instead of every two years. 'We had', it was said, 'lost contact with the various members because of stop orders — there were no more Annual General Meetings and even the shop stewards had lost contact with their members because they do not collect the subscriptions any more.'[34] The chairman of the IMS then pointed out that there was no contact to be made as there were hardly any branches left:

The Cape Town branch had closed down in 1971, East London branch in 1975 and if the branch chairman retired in Durban they would have to close that down because there was no one available to take his place. The same thing goes for the Pretoria branch if the chairman retires. The Uitenhage organizer had reported that at his last meeting with the branch in Uitenhage only four members attended.[35]

Thus by the end of the decade only two offices were being maintained by the union: the Durban No.1 Branch, manned on a part-time basis, with 1 000 coloured members (800 of whom lived in Johannesburg); and the Johannesburg branch, the head office, with a full-time secretary and national organizer.[36] Accompanying this decline in the number of branches was a decline in membership participation in union affairs. In 1975 the society's constitution was amended to provide for the appointment of a full-time official by the NEC rather than by a ballot, as had been the practice since the inception of the union.[37] Participation in the Quarterly General Meeting, the only representative meeting open to the rank and file, was poor, the general secretary reported, with attendance amounting to only twenty or thirty members. He suggested that the IMS constitution be amended to provide for half-yearly meetings. By August 1977 it was recorded that only nineteen people attended the Quarterly General Meeting.[38]

The response of TUCSA to the nation-wide work stoppage over the death in detention of Dr Neil Aggett, Transvaal regional secretary of the Food and Canning Workers' Union, in February 1982, illustrated the extent to which these unions had insulated themselves from the struggle of the new unions. In a statement issued a week after Dr Aggett's death, TUCSA 'unhesitatingly distanced itself' from the stoppage, stating that 'we cannot subscribe to strikes not related directly to the employer/employee relationship'.[39] However, this statement was not without consequences: when the National Union of Distributive Workers (NUDW) resigned from TUCSA it gave the Aggett statement as one of its reasons.[40] A year later SABS resigned from TUCSA. Underlying SABS's dissatisfaction was its belief that TUCSA had failed to respond constructively to the emerging unions.

Independent Unions Enter the Industrial Council System

In February 1981 SEAWU became the first independent black union to be a party to the NIC. Although it was only formed in 1979, its roots go back TUCSA's first parallel union, EAWU (see Chapter 5). The lesson EAWU's secretary, Jane Hlongwane, had drawn from the subsequent 'betrayal' by the 'parent' CMBU in the late 1960s was the importance of a black union developing an independent power base.[41] EAWU was able to accomplish this, despite managerial resistance, in the first half of the 1970s. Crucial factors were its links with the IMF (see Chapter 8), the effective use of existing works committees by the union, and the educational assistance of the Urban Training Project (UTP). The heyday of EAWU was the period 1973 to 1974 when the union expanded rapidly on the Witwatersrand. Paid-up membership increased from 400 in 1972 to over 3 000 in 1975, while signed-up membership reached 8 000 in that year.[42]

In 1975 contact had been established with SAEWA when its general secretary was the guest speaker at a weekend seminar held by EAWU.[43] In 1976 EAWU submitted a memorandum to the NIC recommending a narrowing of the wage differential between semi-skilled and unskilled workers.[44] In 1978, however, when SAEWA in anticipation of Wiehahn offered to give direct assistance to EAWU, the latter preferred to 'do all [ts] organizing on [ts] own.'[45] In December 1980 it was to register under the amended Industrial Conciliation Act as a black union without any preconditions, and entered the NIC in February 1981 as an independent rather than a parallel union.

When one considers the various responses made by unions to the deracialization of the industrial relations system, SEAWU remains an anomaly. While Jane Hlongwane had consistently rejected subordination to the CMBU, she had not developed an alternative style of trade unionism — unlike other emerging unions with a similar membership base. It is true that the union had not joined the CMBU, and put forward independent proposals in the 1982 Industrial Council negotiations.[46] However, the union operates with a scattered membership in many different factories, relies consequently on individual shop stewards rather than on a shop steward committee, and has not participated in illegal or legal strikes. Jane Hlongwane's style of unionism expressed the new mood of black self-assertiveness in the early 1970s, but she was unable to survive the 'challenge from below' in the post-1976 period in her own union.[47] In 1978 she was dismissed as secretary of EAWU and founded SEAWU. Only a strong shop-floor unionism is likely to challenge the control of the CMBU over the unions party to the NIC.

Table 11: *Trade Unions Party to the National Industrial Council*
for the Engineering Industry in 1982

Trade Union	Membership	Affiliation	Race Composition
1. A E U	34 000	—	whites
2. A S W	20 758	—	whites
3. E A T U	9 500	—	coloureds
4. *E & A W U* (parallel)*	3 500	—	Africans
5. E I W U	14 000	TUCSA	coloureds
6. I M S	3 100	TUCSA	'mixed'
7. *N U E I A W* (parallel)	3 100	—	Africans
8. R T E A W U	1 435	TUCSA	coloureds
9. S A B S	53 000	TUCSA‡	'mixed'
10. S A E W A	20 000	—	whites
11. S A Engine Drivers	6 990	SACLA	whites
12. Y & S	39 132	SACLA	whites
13. *S E A W U* (indepent black)	8 665	CUSA	Africans
14. *T R T E A W U* (parallel)	560	—	Africans

Note: Those in italics are the new black unions who have joined the NIC.
* In 1983 E and AWU severed its links with its 'white parent'.
‡ Resigned in 1983.

Source: Survey among union officials with significant membership in foundries in the Transvaal.

By the beginning of 1982 the incorporative strategy had led to the expansion of the membership of the NIC from ten to fourteen (see Table 11). The four new unions represented on the Industrial Council included three parallel unions and one independent black union. However, the challenge from below in the period 1981-1982 had led to proposals from the CMBU to restructure the industrial councils. By 1982 it had become clear to a growing number of employers, Department of Manpower officials, and established unions that the experiment had failed to take into account the essential feature of the emerging unions — their shop-floor presence and consequent demand for factory-based bargaining. SABS had, for some years, been developing a greater sensitivity to shop steward structures. In 1981 a separate section of the society was established to provide for the training of shop stewards, officials and office bearers. In other words, SABS was realizing that it was increasingly unable to maintain control over the job by limiting intake, and was now trying instead to expand and build up strength on the shop floor.[48] This was to culminate in a number of cases of joint SABS and MAWU plant bargaining over wages during 1984. Nicholson of SAEWA had also put forward proposals in 1981 to decentralize the NIC by dividing it into different sectors and allowing the shop stewards to administer (not police) the agreement.[49]

Feeling less able to rely on the state, the Y & S has also begun to stress the importance of workplace organization. Announcing a course for union officials and shop stewards aimed at upgrading their bargaining skills and knowledge of unionism, Borman said that

> the white worker had always been protected by job reservation. But since that has been abolished, officials of white unions had to be trained on how best to bargain for their members. Independent — mainly black — unions have long placed a strong emphasis on worker education and on building up shop steward bargaining skills. But because white workers have been protected by job reservation, their unions have generally not relied on tough bargaining on the shop floor and have paid little attention to bargaining skills.[50]

Responding to the withdrawal of state support, 25 members of the Y & S in Volkswagen resigned from their union, joining the predominantly black motor union, NAAWU, in FOSATU.[51] There is a realization, Roux suggests, among the Y & S workers in the motor plants that inevitably blacks will claim a larger share of the more skilled occupations:

> . . . these workers perceive a growing distance between the interests of the state and the white workers — they are aware that the state is no longer prepared to intervene on their behalf.[52]

The majority of white workers, however, are likely to try and win back some control over the state, either through the Nationalist Party or by giving their support to its far-right opponents, the HNP and the Conservative Party (CP).

Thus the initial opposition of the Y & S to the Wiehahn proposals to deracialize the NIC has become a reluctant acceptance of this change. Those unions which amended their constitutions to include blacks are faced by distrust of this strategy of 'reform from above' — whether black workers are invited to join parallel unions or 'mixed' unions with separate racial branches.

Unions such as SABS, with separate racial branches, have had greater success in breaking down this distrust than those unions which have established 'parallels'. In November 1983, for example, the E & AWU, an African parallel union, and the Electrical and Allied Trade Union, a coloured parallel union, severed links with their white 'parent', SAEWA, in an attempt to establish a more independent position. A more important factor contributing to the relative success of SABS in recruiting black workers is its greater effectiveness in transforming the union into an industrial union with shop-floor structures.

The decision in 1983 by MAWU, the largest of the emerging unions in the metal industry, to participate in the NIC was interpreted by supporters of the Industrial Council system as a victory for their incorporative strategy. Such an interpretation is incomplete as it ignores the very different conditions under which MAWU has entered and participated in the NIC. In particular it has continued to involve its shop-floor structures and to demand factory-level wage bargaining. The significance of its participation in the NIC during the 1983 and 1984 wage negotiations is that it has opened up important divisions inside the established union caucus (the CMBU) between those unions with a base largely or exclusively among white workers (such as the AEU) and those (such as SABS), who are attempting to recruit large numbers of African workers. Whether MAWU will be able to transform the NIC depends on the extent to which it is able to consolidate the rapid organizational gains made in the post-Wiehahn period. This will be the subject of the next chapter.

Notes

1   Wessels Borman, general secretary of the Y & S, 'Some Reactions to Wiehahn', *South African Labour Bulletin* (*SALB*), V, 2 (August 1979), p.82.

2   For similar arguments on the need for the union to control the pace of change, see Greenberg's interviews with the Y & S. S. Greenberg, *Race and State in Capitalist Development* (Ravan Press, Johannesburg, 1980), p.320.

3   In this case the Y & S machinist interviewed was prepared to accept working side by side with a black in the same job, provided there was a physical barrier separating him from the newly promoted black machinist. This proved very cumbersome and, desperate to employ an African as there had been seventeen white men in seven months in that job, management was able to persuade the white worker to accept a

yellow line drawn between them on the shop floor. The line had all but completely faded by the time the author visited the plant. Interview with M Zariffs, production manager, Cast and Iron Machine Shop, GEC Machines, February 1980.

4   Interview, W Borman, Pretoria, September 1981.

5   Wessels Borman, 'Some Reactions to Wiehahn', p.83.

6   Interview, W Borman.

7   *Ibid.*

8   E. Robinson, Y & S shop steward in GEC Machines. This was the only Y & S shop steward the author was able to interview. He had qualified as a tool and die maker after five years of apprenticeship and joined the Y & S in 1956. He is now a supervisor and said he had been appointed as a shop steward by the foreman four and a half years ago.

9   Borman, 'Some Reactions to Wiehahn', p.84.

10   In the 1979 Ford dispute white workers reacted in racist ways to the assertiveness of black workers. M. Roux, 'The division of labour at Ford', *SALB*, VI, 2 & 3 (September 1980), pp.34-35.

11   S. Miller, 'Trade unionism in South Africa 1970-1980. A directory and statistics', SALDRU Working Paper No.45, p.27.

12   13th Biennial Conference, IMS, November 1959, A1008 F.

13   S. Greenberg, *Race and State*, chapters 12, 13 and 14.

14   The danger of too sharp a distinction between 'craft' and 'industrial' is also seen in the equivocal response of the AEU, a classic craft union in origin which still draws forty percent of its membership from journeymen. It has not opened its membership to blacks, nor is it a member of SACLA.

15   *Rand Daily Mail*, Johannesburg, 3.8.1973.

16   A. Grobbelaar, 'The parallel trade union', *SALB*, III, 4 (January/February 1977).

17   Similar approaches had been made to MAWU by SABS. See Chapter 6.

18   GEC Machines, liaison committee minutes, 15.8.1979.

19   *Ibid.*, 12.9.1979.

20   *Ibid.*, 14.11.1979.

21   *Ibid.*, 5.3.1980.

22   *Ibid.*, 17.3.1980.

23   *Ibid.*, 5.3.1980.

24   'Report on parallel union activity in GEC Machines, Benoni', *SALB*, V, 6 & 7 (March 1980), p.90.

25   Interview with Ben Harris, National Organizer, IMS, September 1981.

26   See Appendix B, E1. This was confirmed by the one black member of the IMS that the author was able to interview. 'Management said we must join the IMS or we will lose the job that we are now doing'. Interview in Vosloorus hostel, January 1981.

27 Suspicion towards the diluted craft unions is reinforced by what blacks see as discriminatory treatment in apprenticeship training. 'Young blacks were avoiding the trades as they felt that they offered no release from permanent inferiority. Until blacks felt that they belonged in the mainstream of society, this would persist.' W. Baqwa, Group Labour Relations Manager, Roberts Construction. Minutes of the Southern Transvaal SAIRR, 15.11.1978. GEC Machines, for example, introduced a one-year pre-artisan aid training for blacks to overcome white union resistance to black apprentices. This pre-artisan training demands a higher entrance qualification (Standard 10) than whites must possess, and is offered at a separate institution — St Anthony's — and not at the National Technical College. GEC Machines Artisan Aid Training Scheme for Blacks, February 1980.

28 Background material on SABS released by the union.

29 *Ibid.*, pp.4-5.

30 *FOSATU Worker News*, July 1982.

31 Often underlying this strategy is the argument that Africans are not 'ripe' for trade unionism as they are not yet at that stage of industrial development. Hendler believes that the secretary of SABS, Van der Watt, exemplifies this 'stages of growth argument'. P. Hendler, 'The organization of parallel unions', *SALB*, V, 6 & 7 (March 1980), p.110.

32 Reported in the *Garment Worker*, 15.10.1982.

33 S. Greenberg, *Race and State*, p.310.

34 IMS, NEC Minutes, 5.7.1977. These minutes have not yet been transferred to the University library and are consequently unclassified.

35 IMS, NEC Minutes, 29.9.1977. In February 1978 it was reported that the Pretoria secretary, Plunkett, had died, and that the Pretoria branch would therefore close. (IMS, NEC, 27.2.1978). When interviewed by the author in August 1981, the secretary of the Durban branch was 75 years old.

36 Interview with Bronkhorst, general secretary of the IMS, and B. Lawrence, secretary of Durban No.1 Branch.

37 IMS, NEC Minutes, 24.2.1977.

38 *Ibid.*, 25.8.1977.

39 *The Star*, Johannesburg, 18.2.1982.

40 *The Garment Worker*, Johannesburg, 18.6.1982.

41 Interview with Jane Hlongwane, secretary of SAEWU, Johannesburg, August 1981.

42 Jane Hlongwane, 'Emergence of African unions in Johannesburg with reference to the Engineering Union', in J A Grey Coetzee, *Industrial Relations in South Africa* (Cape Town, 1976), p.207.

43 *Ibid.*, p.208.

44 *Ibid.*, p.208.

45   R La Grange, 'A general overview of the relationship between the registered trade unions and the labour process in the engineering industry after World War Two', Industrial Sociology honours dissertation, University of the Witwatersrand, Johannesburg, 1980, pp.109-110.

46   *Rand Daily Mail*, Johannesburg, 5.3.1982.

47   P Bonner, 'Focus on FOSATU', *SALB*, V, 1 (May 1979), pp.17-18.

48   Interview with I van der Watt, general secretary of SABS, Johannesburg, August 1981.

49   Interview with C Nicholson, general secretary of SAEWA, Johannesburg, August 1981.

50   *Rand Daily Mail*, Johannesburg, 9.1.1982.

51   'Perhaps the most striking development between November 1980 and November 1981]comes from the Volkswagen plant in Uitenhage. There, as a result of NAAWU shop stewards resolving the problems of white workers, about 25 white workers have resigned from Yster en Staal to join NAAWU. A general meeting of 3 600 Volkswagen workers recently took the decision to admit them, and they have since attended more general meetings in Uitenhage, KwaNobuhle township.' 'FOSATU Report, November 1980 to November 1981', *SALB*, VII, 4 & 5 (February 1982), p.108.

52   M Roux, 'The division of labour', p.34.

CHAPTER 11

The Challenge From Below: The Rise of the Shop Steward Movement

All three responses to deracialization in the post-Wiehahn period dealt with in Chapter 10 — the racial exclusivity of the Y & S and the AEU, the multi-racial approach of SAEWA, the IMS and SABS, and the formation of the independent, black SEAWU — share a commitment to the maintenance of the Industrial Council system. The responses dealt with in this chapter are different in that they oppose the present Industrial Council system and aim instead at direct involvement of the shop floor in industrial relations. Unions which share this approach differ as to how it can best be conducted — and these differences exist within as well as between unions. In particular, divergent views exist on what the relationship ought to be between the work place and the wider popular struggle in South Africa — as can be seen in the various strategies of the GWU, GAWU, BAWU and now UMMAWOSA, all of whom have members in the engineering industry.[1] However, the great majority of organized black foundry workers, an estimated 25 percent of the industry, belong to MAWU, the largest of the expansionary unions. We will focus in this chapter on the strategy of MAWU in the post-Wiehahn period.

Industrial unions, it was suggested in Part II, are forced to rely on numbers rather than on skill and are expansionary by nature. Their members are mostly unskilled or semi-skilled workers drawn from the secondary labour market described in Chapter 9.

Table 13. MAWU Membership by Skill Level (1975)

Unskilled	47%
Lower semi-skilled	41%
Higher semi-skilled	6%
Lower skilled	6%

Source: Union Membership Survey

Most members joined the union out of a desire to defend workers' rights against what they saw as arbitrary or unfair treatment by management.

Table 14. Reasons for Joining MAWU (1975 and 1982)

Year survey conducted	Benefits	Improved wages	Defend worker rights
1976	20%	9%	71%
1982	0%	23%	67%

Source: Union Membership Survey and Shop Steward Survey

Some of the reasons given by shop stewards for joining MAWU were:

I joined the union because workers are not treated like human beings by management.

I joined the union because I was dismissed for being absent from work for three months. I had in fact been admitted to hospital where I was being treated for swollen feet caused by working in the furnace. I was later reinstated after my case had been heard.

We were forced to eat food sold by the company. This was then deducted from our wages regardless of whether we ate the food or not. It was deducted even when a worker was on leave. Workers used to be dismissed without a reason.

In Chapter 6 it was shown how after overcoming considerable management and state resistance MAWU had entered 'the third stage' — negotiating and maintaining an agreement — in the post 1980 period. This is reflected in MAWU's rapid membership growth between 1980 and 1982 (see Table 15). By May 1982 the union had offices in fourteen different centres, four branches, and twenty full-time officials.

Building Shop Steward Structures

Three organizational principles underlie MAWU's structure and policies — building shop steward structures, factory-level bargaining and worker control. The first principle emerged in the early stages of MAWU's history when it shifted from a strategy of mass mobilization

Table 15. MAWU Membership Growth 1974-1982

1974	3 900
1975	5 000
1976	6 700
1977	6 700
1978	6 700
1979	6 700
1980	10 000
1981	24 300
1982	30 000

Source: Union Records (1974-1982)

to a concentration on building shop steward structures in a few selected factories. By 1980 shop stewards and their committees had become the pivot of the organization. The intrenchment of these committees in the constitution of the union was a significant innovation in South African unionism. (See Section 11 of the MAWU constitution.) The union now has 464 shop stewards elected annually: a ratio of 65 signed up members to every shop steward (58:1 in 1975). Members in the foundry elect shop stewards from every department: these elections take place at work, at the union office, or in the hostels. A union organizer said:

> As soon as we have the majority of workers being MAWU members in one foundry, and we are quite sure that the people understand what unity means, then we call a general meeting of all workers in that particular foundry. They nominate people they would like to see on the shop steward committee and then we decide by voting.

Those elected to the position of shop steward tend to be below 40 years of age, have worked for some time in the same firm, and have little formal education (see Chapter 9).

Well-organized shop steward committees meet once a week in the foundry and once a month at the union office or the hostel with the union organizer. The shop steward's task is to represent the interests of the union members in his department, to protect the rights of workers against management and, if necessary, to challenge management decisions. As a member of the Shop Stewards' Committee he plays a role in negotiating for the whole plant on things like wages and working conditions and, where an agreement exists, he must see that it is followed. He is also the link between the full-time union officials and the members (see Diagram 3).

Diagram 3: The Shop Steward as the Link Between Membership and Officials

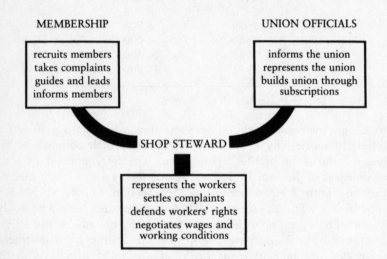

MEMBERSHIP

recruits members
takes complaints
guides and leads
informs members

UNION OFFICIALS

informs the union
represents the union
builds union through
subscriptions

SHOP STEWARD

represents the workers
settles complaints
defends workers' rights
negotiates wages and
working conditions

Shop stewards and union officials are dependent upon each other. The union officials need the shop stewards to perform certain key functions in the foundry. Every week or every month at the factory gates shop stewards collect the members' subscriptions which are then taken to the union offices. Although the union is increasingly establishing payment by stop order in an attempt to stabilize the organization, collecting dues still remains a crucial task of the shop stewards in most foundries. They also provide the union official with vital information about the foundry — a new foreman, the grievances of the workers, the state of negotiations. They settle grievances that emerge in the day to day activities of workers. One organizer gave the following example:

> If the safety guards have been taken off, then it will be the task of the
> shop steward to challenge management to replace these safety guards.

Shop stewards convey the policy decisions of the union to its members, and recruit new union members within the factory.

The shop stewards, in turn, need the union officials. 'If a shop steward cannot solve a problem in his department', one union organizer said, 'he must refer the matter to a shop steward committee for discussion. If after such discussions the matter is not resolved the organizer must be consulted for advice. The organizer then contacts management for a meeting with the negotiating committee.' Or more graphically, in Josias's words:

> When it is difficult I go to the union office and I tell them, *aikona*, there is a difficulty in the company and other people are having difficulty with this thing. They explain to us and I understand — they give us an education so that we can speak to the workers. So that we don't talk nonsense; that we can satisfy our people very well, and help them out of hardship.

The union provides shop steward training in negotiating skills, how to use the agreement, how to handle workers' grievances in a department, and a working knowledge of such matters as dangerous work conditions in foundries.[2] It provides services such as legal advice when workers are charged with illegal striking, or expert back-up in the case of a fatal injury in the foundry.[3]

The shop stewards' function, as they understand it, is to establish a stable relationship between management and worker — a perception which contrasts with management's stereotype of shop stewards as trouble makers. As representatives of the workers in their departments, it is their task to resolve grievances that are brought to them.

> When workers have grievances they tell me about them and I discuss with management about these grievances.

Another shop steward said:

> A shop steward serves as a link between workers and management to ensure harmony between workers and management.

This includes, in their eyes, maintaining discipline amongst workers in the establishment:

> A shop steward is a representative of the workers at the factory. His job is to maintain discipline among the workers under him, and to take worker grievances to management, and to report back to the workers.

Their function includes, for some, encouraging work discipline amongst members:

> We are taught not to go to work in a drunken state and dodge work by remaining too long in the toilets.

The shop stewards are rooted in the work place and their power and positions are largely dependent on the continuing support of the members. Any suspicion that a shop steward has been 'bought' is likely to lead to instant rejection by workers. Quite often, as happened in stoppages on the East Rand, workers have demanded that management remove a shop steward from the foundry because he has become an *impimpi* (an informer). Clearly, shop stewards are exposed to potential cooptation through promotion.[4] Sipho, for example, had recently been promoted to supervisor when he was asked what the workers felt about this.

> Me, I don't control the workers. Only the foreman of the department does . . . I cannot correct someone, for example, if he has made a mistake in closing a box or closed it badly and battered it.

He believes that he has the support of workers because the things that he does are honest:

> I do not favour anyone. Their welfare is the same to me. If there is fighting among the workers, I solve the dispute in the same way.

The workers' power to decide whether a shop steward can continue to represent them was underlined by a union organizer:

> It happens sometimes that management tries to divide the shop steward committee by promoting some of the shop stewards into supervisory jobs and promising to give them tremendous wage increases.

He then gave an example of a shop steward who had accepted promotion and then been forced to resign by the workers.

> He no longer plays any role in representing workers to management because workers have lost confidence in him due to the signs that he has shown. I can say that he showed the weaker side of himself by trying to put himself on management's side.

Shop stewards are directly accountable to the shop floor. It is, in other words, a form of direct democracy. The strength of the shop steward's position depends entirely on the degree of organization on the shop floor. One organizer said:

> In the factories that are not well organized, or the factory where the workers are not really united, then it is a helluva risk for a shop steward to take up serious issues with management. But in factories where management is convinced that the workers are really united, then there is no risk about the shop steward representing the workers because management knows that once it starts pointing fingers at the shop steward, the workers will completely reject that. There is no way that shop stewards can be victimized in a factory that is well organized.

This point was dramatically illustrated in a number of the stoppages where workers successfully forced the reinstatement of a dismissed shop steward.

Although constitutionally the shop steward committee elects two members to represent it on the Branch Executive Committee (BEC), which controls the branch of the union, the shop stewards have increasingly established their own structures — the shop stewards' councils — outside of the constitution in certain areas such as Germiston. The Germiston Shop Stewards' Council emerged in April 1981 and is comprised of shop stewards from the Wadeville/Katlehong area, most of the 23 factories represented being metal factories. They meet every Thursday night to share their demands and combine their power through common action. The strike action in 1981 spread by an imitation effect through the Shop Stewards' Council. The organizer described the process as follows:

> The feeling that management must negotiate was all over Wadeville in this period. The Shop Stewards' Council started to meet in April to plan further developments. They hear about other factories and they share their grievances. Through the organizer in all these factories and not just one they feel strengthened.

It is, in other words, an attempt to bring together different factories from different industries and provide a focus for workers around issues that go beyond the workplace in that area — such as rents. At the 1982 FOSATU Congress, the constitution was amended to allow councils to be formally linked to FOSATU structures through the Regional Executive Council (REC) at local level. However, the main aim of the Council and the reason why it was formed was to involve the shop stewards in organization work. The whole Wadeville area had only one organizer, and the practical problems were enormous:

> 'The organizer can't go to all the factories', it was explained. So we sat
> down and thought, let's change our strategy and give the job to the shop
> stewards. They are now doing the organizing.[5]

The growth of the shop steward movement in the metal industry has
led to two further innovations: the establishment of shop steward
'combine committees', uniting representatives from the various
establishments of multi-national companies; and the establishment of
shop steward councils for a particular sector such as foundries. The
purposes of the former vary considerably: from the simple exchange of
information to the coordination of mutual support, the formulation of
common objectives, and even joint conduct in negotiations. Hendred-
Fruehauf is a case in point; it has plants in Driehoek, Wadeville,
Pinetown and Isithebe, all with different wage levels. The shop
stewards in these plants have now established a shop stewards'
combine committee which negotiates wages at all the plants.

Factory Level Bargaining

Building shop steward structures emphasizes factory level bargaining
— negotiating, policing and enforcing a factory agreement on the shop
floor. It is not surprising, then, that the recommendations of the
Wiehahn Commission in 1979 were seen by MAWU as an attempt to
pre-empt the strategy of factory level bargaining. In the MAWU view,
while the Wiehahn Commission recognized that employers had to
accept unions of African workers, it attempted to impose the condition
that unions would be excluded from the plants.[6] During 1979 and
early 1980, a determined attempt was made to pre-empt MAWU's
emerging shop floor structures through what union leaders called a
two-tier strategy. The strategy envisaged by state and management
involved two elements: firstly

> all domestic problems would be handled by in-plant works councils.
> The unions would have no direct access to these councils. The Wiehahn
> Report recommends that the councils be modelled on the totally
> discredited liaison committees.

And, secondly,

unions would participate directly only in industry-wide bargaining in the industrial councils.[7]

This two-tiered strategy, said MAWU, had been most clearly defined in relation to the metal industry.

The employers' association, SEIFSA, issued guidelines to its members late in 1979 on trade unions for African workers.[8] Companies were advised to have no dealings whatsoever with unions other than through the employers' association at the Industrial Council level, and warned against assisting trade union organization in any way. They were directed not to allow any plant agreements — even with fully registered unions — on any issue falling under the purview of the Industrial Councils. At the industry level there would be, in place of plant negotiation, 'in-plant consultative systems' consisting of works councils catering solely for communication of grievances. These consultative systems aimed to cater for workers 'irrespective of their membership or otherwise of trade unions', and shop stewards were explicitly warned that to grant stop-order facilities to unregistered unions was illegal in terms of the Industrial Council agreement.

In order to ensure that employers only dealt with unions which accepted the two-tier structure, employers actively encouraged the organization of African workers by the established registered unions of white and coloured workers — a strategy discussed in Chapter 10. MAWU felt the impact of this strategy in late 1979 and early 1980 in the plants which they had organized on the East Rand. In Hendred-Freuhauf, for example, where 264 of the 316 black workers were members of MAWU, the Motor Industry Combined Workers' Union was invited to address the workers in early 1980. The shop stewards present recorded what happened:

> Webb [secretary of the parallel union] was called in to address the workers asking them to join his parallel union. The meeting was held on the factory premises during working hours. The workers emphatically rejected him. Management also tried to persuade workers to either choose Webb's parallel union or a company union rather than MAWU. Webb also informed management that MAWU caused strikes, sought disruption and received money from Russia and East Germany. The workers refused to resign from the union.[9]

As part of the two-tier strategy Salcast (Vosa Valves, AMF and Salchain) proposed a works council in February 1980. Drawn from the standard model distributed by SEIFSA its objectives were defined as:

> resolve grievances,
>
> create greater commitment from employees to the objectives of the company,
>
> improve and maintain plant efficiency, productivity and morale . . . .
> Works Councils are primarily advisory and consultative bodies and cannot by resolution or otherwise reverse or amend any instruction given by management. Nor can they interfere with disciplinary measures.

MAWU had started organizing in Vosa Valves in October 1976 and at AMF in 1978: by February 1980, 95 of the 105 workers at Vosa Valves and 600 out of the 1 400 workers at AMF had joined the union.[10] At a meeting with management in March 1980, the shop stewards stated that:

> workers did not accept the works council. They believed it was not different from the liaison committee. They felt it was controlled by management through the appointment of the chairman and secretary. It was also not independent because workers did not have access to union officials. In addition, worker representatives would be paid an allowance by management . . . because of these reasons workers felt they had to reject it as a whole.[11]

A final aspect of this two-tier strategy was a refusal to negotiate with a union unless it was registered. At Zinchem, an Anglo American subsidiary, management had agreed to allow access to union officials once they could prove that 30 percent of the workers had joined. It then changed its policy, refusing to deal with the union until it was registered.[12]

It was in the context of this two-tier offensive to pre-empt the emerging shop floor structures of MAWU that the debate as to whether the union should register in terms of the Industrial Conciliation Act took place. Extensive discussions were held inside the central committee of FOSATU and the MAWU leadership on the pros and cons of registration.[13] In these discussions some members of the NEC felt they would be 'giving in to the state' if they registered. They pointed out that in return for registration African trade unions would be subject to the power of investigation and regulation under the Act. This involved the vetting of the union's constitution; submission of audited financial statements and a list of members and office-bearers; and, in the case of 'abuse', investigation by the registrar. Others felt that the actual controls involved were insignificant and that, provided the union retained its commitment to worker control, these could be overcome. Consensus was eventually reached in the NEC to apply for registration on condition that it was granted on a non-racial basis. An earlier MAWU condition for registration — that the union's right to organize migrant workers should be recognized — had already been conceded by the state in September 1979. The high proportion of migrant workers in MAWU made this concession a crucial victory for the union.

Four advantages of registration were identified by the union:

> It will take away the excuse that many managements have used to avoid negotiation with us in the past when they have said that they cannot talk to an unregistered union.

> We could get stop orders in factories which would help to make the union more financially secure and independent.

> Many workers who have been afraid to join us in the past will now lose their fear.

> We will be in a better position in the long run to fight the parallel unions which are going to try and start organizing with the help of management.

The decision to register was made for tactical reasons: the leadership believed that the controls involved in registering were ineffectual and that registration would help the union to survive in the face of the two-tier strategy.[14]

MAWU's tactical approach to the issue can be seen from subsequent developments. In March 1980 the union applied for registration and in June it was informed that it would be permitted to apply for registration on a non-racial basis.[15] However, registration was eventually granted on condition that the union would represent black workers only. MAWU challenged this decision, appealing first to the Minister of Manpower and then to the Supreme Court. It announced publicly that it would deregister if it lost the appeal.[16] The appeal was, however, successful in April 1983.[17]

The decision to register by MAWU and other FOSATU affiliates was to lead to strong criticism from those unions that refused to register. In particular it was argued that state control would render these trade unions undemocratic.[18] The MAWU denial of this charge was supported by the surge of militancy among metal workers on the

East Rand in 1981-82 which bore dramatic testimony to the continuing efficacy of shop floor control. Registration, the leadership believed, was not a central issue:

> MAWU does not feel registration is an issue. We feel that it is largely a red herring. To us it's actually made no difference whatsoever. It was a tactical question.[19]

Although a number of people inside MAWU remained uneasy about registration, it never re-emerged as an issue and no challenge to the decision to register crystallized.[20] The process whereby the decision to register was reached will be dealt with later in this chapter.

The amendment to the SEIFSA guidelines in April 1980, after representation from the CMBU, showed that the decision to register had created space for MAWU's organizational advance. The 1979 guidelines were slightly modified to allow for automatic exemption from the prohibition on stop orders for unregistered unions, provided that the union was well advanced in its application for registration and undertook to apply for membership of the Industrial Council on registration.[21] However, SEIFSA made it clear that this was not a shift from their two-tier strategy, and MAWU had no illusions that it was.[22] By April 1980, in spite of SEIFSA's guidelines, negotiation for plant agreements had begun in Hendred-Freuhauf and Tensile Rubber (a General Tyres subsidiary).[23] In May 1980 a new surge of shop floor militancy was signalled when the work force of Rely Precision stopped work. The immediate cause of the stoppage was the refusal of management to discuss the dismissal of a member of the union. Underlying the dispute was management's refusal to negotiate with the shop steward committee.[24]

In September 1980 MAWU achieved its first recognition agreement when, in an out of court settlement with Precision Tools, that company agreed to recognize MAWU in its Johannesburg factory.[25] Further agreements were signed in October 1980 with Tensile Rubber (a company which resigned from SEIFSA in September 1981) and in August 1981 with Hendred-Freuhauf (only one tenth of this factory's operation falls under the NIC). These two agreements established the following rights:

> Shop steward recognition, which includes time-off for union business, access to the plant by union officials, and stop order facilities;

limitation on managerial prerogatives through a dismissal and grievance procedure;

plant bargaining on the terms and conditions of employment, together with the right to report back to members;

other benefits such as retrenchment provisions and health and safety committees.

These agreements were the first concrete evidence of differences among employers on how best to respond to the challenge from below.

Further signs of division in employer ranks were evident from September 1980 in statements by the Federated Chamber of Industries (FCI) and Barlow Rand.[26] Meanwhile the dramatic increase in work stoppages among MAWU members on the East Rand between July and November 1981 transformed the context of industrial relations in the foundry. Between 1980 and 1981 MAWU had almost tripled its membership — the AGM increased from an attendance of 200 in 1980 to a thousand in 1981, and reached 5 000 in 1982. During the second half of 1981 eleven percent of the total work force in the metal industry on the East Rand was involved in 24 stoppages. The stoppages lasted an average of one and three-quarter days, 50 percent lasted one day or less, and three for two hours or less. In twelve of the stoppages the demand for the reinstatement of dismissed workers was made. In a further six stoppages workers demanded the removal of managerial employees accused of exercising control in an arbitrary fashion, or worker representatives thought to have been 'bought' by management. The other six stoppages involved wage demands. Since the primary purpose of these demonstration stoppages was to call attention to the urgency of workers' feelings of grievance, they were usually willing to return to work to permit negotiations to take place, even before concrete concessions had been granted. In twelve of the stoppages the demands made by workers were fully met. In eight no demands were met, even though the union leadership had made the expensive gesture of calling for a return to work.

The renewed challenge from bmlow led to the first significant shift in employers' attitudes to shop floor negotiation, a process captured in the following mxcerpts from an interview. An industrial officer in one of the larger foundries hit by the strikes was asked, 'Why did management change its attitude towards the union?' He replied:

I told them all along that the Liaison Committee had no credibility but they didn't listen to me. But after the September dispute they were forced to start negotiation because there was no one to talk to. They asked to speak to the shop stewards but they [the shop stewards] said they were not prepared to talk unless they were recognized.[27]

However, top management held to its policy of undermining the union, using tactics discussed in Chapter 6. The informant gave as his example the attempt to blacklist union leaders who were on the call-in card system. Furthermore, he said, when they do negotiate

they feel they are losing control. They get together among themselves and talk about kaffirs. They think communists and the ANC are behind the union.

But, he was asked, why then do they bother to negotiate at all?

Oh, they feel they have no alternative. They would rather talk to the shop stewards than a mass of workers. They are dead scared of a mass of people. They feel they can't control it. Besides, we have to meet a tight production schedule.[28]

This ambivalence towards the union is reflected in the November 1981 guidelines of SEIFSA, in which the association recognized for the first time that the NIC would have to become more responsive to the shop floor if it was to survive as an industry-wide bargaining institution. It recommended that employers should allow shop stewards time off for training, and include them in the company's disciplinary and grievance procedures. SEIFSA's horizon, however, was limited to the incorporation of the unions in the NIC. Negotiation over wages at plant level was not one of the changes it envisaged.[29]

The issue of shop-floor bargaining came dramatically to the fore the following year when in the first thirteen days of March 1982 seventeen stoppages took place in the East Rand metal factories, fifteen of them in Wadeville. A further three stoppages had occurred in Wadeville earlier that year, making a total of twenty in the first three months of 1982. The central demand in eighteen of these was for an increase in wages. Inflation, workers argued, had cut into their wages and they had to work progressively longer overtime hours to maintain their incomes.

Whereas the stoppages in the second half of 1981 were demonstrations, those of early 1982 began to shape up as a trial of strength.[30] For example, the 1982 stoppages were longer (two and a half days) than the 1981 stoppages (one and three-quarter days). More significantly, whereas in the 1981 stoppages 50 percent of demands for the reinstatement of workers were met in full, in the March stoppages only 20 percent (four) were met in part or fully. In the majority of cases (60 percent) management refused to negotiate, gave workers a deadline to return to work and selectively rehired those who did. While this meant, on a number of occasions, that all workers were rehired, it was, of course, on management's unilateral terms and without the initial grievances being removed. These wage demands became a central issue when management refused to negotiate wages at plant level, insisting on bargaining through the highly centralized NIC.

Clearly the battle lines were being drawn for a contest over the nature of industrial relations in the metal industry. Initially MAWU had a majority presence in only a third of the factories involved in the stoppages. In five factories it had no members at all. In the course of the stoppages, however, MAWU membership increased significantly. The union had rejected an NIC invitation to attend as an observer the annual wage negotiations that began in March, making it clear that it viewed the NIC structure as unrepresentative and favoured plant level bargaining.[31]

While at least four companies broke ranks and gave limited wage increases in March, battle was not yet joined. With the exception of McKechnie Brothers, the companies involved were small to medium sized firms — employing an average of 223 workers — and the large firms remained untouched by the wave of stoppages. Just as SEIFSA had responded to the challenge from the shop floor in its November guidelines, so the unions party to the NIC now increased their wage demands, hoping to encourage MAWU to enter the NIC.[32]

These tactics did not prevent a trial of strength in the industry. One of the key battles took place in April at Scaw Metal, the largest of the foundries on the East Rand, when management refused to negotiate a modest ten cents wage increase at plant level. An important source of MAWU membership, Scaw was also under the autocratic directorship of Graham Boustred, a pillar of the NIC and a powerful defender of SEIFSA's strategy.[33] Rather than compromise on what was no more than a nominal wage demand, Boustred decided to fight the rise on the principle of the form of bargaining that was to obtain in the industry. All workers were dismissed and then selectively rehired. After eleven days the police broke the strike when they were called in to prevent workers from re-occupying the compound. The defeat of the Scaw workers, followed by similar worker setbacks at factories such as Transvaal Malleable Foundries and National Springs, turned the tide in management's favour.

After battling for three and a half years for wage bargaining at factory level, MAWU was forced to retreat. The union was to apply for membership of the NIC in February 1983,[34] having failed to escalate the dramatic strike wave in the East Rand metal industry in 1981 and 1982 into an industry-wide challenge.[35] Employer resistance had defeated the worker offensive.

MAWU needed to consolidate its rapid growth, having increased its membership between 1980 and 1982 from 10 000 to 30 000. This was the theme of the secretary of the Transvaal branch of MAWU in his AGM report to 5 000 members at the Wadeville soccer stadium in May 1982.

> The union has grown very fast. Membership has grown by 200 percent in a year. But this has led to big problems, too: because so many new factories are joining, the organizers have not been able to train shop stewards and meet and plan with members and shop stewards. So many workers have joined without being clear what the union is.[36]

The magnitude of the problem facing the union was underlined further by the onset of recession and the beginning of large-scale retrenchments in the metal industry. The union's strength on the East Rand is rooted in the hostels and the union leadership was quick to realize the vulnerability of migrant workers to being 'endorsed out' in the wake of retrenchment. By the end of 1982 East Rand metal firms were retrenching an estimated 18 percent of the workforce, and at some factories such as Salcast the figure was as high as 25 percent.[37]

It was in this context of successful employer opposition to bargaining outside the NIC, and MAWU's failure to coordinate worker resistance in individual factories, that discussions on the need for industry-wide bargaining took place inside the union in the second half of 1982. It was argued that entry into the NIC, like registration, was a tactical question. Provided certain conditions were met, MAWU's principles could be retained inside the NIC. MAWU could still fight for the right of workers to negotiate at their own factories. When it bargained for union wages at the NIC it could insist that the factory-based structures on which the union was built be involved. Through the system of mandates and report-back meetings at all levels of the organization, MAWU could retain democratic control, thus frustrating management's unspoken aim of divorcing bargaining from the shop-floor. It was important, the leadership argued, that MAWU's voice be heard in the 1983 negotiations. Many members had expressed anger at the way in which other unions party to the NIC took up demands originating from MAWU — such as shoop floor recognition, retrenchment procedures, lay-offs, etc. — and then negotiated these in a manner unacceptable to MAWU. The union also made it clear to its members that it could withdraw from the NIC at any time, and would not sign any agreement that was rejected by the membership.

When MAWU failed to win significant wage increases in the 1983 negotiations, it refused to sign the agreement and successfully mobilized the membership nation-wide behind a demand for a minimum wage of R90 a week. During 1984 MAWU again refused to sign the industrial council agreement, condemning SEIFSA's call to its members to resist union pressure for plant bargaining. More significant was the strike ballot organized jointly between MAWU and SABS over a wage demand at Highveld Steel.[38] This shop-floor cooperation between the two largest unions in the metal industry, if cemented into a working alliance and widened to include other metal unions in the IMF Coordinating Council described in Chapter 8, could yet break the hold of the CMBU over the NIC.

Worker Control

MAWU's two primary principles — shop steward structures and factory level bargaining — are contained in its third principle: workers' control over the union.[39] To what extent can it be shown that there is active participation in and control of decision-making by the rank and file? Both in the process of negotiating an agreement, and in the form it finally takes, the principle of accountability by the negotiating committee to the rank and file has been stressed by the union. Furthermore, the agreements negotiated are not seen as a substitute for strong shop-floor organization so much as a means of securing minimum rights which can be added to by informal bargaining. As an organizer observed, an agreement on its own is not worth the paper it is written on. Equally, I think it serves a useful purpose both psychologically and legally, because management is felt to be bound by certain rules. And at times when we are weak, it serves as a defence because it becomes an accepted way of working. Where organization is not developed sufficiently the document cannot be used effectively. You can't have a recognition agreement as a substitute for organization. It has an important psychological effect for both workers and management. For workers it clarifies what they have won and what they have a right to do and they tend to be more confident in doing these things. For management it forms a basic level of what has been accepted.[40]

The complexity of the agreements entered into with management could make the accountability of the negotiating committee to the rank and file formal rather than real. The Hendred-Freuhauf agreement, for instance, is 29 pages long, and has thirteen sub-sections and five annexures. Although subsequent agreements have been simplified and shortened, they are legal documents, and often assume that the reader is well versed in points of law. One agreement contained a reference to health and safety standards set by the Occupational Safety and Health Association of the Department of Labour in the United States. The organizers involved in negotiating the agreement knew nothing about these standards.[41] Reflecting on this issue after leaving the union, one of the white organizers emphasized this problem:

The kind of agreements that we were discussing in the Transvaal were absurdly complex. That was the mistake we made. People were struggling to understand the agreements. The shop stewards could not negotiate the agreements and the African organizers were extremely reluctant to negotiate without the white organizer present. You are on management's ground and management are so good at structuring compromises that you don't initially see their significance.[42]

Sophisticated managements (as distinct from those who agreed to negotiate with MAWU during the stoppages when under pressure, though they retained a unitary perspective) were quick to realize the need to seize the initiative in formulating the terms of these agreements.[43] Some observers were equally quick to observe the change:

Capital's first line of defence was the blanket refusal to negotiate at plant level and to insist that all relations with the trade union be restricted to the Industrial Council . . . . The second line of response was to try and extract counter concessions from the union.[44]

To assist management in this task, model recognition agreements were produced.[45] Management's view was that recognition at plant level was a concession, and it expected the union to agree to restrict workplace sanctions such as strikes in return.[46] However, these model agreements were not concerned simply with formalizing a procedure for recognition; they were interested in formalizing all substantive aspects of industrial relations. Having diagnosed the problem as the emergence of an informal bargaining system outside of the formal Industrial Council system, management became eager to re-establish a highly legalized system, rather than accept that most industrial relations issues involve the relative power of capital and labour.[47]

Initially taken by surprise by the rapidity of this shift in managerial strategy, MAWU later participated in a seminar to discuss agreements. The objective of this seminar was to attempt to derive a common general strategy in the face of management's attempt to seize the initiative on agreements. Companies were attempting, FOSATU said, to tie the hands of the unions by including restrictive clauses in agreements and by drawing up model agreements which contained the least favourable among the clauses which had been accepted by FOSATU unions.[48] The seminar led to a greater awareness of the need to involve the shop steward at all stages in the process of implementing and maintaining the agreement:

> Take a disciplinary agreement. We tried to entrench certain principles. Now if you've got a bloody-minded management and weak shop stewards they'll give a guy three warnings and he's out in terms of the rules [of the agreement]. What we try to ensure is whenever a worker is given a warning, a shop steward is present. Then we ran into another problem. The foreman would write out a warning and tell the shop steward to sign it. If the shop steward isn't on the ball then he would sign it. Now we try to ensure that the shop steward is present to discuss this before anything is written down, so we've learnt a lot. One wants to ensure that the purpose of the warning is to give the worker the choice to fight back.[49]

Retaining the participation of all members in the organization remains a difficult task. The growth of MAWU has led to calls for a further division of labour. In January 1982 a full-time administrator was appointed by the Transvaal BEC because, they said, 'not everyone

must be an organizer'.[50] The increasing need for skilled negotiation
had also become apparent. The danger inherent in such a trend is well
documented in the sociological literature. A substantial body of this
literature takes as its point of departure the basic thesis developed by
Michel that the labour movement, despite its democratic origins and
objectives, is as prone as any other organization to an iron law of
oligarchy. This point is made forcibly by Ross:

> As an institution expands in strength and status, it outgrows its formal
> purpose. It experiences its own needs, develops its own ambitions, and
> faces its own problems. These become differentiated from the needs,
> ambitions, and problems of its rank and file. The trade union is no
> exception.[51]

Such a tendency is more likely where a proportion of the full-time
organizers have non-working class social backgrounds.[52]

There is evidence that decisions that go beyond the immediate
concerns of the shop floor are made at leadership level with limited
participation outside of this group. The clearest illustration of this is
the nature of decision-making over registration. This issue was first
discussed in the NEC, and the national organizer led the discussion on
the pros and cons of registration. It was then referred to the BECs and
some delegates discussed it with the shop stewards. The final decision
was made at the NEC where consensus was established to register
conditionally. Although a discussion took place at the 1979 AGM, no
decision was made there. Only 200 people attended. This tendency to
concentrate participation on certain issues in the hands of a small
number of people was increased further once the decision to register
was made. The Transvaal regional secretary (a white official) was able
to participate in the administrative work that followed registration,
said national secretary June-Rose Nala,

> because he had been trained as an intellectual and had the ability to sit
> down and read the constitution . . . I don't think Makathini [a factory
> worker who had been made an official] could have done it as Natal
> secretary at the time.[53]

Yet to analyze decision-making as a self-contained area is to ignore the
context of the other institutions of power with which a trade union
interacts. The lack of education among members makes informed
decisions difficult. These broader structural determinants have led

some to argue that the restricted nature of debate over registration was a necessity imposed by the power of the state and capital and the relative powerlessness of workers.[54] More significantly, perhaps, an emphasis on the formal mechanisms of decision-making prevents adequate attention being given to certain countervailing tendencies to those discussed by Michel.[55]

The first and most important of these is the emergence of the shop steward movement on the East Rand. In both 1981 and 1982 the union officials were brought in after mass action to negotiate and found themselves obliged to give backing to these movements. The ambivalence of the trade union official's role in this process has been captured by C. Wright Mills's characterization of the union leader as a 'manager of discontent':

> During mass organization drives, the labour leader whips up the opinion and activity of the rank and file and focuses them against the business corporation as a pedestal of the system and against the state as the crown of the system. At such time, he is a man voicing loudly the discontent and the expectations of the people next to the bottom, and he is seen and recognized as a rebel and an agitator . . . . Yet even as the labour leader rebels, he holds back rebellion. He organizes discontent and then he sits on it, exploiting it in order to maintain a continuous organization: the labour leader is a manager of discontent.[56]

A second factor is the prevalence of assumptions that trade unions ought to be controlled by workers: this sets significant limits to the oligarchic tendencies in the union. On the one hand the union has had to struggle to establish its representativity in the eyes of managements anxious to demonstrate that union leaders are unrepresentative of the wishes of their employees. In Chapter 6 the struggle against the liaison committee and its rejection by workers as unrepresentative was discussed. In this process of struggle, norms of democratic practice have become deeply entrenched among rank and file activists who inter-act regularly with their officials. Shop stewards have been socialized into defining their role as controlling the union.[57] Those officials who continually refuse to change their actions in the face of criticism by the shop stewards are removed from their positions.[58]

A third important criticism of Michel's thesis is the fact that he focuses on the national level where decision-making is likely to be most centralized. This is likely to be of particular importance in the case of MAWU because of its link to the 'tight federation' structure of

FOSATU.[59] Membership participation at this level is likely to be limited. However, if we focus on membership involvement on the shop floor, the limits of Michel's thesis become clearer. The emergence of workplace organization as the principal means of MAWU's workers' struggle has been emphasized in this chapter. The union's rejection of arbitrary control by management — demands for the reinstatement of dismissed workers, for example — was the central theme of the 1981 stoppages. This demand eroded managerial control at the point of production and there is evidence that active membership participation generated the demand, with the shop steward acting as the crucial link between the members and the union officials. Recent experience on the East Rand suggests that the rank and file has established considerable influence over (or else acts independently of) leadership policies and decisions.

It is important that the issue of workers' control should not be reduced to a problem of participation only, as this tends to obscure the structural dilemmas which have to be resolved in building worker organization. Democratic participatory structures are most effective where the unit is small and operates at local level.

> You can only have participation, an organizer said, where people know those standing for election. Otherwise a good speaker gets in — you have to know the person personally; whether he is hard-working, reliable. You only know if he is in your factory. Direct participation is best at the factory level at present. AGMs are hopeless.[60]

The attempt to discuss the issue of entry into the NIC at the May 1982 AGM was unsuccessful because a mass meeting of 5 000 people is not an arena in which effective participation can take place.[61]

The shop steward councils that emerged spontaneously in Wadeville in 1981 come closest to providing such a structure. Anderson, who was involved in an attempt to establish a shop steward council in Benoni in 1976, captured the potential of these councils when he described them as follows:

> The shop stewards could become the main policy-determining body of the union. All matters of general policy could be decided there. The BEC could be concerned with the day-to-day running of the union but it would be the shop stewards that would have the final say. This is what worker control of the union means — a union run completely by workers.[62]

In spite of the romanticism underlying this theory of worker control, it is significant for two reasons. It challenges the thesis that an institutional logic leading to oligarchy is inherent within trade unionism. And, more importantly, it points to the organizational base upon which the working class can assert its political independence — not in opposition to the wider popular struggle, but located within it.[63] How best the shop steward councils can articulate with existing trade union structures on the one hand, and the wider popular struggle on the other, is a matter that has not yet been resolved.

The emergence of 'technical control' linking together the foundry's work force — so that when the line stopped every worker necessarily joined — was a key factor facilitating the growth of rank-and-file militancy reflected in the rise of the shop steward movement. In one stoppage on the East Rand, for instance, the furnace men were able to bring production to a standstill when they stopped work, leaving the hot metal in the furnace.[64] In a large integrated manufacturing operation such as the auto industry, a relatively small group of workers can cripple an entire system by shutting down a part of the line. The company spokesman for General Motors in Port Elizabeth made this point when he said that 'operations were interrupted when certain employees walked off the assembly line, thus curtailing production in the vehicle assembly plant'.[65] Similarly, Volkswagen in Uitenhage reported that a go-slow in the press and body shop halted production at the point of final assembly and machining.[66]

The growth of an organized challenge from the shop floor has widened the terrain of negotiation and pushed forward the invisible frontier of control in the workplace.[67] The reduction in the formal powers of the employer has threatened management's traditional presumption that workers have no right to participate in the conception and planning of production. Two types of demands can be identified. The first type — epitomized by demands for financial disclosure — challenges management's prerogative in the sphere of production. The second type goes beyond production to wider issues related to the reproduction of the workforce. Examples of this type include demands that management pressurize the East Rand Administration Board to refrain from demolishing shacks in Katlehong and demands for worker control over pension funds. In 1983 black unions in the metal industry won the right to sit on the industry's R800 million Pension Fund Board. They have proposed that, instead of investing in defence bonds, the Fund explore ways of investing in government housing stock in ways that enable its members to benefit by housing loans.

The significance of these latter demands is that they are moving beyond the factory. As one union organizer remarked:

> Low wages in South Africa are associated with the fundamental inequalities of our society . . . . Inevitably, therefore, better wages become a political demand and workers do not confine their perceptions of wages to the narrow economics of the factory.[68]

In fact workers in some metal factories have demanded precisely this: they have claimed wage increases well beyond the increase in the cost of living on the grounds that to maintain their overall standard of living, wage increases must take into account the added burden of unemployed dependants. As they made clear in a letter to management:

> The workers in the company are from the rural area but they also have a home in town . . . . The situation is compounded by the present economic situation which has meant high unemployment which increases the number of dependants who have to be catered for by the worker.[69]

While management, of course, rejected this demand, the workers had common sense on their side: without adequate unemployment benefits for the population at large those in employment, because they have links to the unemployed in the countryside, will experience a decline in living standards. Workers were doing no more than pointing to the role of social security in maintaining the living standards of families during periods of economic hardship.[70] The social penalty paid by retrenched metal workers forced to return to the 'homelands' has been devastating. In a study of fifty workers retrenched from Dunswart Steel in Benoni who were forced to return to KwaZulu in January 1983, the researchers found that only three percent had received Unemployment Insurance Fund (UIF) benefits. Seventy-five percent of the families had no income coming into their households and were on the verge of starvation. Children had to be taken out of school and sent to the nearest towns to beg; families were ultimately forced to sell cattle and borrow money in order to buy food. The men who did apply for UIF had in some cases become too weak to walk to the nearest labour bureau, often situated some twenty kilometres from their homesteads.[71]

The importance of these social security demands is that they are crossing the crucial boundary in the industrial relations system between what Thompson calls the *politics of production*, concerned with the wage-effort bargain, to *global politics*, concerned with ownership and distribution of the product at the level of capitalist society as a whole.[72] The demand for what has been called the social wage is now being put on the bargaining table and in the process a new form of workplace organization is in the making.

What has emerged on the shop floor in the metal industry, then, is a type of trade unionism that has not existed before in engineering — the national mass-based industrial union. Its central features are not those of the industrial unions of syndicalist theory, or the 'business unionism' of social democratic practice: instead, emerging shop-steward structures rooted in a theory of worker control are at the heart of the promise of the new unionism.

In practice though, as we have suggested, worker control is most effective in smaller units. It often remains more formal than real at the higher levels of decision making. This has created tensions inside MAWU over the meaning and practice of worker control. 'We outgrew our resources', one organizer admitted, 'and didn't develop the structures to facilitate [growth]'.[73] The tenuous nature of these structures has meant that when conflicts have emerged, dissatisfied groups such as UMMAWOSA have broken away rather than resolve their differences within the union. The challenge facing MAWU as it grows in size is to build representative structures which can be made accountable in a real way to the rank and file.

Notes

1   For an example of strong emphasis on the necessity for links with the community, see interview with Samson Ndou, chairperson for the General Allied Workers' Union (GAWU), *Labour Focus* I, 3 (August, 1981). UMMAWOSA, the group which has broken away from MAWU, has given as a reason for leaving that no distinction can be drawn between the problems black workers face in the community and on the shop floor. *Financial Mail*, 26.7.1984.

2   The question of participation is closely linked to the perceived need to transmit knowledge and skills. FOSATU has the most advanced educational programme for shop stewards. See 'Manpower Survey', supplement to *Financial Mail*, 27 August 1982, p.56. In addition MAWU runs

its own seminars for shop stewards. An example of one held for a large foundry is the following: Tuesday — functions of the shop stewards, procedures, union history. Wednesday — grievance handling. Thursday — negotiation, Industrial Council, industrial laws.

3   Support from intellectuals outside the organization was crucial in the case of Rely Precision, both in the provision of legal services and in popularizing the struggle inside the foundry in the play *Ilanga*. See *South African Labour Bulletin (SALB)*, VI, 6 and VI, 8.

4   Tony Lane, *The Union Makes Us Strong* (Arrow Books, London, 1974), pp.204 and 207.

5   See J. Baskin, 'The Germiston Shop Stewards' Council' *SALB*, VII, 8 (July 1982) for a detailed discussion of the emergence of this council.

6   'Anti-union campaign', report written by B. Fanaroff to the IMF Central Committee, March 1980. Records of IMF SACC, Durban.

7   *Ibid*.

8   SEIFSA, 'Guidelines for SEIFSA's members as to the development and participation of blacks in trade unions in the metal industry', November 1979.

9   Document headed 'Report on progress in MAWU, March 1980', records of IMF SACC, Durban.

10   Document headed 'Memo on Vosa Valves', personal collection.

11   Document headed 'Report to the Executive Committee of MAWU on a meeting between MAWU and Stewarts & Lloyds Management, March 1980', personal collection.

12   'Report on progress in MAWU, March 1980'.

13   For FOSATU's statements on registration, see pp.10-17 of *SALB*, V, 6 & 7. For MAWU's position, see document headed 'Registration' and interviews with Rodney Mwambo, Bernard Fanaroff, June-Rose Nala, John Stanwix and the union lawyer, John Brand. All in personal collection.

14   The argument that registration was necessary for survival was articulated at the time. See letter from Fanaroff to IMF Central Committee on 22.11.1979: 'For at least the next five to six months we will all be completely occupied with the struggle to obtain registration and to survive in the face of attacks from the parallel unions.' This interpretation is confirmed by the interview with Stanwix: 'The registration issue was presented as a necessity. If we don't register then we face a full frontal state/management/parallel union attack. The way in which the issue was presented was a case of looking at the issue and seeing how we could survive.'

15   MAWU, *A Brief History* (Durban, 1980), p.18. For an analysis of the registration debate, see *SALB*, VII, 1 & 2, pp.30-35.

16   *Ibid.*, p.20. See also interview with Rodney Mwambo.

17   *Survey of Race Relations, 1983* (SAIRR, Johannesburg, 1983), p.179.

18 The clearest statement of the opposition to union registration was in the Western Province General Workers' Union memo to the *SALB*, V, 4. The debate was continued in a full edition of the *SALB*, V, 6. See Fine, de Clercq and Innes, 'Trade Unions and the State: The Case for Legality', *SALB*, VII, 1 & 2, for defence of registration.

19 For interview with Fanaroff, see Dobson, 'The National Industrial Council for the engineering and metallurgical industry: a case study', Sociology Honours Dissertation, University of Cape Town, 1982, p.142.

20 For an account of this critique from a perspective outside the union's, see Morris, *SALB*, VII, 1 & 2.

21 *Financial Mail*, 18.6.1980; for a statement of SEIFSA's position see *Rand Daily Mail*, 15.5.1981. For MAWU's response see B. Fanaroff, 'Anti-union campaign'.

22 *Umbiko we MAWU*, Johannesburg, April 1980.

23 *Ibid*.

24 For a description of the background to this strike see P. Stewart, 'A worker has a human face', Honours dissertation, University of the Witwatersrand, 1981, pp.107-122. For the subsequent trial and a report on the successful assault case against the police, see *SALB*, VII, 8, pp.15-18.

25 *Rand Daily Mail*, Johannesburg, 12.9.1980.

26 See Morris in *SALB*, VII, 1 & 2 for a development of what he calls the 'carrot' approach to trade unions by FCI and Barlow Rand.

27 Interview with an Industrial Relations Officer, East Rand, 4.11.1981.

28 *Ibid*. For a similar account of the ambivalent nature of a unitary frame of reference, see A. Fox, 'Management's frame of reference', in A. Flanders, ed., *Collective Bargaining* (Penguin, Harmondsworth, 1969), pp.390-409.

29 For an analysis of the guidelines, see *SALB*, VII, 4 & 5 (February 1982), p.11.

30 For a discussion of the distinction between demonstration stoppage and trial of strength, see R. Hyman, *Strikes* (Fontana and William Collins, 1972), pp.19-24.

31 *The Star*, Johannesburg, 30.10.1981.

32 *Rand Daily Mail*, Johannesburg, 30.3.1982.

33 See Craig Charney's interview with Boustred, in 'Only The Strong Survive', *Management*, April 1983, pp.19-20.

34 For a more detailed account, see E. Webster, 'MAWU and the Industrial Council', *SALB*, VIII, 5.

35 E. Webster, *ibid*.

36 E. Webster, 'The labour process and forms of workplace organization in South African foundries', Ph.D. thesis, University of the Witwatersrand, 1983, Chapter 11.

37 I. Obery, 'Recession and retrenchment: responses by capital and labour in the East Rand metal industry, 1982', Honours dissertation, University of the Witwatersrand, 1983.

38 'SEIFSA heads for collision with metal workers', *FOSATU Worker News*, August 1984.

39 MAWU, *A Brief History*, p.11. 'Our union fights for the principle that workers must control the organization. We believe that workers alone know what they want. We will not allow people with other interests to control our organization'.

40 Interview with Fanaroff in T. Sideris, 'Industrial Councils and Union Democracy', Industrial Sociology Honours Dissertation, University of the Witwatersrand, 1982.

41 Meeting between organizers and shop stewards of Boksburg foundry, August 1981.

42 Interview with John Stanwix, August 1981.

43 A courageous and articulate exponent of sophisticated managerialism, Theo Heffer, described his decision to negotiate an agreement with SAAWU, in spite of the state's orchestrated attack on that union, in these terms: 'To refuse to deal with a representative union, even if it is not registered, would . . . fly in the face of reality. If a union reflects the true representatives of the workers, then one is courting disaster to refuse to deal with that union.' *SALB*, VII, 4 & 5, p.91. Heffer's argument fits clearly into the classic pluralist approach to industrial relations.

44 'Recognition agreements — a response', *Work in Progress*, 21, 1981, p.20.

45 Recognition guidelines, January 1982, Institute of Industrial Relations, Johannesburg.

46 See Hendred-Freuhauf recognition agreement, Clause 10. In return for this concession by the union, management agreed not to dismiss a worker who went on strike, provided the strike did not last for more than 24 hours.

47 For evidence of the extent to which informal bargaining takes place, despite the extension of procedural agreements that formerly ruled out the use of sanctions to settle day-to-day grievances in the work place, see James W. Kuhn, *Bargaining in Grievance Settlement* (Columbia University Press, New York, 1961) p.47.

48 Document on a FOSATU agreement seminar, 28-30 August, 1981.

49 Quotation from Fanaroff in Dobson, 'The National Industrial Council', p.49.

50 Transvaal BEC Minutes, 31.1.1982.

51 A.W. Ross, *Trade Union Policy* (University of California Press, Berkeley, 1948), p.53. For a summary of this sociological literature see R. Hyman, *Marx and the Sociology of Trade Unionism* (Pluto Press, 1972).

52 The role of intellectuals within the workers' movement is a complex question which I have not been able to explore systematically in this study. For a controversial critique claiming that a group of white intellectuals controls FOSATU, see Calvin Nkabinde, general secretary of EAWU, on his expulsion from FOSATU in *Sowetan*, 30.3.1982; for a critique claiming that petty bourgeois intellectuals dominate FOSATU, see unnamed document, 'Social background of working class leadership', submitted in the state versus Hogan, September 1982; for a similar critique, see the interview given by Andrew Zulu at the time of the breakaway of UMMAWOSA, in *City Press*, 29.7.1984; for a statement of the contradictory nature of the intellectual within the class structure, see Eric Olin Wright, 'Intellectuals and the working class', *The Insurgent Sociologist* VIII, 1 (1978).

53 Interview with June-Rose Nala.

54 This position was stated by Cheadle in a letter to the *SALB*, V, 6 & 7; for a sharply critical reply see letter by General Workers' Union, *SALB*, VI, 1.

55 This critique is drawn from Hyman, *Strikes*, pp.29-32.

56 C. Wright Mills, *The New Men of Power* (Harcourt, Brace, 1948), pp.8-9.

57 In interviews with shop stewards, January 1982, this was strongly identified as a practice inside the union. Similarly in the UMMAWOSA breakaway both sides accused each other of undemocratic behaviour.

58 Shortly after the survey was conducted the Transvaal regional secretary of MAWU was dismissed by the Branch Executive Committee for alleged corruption.

59 For the argument stating the tight nature of FOSATU as a federation, see P. Bonner, 'Focus on FOSATU', *SALB*, V, 1, p.23.

60 Interview with B. Fanaroff, 9.11.1981.

61 For a critique of the attempt to establish participatory democracy through mass meetings in SAAWU, see Maree, 'SAAWU in East London, 1979-1981', *SALB*, VII, 4 & 5 (February 1982).

62 G. Anderson, banned MAWU organizer, interviewed September 1981.

63 For a development of this argument, critical of the attempt to incorporate the shop steward councils into FOSATU, see Mark Swilling, 'Workers Divided: a critical assessment of the split in MAWU on the East Rand', *SALB*, X, 1 (August/September 1984).

64 *Rand Daily Mail*, 7.7.1981.

65 *Ibid.*, 4.8.1982.

66 *Ibid.*, 3.8.1982.

67 This argument is developed further in E. Webster, 'A new frontier of control? Changing forms of job control in South African industrial relations', paper no.111, Second Carnegie Inquiry into Poverty and Development, University of Cape Town, April 1984.

68   *Ibid.*, p.12.
69   *Ibid.*, p.11.
70   This is stated clearly in the ILO's *World Labour Report 1: Employment, incomes, social protection, new information technology* (International Labour Organization, Geneva, 1984). 'Over the past 35 years the industrialized countries have been profoundly influenced by their social welfare systems. The objective of these systems has been first and foremost to give individuals and families a share of security, to reassure them that the vagaries of social, economic, and human affairs need not cause any significant decline in their standards of living. They correspond to a deep-rooted preoccupation of modern society. Social security was recognized as one of the rights of man in the Universal Declaration of Human Rights adopted by the United Nations General Assembly in 1948.'
71   Georgina Jaffee, 'The retrenchment process and some explanations' *South African Review 2* (Ravan Press, Johannesburg, 1984).
72   Paul Thompson, *The Nature of Work* (Macmillan, London, 1983).
73   Mark Swilling, 'Workers Divided'.

CHAPTER 12

Cast in a Racial Mould:
The Birth of a Working Class Politics

This book has shown how capital's attempt to homogenize and deskill
the labour process in South African foundries was resisted by workers,
and how a key role was played by the craft unions through the
mechanism of social closure. In South Africa craft workers possessed
institutional leverage in the industrial relations system and were able
to use this privileged access to entrench the exclusivity inherent within
craft unionism. The specificity of the South African labour process lies
in the explicitly racial form taken by social closure. Capitalist development did not, in the short term, lead to an undermining of the racial
order; instead it led, as shown in Part I, to an intensification of the
racial division of labour in the foundry.

However, the contradictions generated by capitalist development,
and in particular by the transition to monopoly capitalism, created a
crisis of control in work relations. Changes in the labour process led to
a shift in the balance of power: the decline of the 'labour aristocrat'
saw the rise of the production worker. As a consequence a new form
of workplace organization emerged — the industrial union, which
through the strategic location of its members in the labour process was
able to challenge the traditional forms of control in the foundry. Faced
by the challenge described in Part II, the state withdrew formal support for racial exclusion and embarked upon an experiment to incorporate black workers into the industrial relations system (the Wiehahn
solution). Part III showed how this incorporative strategy has been
challenged 'from below' by demands that the shop steward structure
be involved in negotiations and that factory-level bargaining take
place. These demands have now widened, moving the frontier of control beyond production to the reproduction of the workforce — from
the politics of production to global politics. This raises the difficult
and unresolved question of the relationship between workplace
organization and the wider popular struggle. To illustrate the complex

nature of the interaction between divisions within the working class, the labour process, and workplace organization, we need to return to the 'five faces' introduced in Chapter 1. Through these five working lives — Bob, Len, Morris, Sipho, and Josias — we hope to provide an illustration, in capsule form, of the main themes of the study.

In Chapter 9, following Edwards, it was suggested that the racial and occupational distribution of the workforce in the foundries consists of three racially segmented labour markets — the independent primary, the subordinate primary, and the secondary. About ten percent of the foundry workforce are members of the independent primary labour market — predominantly white, skilled, and relatively secure in their jobs. They are illustrated in this chapter by Bob and Len. Forty percent of the workforce are members of the subordinate primary labour market. These machine-based, semi-skilled jobs are occupied largely by coloureds, although an increasing number of Africans are being taken on. Morris, a coloured production moulder, illustrates this segment. The secondary labour market (50 percent of the workforce) consists almost entirely of Africans, many of whom are migrant workers living in the hostels. They are illustrated in this chapter by Sipho and Josias.

Bob: Craftsman Turned Rate-Fixer

In the early years members of the IMS successfully struggled to maintain their privileged position as a labour aristocracy through the mechanism of the closed shop and the apprenticeship system (Chapter 2). Bob, a skilled moulder apprenticed from 1922 to 1929, illustrates this phase of workplace organization. While the concept of 'labour aristocracy' captures the privileged aspect of the lives of skilled craftsmen such as Bob, it neglects a central aspect of craft work, namely the degree of control a craftsman exercised over his job.[1] The autonomy of these early craft moulders was embedded in craft rules, amounting to a moral code which defined the moulder's notion of economic justice. Bob enforced the code, when necessary, by simply walking off the job if he was dissatisfied.

> I worked there [Scaw Metals] and we were making frames for bicycle seats . . . . When the bicycle seat contract was completed, the foreman gave me another job, and I said to him, 'How many are there of these

frames?' He said, 'Four thousand five hundred.' I said, 'Make them your bloody self.' He said, 'What do you mean?' I said, 'I'm going', and I went. I got a job at the Phoenix Foundry. And I worked there for quite a while. The boss and I had words and I told him what I thought of him. He told me what he thought of me and I went. That's how the foundry worked. Then I got a job at Rowell Jewell.

It would seem that before World War II craftsmen such as Bob relied purely on skill, and not on racial exclusion, to control access to the job.

During the war Bob was one of the 'key men' drafted into Iscor to assist in the production of munitions. The quantities demanded by war necessitated the introduction of mass production rather than the jobbing which had prevailed previously. Most foundries were converted to manufacture heavy armaments supplies, materials, and shell cases. Between 1938-39 and 1944-45 the value of the net output in basic metals rose from £9 285 000 to £25 957 000. But the skilled moulder was not redundant as his skill was required in the production of the larger castings for which mass production was neither economic nor practical. In 1948 Bob joined VECOR, a new parastatal foundry at Vanderbijlpark, to work in the jobbing section. Here the skill of the craft moulder was still required, this time in the casting of large hoists for the mines. However, as we shall see, the process of deskilling had already begun.

Bob was a skilled man and proud of it. As a shop steward in the IMS he jealously guarded the craft skill and autonomy of the moulder when they came under attack in the 1940s (see Chapter 4). Thus when VECOR violated union custom, established in the early years of the union, and appointed a non-moulder as foreman, he brought the shop to a standstill: he refused to work until management agreed to appoint a moulder as foreman. He would only accept orders from his peers. He described the incident as follows:

> I said you are not a moulder, you can't tell me how to mould. I said I had been too long at the trade. He went off and reported me to the boss, the foundry manager, and I was fetched in and hauled over the coals. I got fired, zap, finish and *klaar*. When I walked out of the shop all the moulders walked out behind me.

A union official came down from Johannesburg to settle the dispute. The outcome was an unqualified victory for the union when Bob was reinstated and the foreman replaced by a moulder.

Bob's accident, mentioned in Chapter 4, strengthened the hand of management in VECOR's jobbing section. In 1949 he fell into a pool of molten metal after the mould burst, permanently disabling both his hands, and in 1950 management offered him a job as a 'rate-fixer'. For the men on the floor he had crossed sides: for management he was an ideal choice as he knew the pace of work. After initial resistance to Bob, the moulders were forced to accept his timing of the job.

To fix a rate is to experience the antagonistic nature of capitalist production, rather than the cold rationality of science:

> On the one hand I knew that the moulders would be squealing because I would not allow enough time. On the other hand, if I allowed too much time the manager would be on to me . . . . I was serving two masters. The biggest master is competition. There were times when I felt guilty, but I had to do the job for the benefit of the firm. You can't do that job and be friends with the men. They didn't want to talk to you at all after work because they thought that you were now a rate-fixer, and that you were on the other side.

The men on the shop floor gave visible expression to their antagonism when they refrained from giving Bob a farewell collection when he retired in 1971 to spend the rest of his days on a small-holding outside Van der Bijl Park. He is seriously ill with silicosis, an occupational disease directly related to excessive dust in the foundry. 'I wake up sometimes in the night', he said, 'and I can't breathe. I feel I'm being choked to death.' Whatever benefits Bob's privileged position as a craftsman gave him, they did not enable him to escape from the disease and injuries that affect the lives of all foundry workers. He retains the pride and the scars of the craftsman.

Len: From Craftsman to Supervisor

Len approached the craft of moulding in a more instrumental way than Bob. The late 1940s and the 1950s were years of rapid growth in the East Rand metal industry. A qualified moulder, a man like Len, could make a considerable amount of money at the trade. As he remarked:

> I made a lot of money working overtime in the 1950s. I worked from

7 a.m. until early evening from Monday to Thursday from 1950 to 1958. I banked all my overtime money.

He seems to have moved frequently from one foundry to another, exploiting the demand for moulders to bargain for higher actual wage rates. Consequently he felt that he did not really need a union. He belonged to the IMS because of the closed shop, and had once attended a meeting in Johannesburg, but had no interest in its activities. His only interest, he said, was money.

In the 1950s CO_2 was introduced into many of the more advanced foundries in the Transvaal, reducing the level of skill required in Len's job (see Chapter 5). Len was ambiguous towards this technological change. On the one hand it displaced an important part of his craft. On the other hand, the old skills were laborious and CO_2 lightened his load. More specifically, it enabled him to take advantage of the new supervisory jobs that were opening up in the foundries as routine machine work became the order of the day. In 1964 he joined Salcast as a supervisor. Reflecting on these changes, Len observed:

Nobody is apprenticed anymore. Most of them are coloureds anyway. I told my two sons to go to college and get a proper education. There is no future for the white man on the foundry floor.

Len has been with Salcast for the past twenty years. His experiences during that time typify all the changes that accompanied the transition to monopoly capitalism as discussed in Part II. The company is the outcome of a number of mergers in recent years: its largest shareholder is Stewarts & Lloyds. In the late 1970s Salcast, eager to penetrate the export market, introduced a R14 million 'modernization programme' that has equipped it with the most up-to-date foundry technology in South Africa. However, inflation and the recession have squeezed the company out of its new markets. In 1982 twenty percent of the workforce was retrenched. Increasingly Salcast has found it difficult to compete with cheaper imported castings and has even discussed the relocation of production to the 'border' areas to cheapen wage costs and take advantage of decentralization incentives.

As we have seen in the case of Bob, the moulders' privileged position had always rested on their capacity to maintain control over the job and to negotiate agreements that protected moulding jobs at the annual sessions of the Industrial Council. Indeed, the conclusion drawn from Part I was that craft workers resisted the process of deskilling, and thus retained considerable control over the supply of labour to individual companies and to the industry as a whole. The result was the survival of a higher number of 'craft' jobs than the deskilling thesis would suggest. This, as was argued in Part II, contributed to a crisis of control in work relations in the 1970s. The crisis was in part the result of the new scale of operations in the foundry after the transition to monopoly capitalism in the 1960s (Chapter 6), and its flashpoint was the despotic racial regime that ruled the workplace. Just when management needed to raise the level of control in order to regulate the intensified rate of production, its traditional, hierarchical means of control became less effective as a method of managing the growing workforce.

The inadequacy of this system of racial despotism is revealed in Len's contradictory attitudes towards black workers and in his inability to handle managerial responsibility. Of course the racial division of labour had always existed in the foundry through the widespread practice of employing an African 'helper' to assist the journeyman on the manual side of the job. Len described this practice:

> Every moulder has a boy [an African helper]. Your boy would be with you all the time. He did everything. He would dig the hole. He would mix the sand to make the mould. The only person who can touch the journeyman's tools is his boy, and then only to clean and carry them.

Not surprisingly, these 'hierarchical relations' were reinforced by racist ideas.

> They can take instructions — do this and do that — but they can't think the way you and I do.

For Len, craft work was beyond the intellectual capacity of Africans. Consequently he was sceptical of their ability to hold down skilled jobs after the opening of the union to Africans in the wake of the Wiehahn Commission in 1979.

> They will not be able to do the very skilled jobs. They cannot think properly. They will always need white journeymen moulders. Who will do the big jobbing castings? The blacks are all right for the mechanical repetition jobs but where you have to think, they are not going to be able to do the job.

Here we see the contradictory nature of Len's racial attitudes: on the one hand he believes that Africans are incapable of performing certain tasks in the foundry, yet on the other hand, he feels the need to introduce *de facto* job reservation in order to keep them out of these jobs. In earlier times, when the moulders' skill was intact, such racism had not found its way into formal union rules. It was the 'dilution' of their jobs which brought home to white craftsmen the economic advantage of racism.

In 1968 Len was promoted to the position of foundry manager. He held the job for six years but resigned and went back to the job of supervisor when he found he could not cope. Changing technology in the modern foundry which had superannuated many of the skills of the craftsman, had simultaneously created the need for a higher grade of technical knowledge, learned from books rather than on the job as in craft training.

> Figures were beyond my capacity. They needed university-trained metallurgists.

Len's limited formal technical training was effectively blocking his mobility into management.

Len lives in a comfortable suburban house in Boksburg with a large swimming pool, two cars, and a colour TV set. Unlike Bob, he was never a union stalwart and saw his job as a means to money and social mobility. He was not keen to be interviewed and tried to avoid discussing his past. His wife felt that they had struggled, during the 1950s in particular, to escape the dirt and danger of the foundry. Len has now become deeply committed to the charismatic movement — a Christian sect active among the white population on the East Rand. Whereas Bob saw his change from craftsman to rate-fixer as the unfortunate result of an accident, Len sees his change from craftsman to supervisor as an opportunity that led to promotion and mobility.

Morris: A 'Second-class' Production Moulder

Morris is a coloured man whose experience of race discrimination inside the union and the industry embittered him so much that he eventually left the union and the industry. Morris began his working life as a production moulder in Durban Falkirk (now Defy) in 1946.

The establishment of Durban Falkirk in 1936 as South Africa's first large-scale mass production foundry had opened up a demand for a new type of worker, the machine-operating production moulder, in the foundry.

The creation of a large demand for non-craft moulders at Durban Falkirk precipitated a crisis in the IMS, particularly as most production moulders were coloureds. Should the IMS retain its craft exclusivity, or should it bow to the inevitable and open its membership to non-craft moulders — thus retaining its monopoly over moulding jobs? The traditionalists in the union argued for the status quo, the pragmatists for the need to accept the inevitable. After considerable debate the pragmatists won and the IMS opened its membership to production moulders from Durban Falkirk. When Morris began work there coloured moulders had been active for a decade in the Durban branch of the IMS. Morris recalled these early non-racial meetings where strict discipline was maintained through a system of fines — he was once fined 2s 6d for not attending a meeting. Being part of a closely-knit, exclusive group clearly meant a lot to Morris. By all accounts he was an active member, constantly challenging management on the shop floor when he believed the Industrial Council agreement had been breached. A constant area of conflict was the attempt by management to increase the intensity of work by lowering the piece rate. After he was elected shop steward in 1952, Morris successfully forced management to back down.

The victory of the National Party in 1948 was to threaten, and eventually remove, this important area of equality for coloured moulders in Natal. In 1956 the government amended the Industrial Conciliation Act, forcing all 'mixed' unions to establish separate racial branches under a white national executive. While only five percent of the total IMS membership at the time were coloured, the society was determined to retain a monopoly over moulding jobs. Thus, rather than establish a separate coloured union at the risk of losing control over moulding jobs, the IMS in 1958 decided to establish a separate branch for coloureds at Falkirk, called the Durban No.1 Branch. Morris was very unhappy about this proposal and argued strongly at the time that if the union was going to have separate branches the officials for the coloured branch must be coloured.

We coloureds met to discuss the establishment of a separate branch. The IMS wanted the officials to be white. We have been a very docile people and have trusted the white man, but he has usurped all what belonged to the coloureds. I said to the officials of the IMS that if you people want a separate branch then we must have coloured officials. I said there were capable people in this hall that might know who could do the job. I put it as a proposal and it was unanimously accepted.

Morris was later elected secretary of the Durban No.1 Branch.

What came to be regarded as a constitutional issue broke out later when Morris signed on four Transvaal coloured production moulders as members of the Durban No.1 Branch. He was hoping to give them an opening to work as moulders in the Transvaal. Until 1970 the IMS was to ensure that moulding remained a white job in the Transvaal, although coloureds had been members at the coast from the beginning of the century. Consequently the IMS opposed Morris's decision, suspending him as secretary. Then, finding that no one else was prepared to accept nomination, they were forced to instruct Morris to continue.

For Morris this attempt to thwart his efforts to give Natal coloureds openings in the Transvaal foundries was the last straw. He also felt that the union executive had not given him sufficient backing in his struggle with management at Durban Falkirk. In the mid 1960s he resigned from Durban Falkirk and from the IMS, a deeply embittered man. He was eventually able to obtain a job in marine engineering and became active in the South African Boilermakers' Society (SABS). Although the roots of SABS also lie in craft exclusivity, this union had been able to respond to the challenge of non-craft and non-white workers more effectively than the IMS. It has encouraged strong shop floor leadership on a multiracial basis. In fact, SABS left TUCSA in 1983 because the union felt that the established unions were not sufficiently responsive to the needs and demands of black workers.

Morris has become convinced of the effectiveness of the SABS philosophy towards race relations. SABS has organized the union around separate racial branches in order, they argue, to provide for 'equal opportunity' for each racial group. Morris believes that, provided coloureds are in control of their branch and properly represented at the National Executive, they can be 'equal partners' with whites and with Africans. Africans will also, he believes, benefit by a system of separate racial representation as they are not as experienced as whites are. It is only through allowing racial groups to organize separately inside one union that each group will find 'justice'.

Unlike Bob and Len, who have established comfortable homes, Morris lives in a small house with his family in the coloured township of Wentworth. Because of the housing shortage among coloureds he is forced to share his small house with his two grown-up sons and their families. He was reluctant to speak to me about his situation as it reminded him of past and present experiences of race discrimination. He is sceptical of the government's new dispensation towards coloureds. 'We coloureds', he said to me as I left his house, 'almost always get short-changed by the whites. You can't trust the white man.'

For Morris it is the colour of his skin that prevented him from being apprenticed many years ago in Pietermaritzburg and that now forces him to live in an overcrowded ghetto in Durban. Although he feels his voice is now being heard inside the union, he retains a bitter conviction that his working life would have been more comfortable and rewarding if he had been a white and not a coloured worker.

Sipho: 'Cast-boy' and 'Temporary Migrant'

Sipho and Josias are both Zulu-speaking workers whose families live in KwaZulu. This affects their response to trade union organization in a direct way; in fact for Sipho and Josias the union is not merely their representative at the workplace — it is a vehicle for their wider social and political objectives. As members of the secondary labour market they are the most vulnerable section of the workforce. It is by building unity between workers, they believe, that they can bring about change in their lives. Sipho has worked sufficently long in Boksburg to acquire Section 10/1(b) rights, but he lives in the Vosloorus hostel and his wife lives on their plot of land in KwaZulu. He does not want his wife to join him — he has no town home anyway.

> I have no wish of bringing my wife to the urban areas. We only bring our wives to the urban areas when they get sick — bringing them here is bringing them to the doctors.

He is deeply dissatisfied with conditions in the hostel. Run by the East Rand Administration Board (ERAB), it houses nearly 15 000 inmates. The first and most immediate grievance was that the hostel was dirty and inadequately serviced. Sipho described conditions as follows:

The hostel is never clean. The dirt concentrates on the roof inside [because of steam cooling inside the room]; the windows are dirty and some are broken with no one to repair them. We use cardboard boxes to close the broken windows. Nobody washes the floors. When the roof leaks we use more cardboard to stop the gaps. The last time the hostel was cleaned was when the hostel was built. Things are getting worse and the cause is that there is no repairs. There is no person who represents people's grievances. The toilets have no electricity. There is nobody who cleans them. It is always dirty.

Sipho's deepest grievance was the presence of the 'black-jacks' and their associated system of spies, the *impimpi*. They are the front line of state control over migrant workers, constantly searching for illegal hostel residents and those who have not paid hostel rents. Black-jack raids — they wake workers in the middle of the night, banging on the metal doors — are fiercely resented.

A sense of having being deprived of a stable social life underlies complaints about the lack of privacy (16 to a room), having to cook their own food after a long day at work, stealing, excessive drinking over the weekends, and violent assaults. Accompanying this sense of deprivation is the acceptance of certain social consequences. As Sipho remarks:

There are times when you need a woman, but you know you have come with one aim. Then that fades away. You can sometimes buy a woman with money. There is a lot of them [prostitutes], you can pick them up all over Vosloorus and Boksburg. But you can't have a woman without having money; the township woman will desert you when you are in trouble. These women don't love you, they love your money.

Another aspect of this deprivation is the decline in the parental authority of the migrant man when he returns to his family in the reserve:

When a man comes home there is no respect for him anymore because he has been away for such a long time.

Sipho works as a 'cast-boy'. His job consists of manoeuvring an overhead ladle full of molten metal and pouring the metal into moulds. The job is very dangerous: in particular, molten metal can spill onto the worker's feet. The men are given no training.

After two months you get the hang of the job. But before that, many people are sacked because they recoil from the fires. They never sack people because they run away sooner. Migrants don't leave the job. They say it is hard and then they complain and then they are sacked. But they don't just leave on their own account. I would run too if I had somewhere to run to.

Sipho describes the dangers of his job, and the cynical attitudes of employers:

One day we had to lift up a heavy pot very high. While we were pouring it it did not go straight into the hole and the metal spilled. The molten burned the whole of a man's arm. They did not take him to hospital but only bandaged him. They sacked him . . . he was a temporary worker.

Sipho, in sharp contrast to Len's attitude towards blacks, feels resentful that he gets paid considerably less than the white 'supervisors' when he has to train them informally on the job. He illustrates the anger that is built up over the years as white furnacemen come and go, each being to a large extent taught by the 'cast-boy', then exercising authority over him:

I was supposed to do the white man's job, whereas the white man gets more than I get. When he gets employed they say he knows the work. When he is inside the firm I teach him. That made me angry. I don't get the money which he is getting, but I am supposed to be his teacher. How can a clever man be taught by a stupid man like myself.

Sipho feels that the introduction of new technology, in particular the electrically-operated furnace, has increased the intensity of work:

When the electricty is on it's not possible to rest. We have to work all the time. I am controlled by this electricity. At Rely the furnace makes us work fast. You cannot stop once it is on. There is absolutely no time for rest.

The increase in intensity of work at Rely was the result, said Sipho, of a new machine that cast six times instead of twice a day:

When I started at Rely in 1973 we used to work normally. For maybe two or three hours we used to work hard. Now when they brought this new furnace we could no longer dodge. They brought it in 1975 and when it came we rejoiced because we didn't know it. But after some time, when we saw the way it worked, we were deeply saddened.

The new machine also increased management's control over the labour process:

> Before, we used to be the ones who started the furnace. We knew that if we started it at a particular time it would take three or four hours before you casted. Just like a car [you can control it] by raising and lowering the speed. The previous one used to be like that but the present one controls itself.

In July 1979 Sipho was among a group of workers from Rely who joined MAWU, which had started recruiting in the Transvaal in 1975. 'I joined the union', Sipho said, 'because workers are not treated like human beings by management.' The men who joined MAWU between July 1979 and May 1980 came from three different districts in KwaZulu, lived in Vosloorus hostel, and consequently shared a common set of grievances. However, it was at the workplace that these men became aware of their common interests. 'The first thing that makes people aware of their unity', said Sipho, 'is that they learn it in the factory.'

In May 1980 Sipho, as a union member, became involved in a strike over the dismissal of a colleague. Management proved intransigent and the police were called, leading to the instant arrest of the strikers. Although they were found guilty and fined R60 for striking illegally, they were able to pursue an assault charge against the SAP, winning R700 damages. Because he has Section 10/1(b) rights, he unlike others, was not 'endorsed out' of the urban area when he lost his job at Rely.

He is now back at Rely after the company had unsuccessfully attempted to employ 'local' labour in the wake of the Riekert Commission proposals. Management found that 'local' labour was not prepared to work in such dangerous and dirty conditions and applied for an exemption to employ migrants. This, Sipho believes, emphasizes how much management needs workers like himself.[1]

MAWU has grown rapidly since 1980 and strikes have become commonplace in the metal industry on the East Rand. Many black workers have won enforceable rights in the factory since then, giving them a sense of dignity and pride. Although Sipho still hopes to maintain himself and his family on his land in the countryside, he has worked intermittently for 25 years in Boksburg and the possibility of his breaking this dependence on wage labour is remote. But his cultural world is still shaped by his rural values: 'I work in Boksburg but my spirit is in Mahlabatini', he says.

Josias: Shop Steward and Permanent Townsman

Josias is the youngest of the faces from the hidden abode. He came to the Reef in 1975 in search of work on the East Rand. As a contract worker he found it easiest to find employment in the foundries.

> I do this work but it is very hot. There is nothing that is easy here, if you work in the foundry. Everything is hot and heavy. It burns your eyes and you wear goggles to keep the dust out of your eyes.

A crucial feature of Josias's position in the labour market is that it offers virtually no job security.

> I came to the Reef because I heard a rumour that the money here was good. When I reached here I found that there was no money. If you want money you have to work overtime, at night, and if you fail to do that the foreman will chase you away.

However, Josias realized that there was no turning back to Nqutu, a resettlement camp where his family had been relocated after being forced off a white farm near Vryheid: he had waited long enough for his first job. He went on to describe how he found another job at a foundry, where the pattern was repeated:

> I found a job for ten months at J and C Malleable foundry, and they registered me. We quarrelled because they said that I must work after I had been injured [he was badly burnt by molten metal]. My skin is like a snake's because of these burns. Even my children do not know my true colour. I was dismissed because they said I did not want to work and should go to the homelands. I still had not got my sick pay from them. If you speak the truth you are dismissed.

The power management has over the migrant worker, and the dependence it creates on the part of workers, is vividly illustrated by Josias:

Our employers don't treat us like human beings but animals because they know that as soon as they fire you, you would have no place of residence, because you would not be able to pay for the hostel fees without the money which they provide. And the pass office is going to be indifferent and will instruct you to go back where you came from. That is very painful.

Josias says he has worked at most of the unskilled and semi-skilled jobs in the foundry. The work almost never requires previous training and many of the tasks do not require any formal education at all. Workers are simply hired, usually by the 'boss-boy' on a trial basis, and learn the task by performing it. He described his introduction to the furnace in these terms:

You are just put there at the fire, even though it is dangerous, and you do what the others do. Some people will take two weeks to get used to the job. Some people never adapt to the fear of the fire in the foundries. They get dismissed.

Even when promotion does take place, it does not lead to the status and remuneration associated with these jobs when they are performed by whites.

I was promoted to supervisor in this job because I can do it. Still the money that I get is not the same as they give a white man, even though I took the job over from the *umlungu* [the white man].

At present Josias is employed at Salcast, the same firm that employs Len. In 1978 he joined MAWU after a dispute with his *induna*.

Whenever we had complaints we told the *indunas*. They would say that the boss said that those who don't want to work can take their jackets and get out of the gate. We used to ask ourselves whether we were in jail or being employed. Then we heard about the union.

In July 1981 they were able to bring production in the whole foundry to a standstill by persuading the furnace men to leave the hot metal in the furnace. This, says Josias, made them realize that their power lay on the shop floor.

Josias was soon elected a shop steward in the foundry and has now served three years as chairman of the shop steward committee. His experiences as a shop floor leader reveal some of the contradictory characteristics of the shop steward which were described in Chapter 11. He is the key link between the rank and file members and the union officials. His standing among fellow workers has placed him in the frontline of potential cooption. However, the persistence of racial discrimination even after promotion has ensured his continued active involvement in shop floor politics.

Although he believes migrants are more responsive to unions Josias believes the union cuts across the migrant/non-migrant divide.

> Both migrants and non-migrants are interested in unions, but more especially the migrants. The migrants do the hardest work in this world. The employer thinks he can do what he likes with them. So they must have somebody to stand up for them. But the locals who join, they just seem few because there are not that many in the foundries.

The vulnerability of migrant workers was revealed in 1982 when those retrenched at Salcast were forced to return to KwaZulu in terms of influx regulations. Many have become destitute because of lack of adequate social security in these areas.

Recently Josias's wife came to join him from Nqutu as he found it difficult to survive and send money back to his family. He built a 'Zozo hut' (corrugated iron shack) in Daveyton for himself and his wife, Veronica. But the interdependence between town and countryside is maintained through the family — Veronica prefers living in her village, Nondweni, where her children live with her mother. She feels a stranger in Daveyton and is an illegal resident there:

> I cannot mix with the people in Daveyton because I am different to them. I do not have rights to be here like they do. The people here have no respect. In Nondweni we teach our children to respect their elders but here they have no respect. They even go so far as to kick their parents out of their houses. They become *tsotsis* because they have no work.

Yet, in contrast to Sipho, Josias remarked:

> My home is now here in Boksburg.

He has begun to see his future in the town. By building a shack for his wife in Daveyton, he has begun to put down roots for his family.

The transition remains tenuous, of course: Veronica is in town illegally and their children are still in Nqutu.

More important, for Josias, is his involvement in the trade union. This has given him a sense of purpose and has provided an outlet for his aspirations and his capacity for leadership. The aspirations go beyond a demand for representation in the workplace: for him the union expresses the worker's struggle for economic and political justice in South Africa, and no sharp distinction can be drawn between the problems black workers face in the community and those they confront on the shop floor.

He is sympathetic to the recent breakaway union from MAWU, the United Mining Metal and Allied Workers' Union of South Africa (UMMAWOSA) as it publicly articulates a more political unionism. 'You can't limit politics in this country to the factory floor', their new secretary said at the public launching of the union, 'you can't say workers must be silent when Katlehong shacks are demolished, rents are increased and electricity bills are eating at workers' wage packets'. Josias is now uncertain as to which union he should follow. His uncertainty reflects the unresolved nature of the central debate inside the workers' movement on the relationship between workplace organization and the wider popular struggle.

Conclusions

These five faces from a hidden abode illustrate the transformation of the labour process and its effect on life and work in the foundry. Bob illustrates the disappearing 'craft conscious' English-speaking worker, while in Len we see the growing embourgeoisement of the white worker. While they differ from each other, however, they also differ from the rest. They are both privileged workers in the foundry and in society. Morris, Sipho, and Josias have in common the fact that they are neither white nor craftsmen, and owe their position in the foundry to the transformation of the labour process. But Morris stands apart from Sipho and Josias through his intermediary status within production and his experience, as a coloured man, of partial integration in the craft union. Although, since 1979, the opportunity for integration into the established unions exists for Sipho and Josias, they have chosen a different path. As African migrant workers they share a distinct form of oppression that accounts for the different form of worker organization to which they adhere. Their involvement in their union goes beyond a demand for representation in the foundry: it has become a struggle against a system of racial capitalism.

The experiences of these five men illustrate the complex nature of the interaction between the labour process, workplace organization, and divisions within the working class. These divisions cover skill, education, region, language, political power, ethnicity, migrancy, and, above all, race. They express themselves in divided worker organizations. The IMS and SABS are established unions which have served the interests of privileged workers. Changes in the labour process, and more recently in state policy, have forced both unions to open their membership to Africans. For SABS this has meant fundamental changes in policy, leading Morris to feel much happier in SABS than in the IMS. MAWU, on the other hand, is an emerging industrial union drawing largely on semi-skilled and unskilled black workers. Rooted in the working lives of the East Rand migrant workers in the metal industry, it has taken on some of the characteristics of a social movement.

The introduction of machine-based production has undermined the traditional division of skill and race in the foundry. It has shifted the balance of power away from the 'labour aristocrat' and his craft union, to the production worker and his industrial union. Through their strategic location in the labour process these workers have been able to challenge the traditional form of control in the foundry. But in spite of this challenge the lives of Bob, Len, Morris, Sipho, and Josias still remain profoundly shaped by divisions within the working class and their organizations.

The transformation of the labour process both undermines traditional divisions within the working class and leads to their reconstitution, often in a new guise. Yet in spite of the persistence of these divisions within the working class, changes in the labour process have created the conditions for a new form of workplace organization. A mass-based, non-racial, industrial union has emerged for the first time in the foundry industry. An important feature of this union is its concentration on building shop steward structures in the foundry.

By establishing independent working class organizations, the emerging unions have created the embryo of a working class politics in South Africa. This can be seen most clearly in the evolving shop steward councils which readily concern themselves with non-foundry issues, pushing unions beyond pure-and-simple trade unionism. But it can also be seen in the growth of an organized challenge on the shop floor which has widened the negotiable issues, pushing forward the invisible frontier of control in the workplace. These demands extend beyond the workplace to include issues concerned with the reproduction of the workforce such as housing and pensions.[2] Now that these wider demands have been placed on the bargaining table a new form of workplace organization is in the making. This emerged most clearly in November 1984 when over half a million workers stayed away from work in protest over issues in the schools, townships and factories. The stay-away marked a new phase in the history of protest against apartheid, signalled by united action involving organized labour, students, and community groups — with unions taking the leading role.[3]

What implications do these conclusions have for an analysis of South Africa in a comparative perspective? The specificity of South Africa lies in the way in which the state has intervened in production, giving labour market segmentation a racial form. This intervention has aimed at maintaining a racial division of labour (through the industrial council system); at confining blacks to secondary labour market jobs (through influx control); and at containing black unions (through their exclusion from the formal collective bargaining system before 1979). In contrast to South Africa, the state does not intervene directly in foundry production in Britain and the United States, though it does, of course, function indirectly to maintain overall capitalist relations of production. Production as a consequence ceases to be an immediate political issue[4]. The roots of 'economism' lie in this separation of production from politics: class struggle now appears not as a political struggle, Wood says, but as a battle over the terms and conditions of work,[5] whereas in South Africa the state's intervention in production makes its racial form clear for all to see. It thus directly links the *politics of production*, i.e. questions of the wage effort bargain, to *global politics*, i.e. the ownership and distribution of the product at the level of capitalist society as a whole. The implications of our argument are now clear: the transformation of the labour process has created the potential for mass-based industrial trade unions, while failing to provide the conditions for their political incorporation. The dilemma facing South Africa's system of racial capitalism lies in the fact that a process of 'deracialization' of the workplace has begun without an accompanying 'deracialization' in society at large. Rather than facilitating a separation of 'economic' and 'political' struggle, the contradictions generated by capitalist development have given birth to a working class politics. The central issue now confronting the organized working class is the form and content of this politics.

Notes

1   Hobsbawm's six major criteria for defining this group do not include control over work. See E. Hobsbawm, 'The labour aristocracy in nineteenth century Britain' in *Labouring Men* (London, 1964).
2   E. Webster, 'A new frontier of control? Changing forms of job protection in South African industrial relations', paper no.111, Second Carnegie Inquiry into Poverty and Development, University of Cape Town, April 1984.
3   The Labour Monitoring Group, 'The November stay-away', *South African Labour Bulletin*, X, 6 (May 1985).
4   E.M. Wood, 'The separation of the economic and the political in capitalism', *New Left Review*, 27.
5   *Ibid.*

Bibliography

A. Books

Aglietta, M, *A Theory of Capitalist Regulation: The US Experience* (New Left Books, London, 1976).

Alridge, A, *Power, Authority and Restrictive Practices, a Sociological Essay on Industrial Relations* (Blackwell, Oxford and London, 1976).

Baritz, L, *Servants of Power* (Wiley, New York, 1965).

Bendix, R, *Work and Authority* (University of California Press, Berkeley, 1974).

Berg, M, *Technology and Toil in Nineteenth Century Britain* (CSE Books, London, 1979).

Beynon, H, *Working for Ford* (Allen Lane, London, 1973).

Bozzoli, B (ed.), *Town and Countryside in the Transvaal* (Ravan Press, Johannesburg, 1981).

Braverman, H, *Labour and Monopoly Capital. The Degradation of Work in the Twentieth Century* (Monthly Review Press, New York and London, 1974).

Bright, J R, *Automation and Management* (Harvard University Press, Boston, 1958).

Burawoy, M, *Manufacturing Consent. Changes in the Labour Process under Monopoly Capitalism* (University of Chicago Press, Chicago, 1979).

Cebula, J E, *A History of the Moulders' Union* (International Moulders and Allied Workers' Union, Cincinnati, 1976).

Cleaver, H, *Reading Capital Politically* (University of Texas Press, Houston, 1979).

Cope, R K, *Comrade Bill — The Life of W. H. Andrews* (Workers Reader).

Davies, R, *Capital, the State and White Wage Earners* (Harvester

Press, London, 1979).

Du Toit, M A, *South African Trade Unions* (McGraw Hill, Johannesburg, 1976).

Edwards, R, *Contested Terrain: The Transformation of the Workplace in the Twentieth Century* (Basic Books, New York, 1979).

Flanders, A (ed.), *Collective Bargaining* (Penguin Books, Harmondsworth, 1969).

Fyrth, H J, and Collins, H, *The Foundry Workers, A Trade Union History* (Amalgamated Union of Foundry Workers, London, 1959).

Gould, W B, *Black Workers in White Unions: Job Discrimination in the United States* (Cornell University Press, London, 1977).

Greenberg, S, *Race and State in Capitalist Development* (Ravan Press, Johannesburg, 1980).

Hinton, J, *The First Shop Stewards' Movement* (George Allen & Unwin, London, 1973).

Hobsbawm, E, *Labouring Men* (Weidenfeld & Nicholson, London, 1964).

Horrell, M, *South Africa's Workers: Their Organization and Patterns of Employment* (South African Institute of Race Relations, Johannesburg, 1969).

Hoxie, R F, *Scientific Management and Labour* (Appleton & Co., New York and London, 1921).

Hutt, W H, *The Economics of the Colour Bar* (Andre Deutsch, London, 1964).

Hyman, R, *Marxism and the Sociology of Trade Unionism* (Pluto Press, London, 1971).

— *Strikes* (Fontana and William Collins, London, 1972).

— *Industrial Relations: A Marxist Introduction* (Macmillan, London, 1976).

Institute for Industrial Education, *The 1973 Durban Strikes* (Ravan Press, Johannesburg, 1974).

Johnstone, F A, *Class, Race and Gold* (Routledge & Kegan Paul, London, 1976).

Katz, E, *A Trade Union Aristocracy* (University of the Witwatersrand Press, Johannesburg, 1976).

De Kiewiet, C W, *A History of South Africa* (Oxford University Press, London, 1966).

Kuhn, J W, *Bargaining in Grievance Settlement* (Columbia University

Press, New York, 1961).

Landes, D S, *The Unbound Prometheus* (Cambridge University Press, Cambridge, 1969).

Lane, T, *The Union Makes Us Strong* (Arrow Books, London, 1974).

Luckhart, K, and Wall, B, *Organize or Starve, the History of SACTU* (Lawrence & Wishart, London, 1980).

Maré, G, *African Population Relocation in South Africa* (South African Institute of Race Relations, Johannesburg, 1980).

Marx, K, *Capital. A Critique of Political Economy*, Vol. I (Penguin Books, London, 1976).

Meier, A, and Rudwick, E, *Black Detroit and the Rise of the UAW* (Oxford University Press, New York, 1979).

Montgomery, D, *Workers' Control in America: Studies in the History of Work, Technology and Labour Struggles* (Cambridge University Press, Binghamton, 1979).

National Productivity Institute Survey, *Productivity of the Iron Foundry Industry in South Africa* (NPIS, 1973).

Nichols, T, (ed.), *Capital and Labour, a Marxist Primer* (Fontana, Glasgow, 1980).

Norval, A J, *A Quarter of a Century of Industrial Progress in South Africa* (Johannesburg, 1962).

Parkin, F, *Marxism and Class Theory. A Bourgeois Critique* (Columbia University Press, New York, 1979).

Patterson, T T, *Job Evaluation*, Vol. 2 (Business Books Ltd., London, 1972).

Poulantzas, N, *Classes in Contemporary Capitalism*, Part 3 (New Left Books, London, 1974).

Richards, C S, *The Iron and Steel Industry in South Africa* (Johannesburg, 1948).

Rimner, M, *Race and Industrial Conflict* (Heinemann Educational Books, London, 1972).

Ross, A W, *Trade Union Wage Policy* (University of California Press, Berkeley, 1948).

Schlemmer, L and Webster, E, (eds.), *Change, Reform and Economic Growth in South Africa* (Ravan Press, Johannesburg, 1978).

SEIFSA, *The Organization and Structure of the Metal and Engineering Industry in South Africa* (SEIFSA, 1968).

South African Institute of Race Relations, *Survey of Race Relations 1956 – 57* (Johannesburg, 1957).

— *Survey of Race Relations 1958 – 59* (Johannesburg, 1959).

— *Survey of Race Relations 1959 – 60* (Johannesburg, 1960).
— *Survey of Race Relations 1961* (Johannesburg, 1961).
— *Survey of Race Relations 1972* (Johannesburg, 1972).
— *Survey of Race Relations 1976* (Johannesburg, 1976).
— *Survey of Race Relations 1978* (Johannesburg, 1978).
Sohn-Rethel, A, *Intellectual and Manual Labour, A Critique of Epistemology* (Macmillan, London, 1978).
Spiro, R B, *Rationalization of South African Industry* (The Knox Publishing Company, Durban, 1944).
Sterling D S, and Harris, A C, *The Black Worker* (Atheneum, New York, 1969).
Taylor, F W, *Scientific Management* (New York and London, 1947).
Thompson, P, *The Nature of Work. An Introduction to Debates on the Labour Process* (Macmillan, London, 1983).
Thompson, E P, *The Making of the English Working Class* (Penguin Books, Harmondsworth, 1963).
Thomson, A G, *The Years of Crisis* (Johannesburg, 1946).
Thomson, D, and Larson, R, *Where Were You Brother?* (War on Want, London, 1978).
Union Statistics for Fifty Years, 1910 – 1960 (Pretoria, 1960).
Whyte, W F, *Street Corner Society. The Social Structure of an Italian Slum* (University of Chicago Press, Chicago, 1943).
Wilson, F, *Migrant Labour* (Ravan Press, Johannesburg, 1972).
Wright, E O, *Class, Crisis and the State* (New Left Books, London, 1978).
Wright Mills, C, *The New Men of Power* (Harcourt Brace, 1948).

B. Published Articles

Alverson, H, 'Africans in South African industry: the human dimension' in C. Morse and C. Orpen, *Contemporary South Africa* (Juta, Cape Town, 1975).
Anonymous, 'Recognition agreements — a response', *Work in Progress* No.21, 1981.
Baskin, J, 'The Germiston Shop Stewards' Council', *South African Labour Bulletin* Vol. 8, No.1, September 1982.
Bonner, P, 'Focus on FOSATU', *South African Labour Bulletin* Vol. 5, No. 1, May 1979.
Bonner, P, and Webster, E, 'Background to the Wiehahn Commission',

South African Labour Bulletin Vol. 5, No. 2, August 1979.

Bozzoli, B, 'Managerialism and the mode of production in South Africa', *South African Labour Bulletin* Vol. 3, No. 8, October 1977.

Brighton Labour Process Group, 'The capitalist labour process', *Capital and Class* Vol. 1, 1977.

Burawoy, M, 'Migrant labour in South Africa and the United States' in T. Nichols, *Capital and Labour, A Marxist Primer* (Fontana, Glasgow, 1980).

— 'Towards a Marxist theory of the capitalist labour process', *Politics and Society* Vol. 13, No.1, 1978.

— 'The politics of production and the production of politics: a comparative analysis of piecework machine shops in the U.S. and Hungary', *Political Power and Social Theory* Vol. 1, 1980.

Castles S, and Kosack, G, 'The function of migrant labour in Western European capitalism', *New Left Review* 73, May/June 1972.

Claasens, A, 'The Riekert Commission and unemployment: the Kwa Zulu case', *South African Labour Bulletin* Vol. 5, No. 4, November 1979.

Copelyn, J, 'And what of Leyland?', *South African Labour Bulletin* Vol. 1, No. 3, June 1974.

Davies, R, 'Capital restructuring and the modification of the racial division of labour', *Journal of Southern African Studies* Vol. 5, No. 2, April 1979.

De Clerq, F, 'The organized labour movement and state registration: unity or fragmentation?', *South African Labour Bulletin* Vol. 5, Nos. 6 and 7, March 1980.

De Villiers, R, 'Clash looms on colour bar', *Rand Daily Mail* Johannesburg, 2 May 1978.

— 'Eveready strike', *South African Labour Bulletin* Vol. 5, No. 1, May 1979.

Elger, T, 'Valorization and "deskilling": a critique of Braverman', *Capital and Class* 7, 1979.

Elger, T, and Schwarz, B, 'Monopoly capitalism and the impact of Taylorism', in T. Nichols (ed.), *Capital and Labour, a Marxist Primer* (1980).

Ensor, L, 'TUCSA's relationship with African trade unions — an attempt at control 1954–1962', in E. Webster (ed.), *Essays in Southern African Labour History* (Ravan Press, Johannesburg, 1978).

Ensor, L, and Cooper, C, 'Summary of the recommendations of the Riekert Commission', *South African Labour Bulletin* Vol. 5, No. 4, November 1979.

Fine, B, *et al.*, 'Trade Unions and the state: the case for legality', *South African Labour Bulletin* Vol. 7, Nos. 1 and 2, September 1981.

Flanders, A, 'What are trade unions for?', in W E J McCarthy, *Trade Unions* (Penguin, Harmondsworth).

Foster, J, 'The workers' struggle — where does FOSATU stand?', *South African Labour Bulletin* Vol. 7, No. 8, July 1982.

Frobel, *et al.*, 'The new international division of labour', *South African Labour Bulletin* Vol. 5, No. 8, May 1980.

Grobbelaar, A, 'The parallel trade union', *South African Labour Bulletin* Vol. 3, No. 4, January – February 1977.

Heffer, T, 'Management strategy at Chloride', *South African Labour Bulletin* Vol. 7, Nos. 4 and 5, February 1982.

Hemson, D, 'Trade unions and the struggle for liberation', *Capital and Class* 6, 1976.

Hendler, P, 'The organization of parallel unions', *South African Labour Bulletin* Vol. 5, Nos. 6 and 7, March 1980.

Hindson, D, 'The new black labour regulations: limited reform, intensified control', *South African Labour Bulletin* Vol. 6, No. 1, July 1980.

Hlongwane, J, 'The emergence of African unions in Johannesburg with reference to the engineering industry', in J A Grey Coetzee, *Industrial Relations in South Africa* (Juta, Cape Town, 1976).

Hobsbawm, E, 'The labour aristocracy in nineteenth century Britain', in *Labouring Men* (1964).

Hyman, R, 'The politics of workplace trade unionism', *Capital and Class* Vol. 8, 1979.

Keenan, J, 'B and S closure: rationalization or reprisal?', *South African Labour Bulletin*, Vol. 10, No. 1, September 1984.

Kirkwood, M, 'The Defy dispute: questions of solidarity', *South African Labour Bulletin* Vol. 2, No. 1, May – June 1975.

Labour Research Committee, 'State strategy and the Johannesburg municipal strike', *South African Labour Bulletin*, Vol. 6, No. 7, May 1981.

Lambert, R, 'Political unionism in South Africa', *South African Labour Bulletin* Vol. 6, Nos. 2 and 3, September 1980.

Legassick, M, 'The record of British firms in South Africa in the context of the political economy', *South African Labour Bulletin* Vol.

2, No. 1, May – June 1975.

Legassick, M, and Innes, D, 'Capital restructuring and apartheid, a critique of constructive engagement', *African Affairs* 76, October 1977.

Lewis, J, 'The new unionism', in E. Webster (ed.), *Essays in Southern African Labour History* (Ravan Press, Johannesburg, 1978).

Maree, J, 'Seeing strikes in perspective', *South African Labour Bulletin* Vol. 2, Nos. 9 and 10, May – June 1976.

— 'SAAWU in the East London area: 1979 – 1981', *South African Labour Bulletin* Vol. 7, Nos. 4 and 5, February 1982.

Marglin, S A, 'What do bosses do? The origins and functions of hierarchy in capitalist production', in A. Gorz, *The Division of Labour, the Labour Process and Class Struggle in Modern Capitalism* (Harvester Press, Brighton, 1978).

Marx, K, 'Manifesto of the Communist Party', in R. C. Tucker (ed.), *The Marx-Engels Reader* (W. W. Norton Co., New York, 1972).

— 'The German Ideology: Part 1', in *The Marx-Engels Reader*.

Meth, C, 'Are there skill shortages in the furniture industry?', *South African Labour Bulletin*, Vol. 4, No. 7, November 1978.

— 'Trade Unions, skill shortages and private enterprise', *South African Labour Bulletin*, Vol. 5, No. 3, October 1979.

Molepo, M M, 'Ilanga le so Phonela Abasebenzi', *South African Labour Bulletin*, Vol. 6, No. 6, March 1981.

Monds, J, 'Workers' control and the historians, a new economism', *New Left Review* 97, May 1976.

Morris, M, and Kaplan, D, 'Labour policy in a state corporation: a case study of the South African Iron and Steel Corporation Part 1', *South African Labour Bulletin* Vol. 2, No. 6, January 1976.

— 'Labour policy in a state corporation: a case study of the South African Iron and Steel Corporation Part 2', *South African Labour Bulletin* Vol. 2, No. 8, April 1976.

Morris, M, 'Capital's response to African trade unions post Wiehahn', *South African Labour Bulletin* Vol. 7, Nos. 1 and 2, September 1981.

Nicol, M, 'Legislation, registration, emasculation', *South African Labour Bulletin* Vol. 5, Nos. 6 and 7, March 1980.

Olle, W, and Scholler, W, 'World market competition and restrictions upon international trade union policies', *Capital and Class* No. 2.

Palloix, C, 'The labour process: from Fordism to neo-Fordism' in *The Labour Process and Class Struggle* (CSE, London, 1978).

Palmer, P V, 'Effects of world socio-economic developments on European foundries and their future foundry technology', *Foundry Trade Practice*, July 1979.

Pattow, K J, 'Is maintenance now the top foundry skill?', *Foundry Management and Technology*, June 1979.

Penn, R, 'Skilled manual workers in the labour process, 1856 – 1964' in S Wood, *The Degradation of Work? Skill, Deskilling and the Labour Process* (Hutchinson, London, 1982).

Prendergast, M D, 'Research into the ferrous metallurgy of Rhodesian iron age societies' in T R Wertine, *The Coming of the Age of Iron* (Yale University Press, New Haven, 1980).

Roy, D, 'Fear stuff, sweet stuff and evil stuff: management's defences against unionization in the South' in T Nichols, *Capital and Labour: A Marxist Reader*.

Roux, M, 'The division of labour at Ford', *South African Labour Bulletin* Vol. 6, Nos. 2 and 3, September 1980.

Rubery, J, 'Structured labour markets, worker organization and low pay', *Cambridge Journal of Economics* Vol. 2, No. 8, March 1978.

Saul, J S, and Gelb, S, 'The crisis in South Africa', *Monthly Review* Vol. 33, No. 3, New York and London, (1978).

Spiegel, A, 'Rural differentiation and the diffusion of migrant labour remittances in Lesotho', in P Mayer (ed.), *Black Villages in an Industrial Society* (OUP, Cape Town, 1980).

Stewart, P, 'Pushing the frontiers of control: a shop floor struggle', *Africa Perspective*, No. 19, 1981.

Turner, H A, 'The morphology of trade unionism', in W E J McCarthy, *Trade Unions*.

Webster, D, 'A review of some "popular" anthropological approaches to the understanding of black workers', *South African Labour Bulletin*, Vol. 3, No. 1, July 1976.

Webster, E, 'A profile of unregistered union members in Durban', *South African Labour Bulletin*, Vol. 4, No. 8, January and February, 1979.

— 'Servants of apartheid? A survey of social research into industry in South Africa', in J Rex (ed.), *Apartheid and Social Research*, (UNESCO, Paris, 1981).

— 'Stay-aways and the black working class: evaluating a strategy', *Labour, Capital and Society* Vol. 14, No. 1, August 1981.

— 'SEIFSA has a new line on black unions', *South African Labour Bulletin*, Vol. 7, Nos. 4 and 5, February 1982.

— 'East Rand stoppages continue', *South African Labour Bulletin* Vol. 7, No. 8, July 1982.
— 'The state, crisis and the university: the social scientist's dilemma', *Perspectives in Education*, Vol. 6, No. 1, July 1982.
— 'New force on the shop floor', *South African Review 2* (Ravan Press, Johannesburg, 1984).
Webster, E, and Sitas, A, 'Stoppages in East Rand metal factories', *FOSATU* Occasional Publication, No.3, 1982.
Wood, E M, 'The separation of the economic and the political in capitalism', *New Left Review*, No. 127.
Woodward, W, 'The economic evaluation of apprentice training', *Industrial Relations Journal*, Vol. 6, No. 1, Spring 1975.
Wright, E O, 'Intellectuals and the working class', *The Insurgent Sociologist*, Vol. 8, No. 1, 1978.

C. Unpublished Papers and Dissertations

Bloch, G, 'The development of manufacturing industry in South Africa 1939-69', MA thesis, University of Cape Town, 1980.
Bosman, V, 'The value of scientific research in industry and the establishment of an Institute for Scientific and Industrial Research', unpublished manuscript, February 1930.
Budlender, D, 'Labour legislation in South Africa, 1924-1945', MA thesis, University of Cape Town, 1979.
Cassim, F, 'Labour market segmentation in South Africa', African Studies Institute seminar paper, University of the Witwatersrand, March 1982.
Claasens, A, 'Riekert and Wiehahn: unions and migrants', Honours dissertation, University of the Witwatersrand, 1980.
Cullinan, M, 'Deskilling, technical and industrial training, and white craft unions', Honours dissertation, University of the Witwatersrand, 1980.
De Villiers, F J, 'The application of science to industry in South Africa with special reference to industrial research', unpublished lecture, University of the Witwatersrand, 1936.
Dobson, P, 'The National Industrial Council for the engineering and metallurgical industry: a case study', Honours dissertation, University of Cape Town, 1982.
Douwes-Dekker, L, 'The development of industrial relations by

companies in South Africa, 1973 – 1977', MA thesis, University of the Witwatersrand, 1981.

Fanaroff, B, 'Collective bargaining in industry at shop floor level', lecture given at the AISEC conference, July 1982.

Greenberg, S, and Giliomee, H, 'Labour bureaucracies and the African rural areas; a field research report', Institute of Future Research, University of Stellenbosch, 1982.

Guy, J J, 'The desctruction of a pre-capitalist economy and the origins of labour supplies: the Zulu case', conference on Southern African labour history, University of the Witwatersrand, April 1976.

Hemson, D, 'Capital restructuring and the war economy', mimeo, 1977.

Hindson, D C, 'The role of the labour bureaux in the South African state's urban policy, with particular reference to the Riekert Commission's recommendations', African Studies Institute seminar paper, University of the Witwatersrand, May 1980.

Innes, D, 'The state, post-war manufacturing and class struggle', mimeo, 1978.

Jankelson, M B, 'The operation of the industrial council system in South Africa', MBA thesis, University of the Witwatersrand School of Business, 1975.

Kaplan, D, 'Class conflict, capital accumulation and the state: an historical analysis of the state in the 20th century, South Africa', D.Phil. thesis, University of Sussex, 1977.

La Grange, R, 'A general overview of the relationship between the registered trade unions and the labour process in the engineering industry after World War Two', Honours dissertation, University of the Witwatersrand, 1980.

Lewis, J, 'Trade unions and the labour process (1925 – 1930)', 1978.

— 'Dilution and the craft union during the Second World War', mimeo.

Maree, J, Ndzekeli, L, and Webster, E, 'Membership participation in two unregistered trade unions on the Witwatersrand', unpublished pilot survey, 1979.

Obery, E, 'Recession and retrenchment in the East Rand metal industry', Honours dissertation, University of the Witwatersrand, 1983.

O'Quigley, A, 'Engineering on the Rand 1914 – 1924', mimeo, 1978.

Oudiz, J, 'Silica exposure levels in US foundries', mimeo, 1980.

Sideris, T, 'Industrial councils and union democracy', Honours dissertation, University of the Witwatersrand, 1982.

Sitas, A, 'Disorganizing the unorganized: registered unions and the black workers, 1962-1980', mimeo, 1980.

— 'Drought in the city'. Paper delivered at the University of the Witwatersrand History Workshop, 1980.

Stewart, P, 'A worker has a human face', Honours dissertation, University of the Witwatersrand, 1981.

Steyn, M, 'The South African Non-European Iron, Steel and Metal Workers' Union (1942 – 1950)', mimeo, 1978.

Tobiansky, P, 'SEIFSA and the industry it represents', Honours dissertation, University of the Witwatersrand, 1980.

Webster, E, 'A new frontier of control? Case studies in the changing form of job control in South African industrial relations', Carnegie Conference, paper No. 111, 1984.

D. *Reports*

Autocast, 'Quality in quantity', company publication, 1980.

Advocate Bassey, 'Legal opinion on Section 35 for MAWU', 1978.

Black Sash National Conference, 'Advice Office Annual Report, February 1981 – January 1982', 1982.

Centre for Applied Legal Studies, 'Foundries', 1981.

Department of Labour, 'Job reservation: its background, motivation and application', government printer, Pretoria, 1960.

Economic Research Committee (ERC), 'Survey among migrant workers in the East Rand', University of the Witwatersrand, 1980.

Economist Intelligence Unit, 'Political currents in the international labour movement', B. K. Busel, Vol. 1, Europe and North America.

Educational Panel, 'Education for South Africa', First Report (Witwatersrand University Press, 1963).

— 'Education and the South African economy', Second Report (Witwatersrand University Press, 1966).

Federation of South African Trade Unions (FOSATU), 'Statement of the Wiehahn Commission Report and the amended Industrial Conciliation Act', *South African Labour Bulletin*, Vol. 5, Nos. 6 and 7, March 1980.

— 'Report on parallel union activity in GEC Machines, Benoni', *South African Labour Bulletin*, Vol. 5, Nos. 6 and 7, March 1980.

— 'Annual Report 1981', *South African Labour Bulletin*, Vol. 7, Nos. 4 and 5, February 1982.

'Manpower Survey', *Financial Mail Supplement*, 27 August 1982.

General and Allied Workers Union, 'Interview with chairperson for the General and Allied Workers Union, Samson Ndou', *Labour Focus*, Vol. 1, No. 3, August 1981.

General Factory Workers Benefit Fund, 'A look at the open trade unions' *South African Labour Bulletin*, Vol. 1, No. 3, June 1974.

General Workers Union, 'Comments on the question of registration', *South African Labour Bulletin*, Vol. 5, No. 5, November 1979.

— 'Registration, recognition and organization: the case of the Cape Town stevedores', *South African Labour Bulletin*, Vol. 5, Nos. 6 and 7, March 1980.

Goldblatt, B, Industrial Sociology III research project, October 1981.

Hearings before Special Committee of the House of Representatives to investigate the Taylor and other systems of shop management, 1912.

Industrial Employers Association, 'Memo on its formation, aims and functions', n.d.

International Metal Workers Federation (IMF), 'Survey on wages and social conditions in the foundry', compiled by B. Fanaroff and E. Webster.

Institute of Industrial Relations, 'Recognition guidelines' (Johannesburg, January 1982).

Johannesburg correspondent, 'Relying on the police', *South African Labour Bulletin*, Vol. 7, No. 8, July 1982.

Metal and Allied Workers Union, 'Report on the Leyland Motor Corporation and the Metal and Allied Workers Union', *South African Labour Bulletin*, Vol. 2, No. 5, 1974.

— 'Conac Engineering and the Department of Labour', *South African Labour Bulletin*, Vol. 2, Nos. 9 and 10, May – June 1976.

— 'Workers under the baton. An examination of the labour dispute at Heinemann Electric Company', *South African Labour Bulletin*, Vol. 3, No. 7, June-July 1977.

— 'A brief history', Durban, 1980.

Miller, S, 'Trade unionism in South Africa 1970 – 1980. A directory and statistics', SALDRU Working Paper No. 45, 1982.

R.S.A. Department of Planning, 'Economic development planning for South Africa, 1964 – 1969' (Government Printer, Pretoria).

SEIFSA, 'Guidelines for SEIFSA's members as to the development

and participation of blacks in trade unions in the metal industry',
November 1979.

South African Labour Bulletin, 'Focus on Wiehahn', Vol. 5, No. 2,
August 1979.

— 'Focus on Riekert', Vol. 5, No. 4, November 1979.

— 'Focus on international labour', Vol. 5, No. 8, May 1980.

South African Journal of Labour Relations, Vol. 2, No. 4, November
1978.

South African Tin Workers Union (SATWU), Silver Jubilee Brochure,
A Brief History, 1963.

Trade Union Council of South Africa (TUCSA), 'Africans in trade
unions', 1972.

United Nations Economic and Social Council, 'In-depth analysis of
the role of transnational corporations in the industrial, military and
nuclear sectors of South Africa', April 1980.

University of Stellenbosch, Bureau of Economic Research, 'A survey
of contemporary economic conditions and prospects for 1961',
1963.

Index